THE FORCE
OF TRADITION

THE FORCE OF TRADITION

A Case Study of
Women Priests in Sweden

BRITA STENDAHL

with an Appendix by Constance F. Parvey

FORTRESS PRESS   PHILADELPHIA

Library of Congress Cataloging in Publication Data

Stendahl, Brita K.
  The force of tradition.

  Includes bibliographical references.
  1. Ordination of women—Svenska kyrkan. 2. Women
clergy—Sweden. 3. Svenska kyrkan—Clergy. 4. Lutheran
Church—Sweden—Clergy. 5. Church and state—Sweden.
I. Title.
BX8071.2.S74 1985   262'.14413   84–48713
  ISBN 0–8006–1808–4

3,859

CONTENTS

ACKNOWLEDGMENTS

Ann-Sofie Ohlander, professor of history at the University of Uppsala, Sweden, encouraged me to undertake the study presented in this volume. Constance F. Parvey, formerly at World Council of Churches, Geneva, Switzerland, and presently at Bryn Mawr College, Pennsylvania, became a teammate who not only contributed a piece of new and original research, the chapter on ecumenical history, but also came to help me organize and evaluate the Swedish material in the light of her international experience. Sten Philipson, docent at the University of Uppsala and an associate pastor in Stockholm, helped design the trial questionnaire, took care of the distribution of the final questionnaire and of the follow-up letter. He organized informal meetings with clergy and let me stay in his home while I was visiting Sweden. Finally, he went over the material, checking for accuracy.

I am in debt to two institutions: first and foremost to the Tercentenary Fund of the Bank of Sweden for giving me a grant that supported me for two years and enabled me to visit Sweden to do interviews and to study; and to the Henry A. Murray Center at Radcliffe College for giving me the perfect place to sit and study the material without being interrupted. For a year and a half I was there, surrounded by enthusiastic yet meticulous scholars in pursuit of diverse projects of which they certainly considered mine not the least esoteric. Here I met Dr. Diana Zuckerman who with her staff advised me in coding the material and did the data processing procedure for me.

Three people went over the material and gave helpful hints: Sr. Marie Augusta Neil, professor at Emmanuel College, Boston, who herself has made an exhaustive sociological study of Catholic sisters and therefore was enamored with the results of the questionnaire in particular; Francine Cardman, professor of theology at Weston Theological Seminary, whose crisp advice I have tried to follow; and Krister Stendahl, bishop of the diocese of Stockholm. The book bears much evidence of his care, courtesy, and skill especially in its concluding chapter. My very special gratitude belongs, however, to the 82% of the Swedish clergy approached who took time to fill in and to return our questionnaire. My fervent hope is that this book in some manner can repay them for their effort.

BRITA STENDAHL

INTRODUCTION

In the latter part of the twentieth century the secular world has adapted to the entrance of women into the public world, but for the churches more is demanded than mere adaptation.

The church, often symbolized as a mother, has always welcomed women into her bosom, and women have gladly let themselves be part of her life. The church gave women protection, quiet, dignity, love, and hope. Countless numbers of women have served the church with devotion and in humility. Some became nuns and sisters, missionaries and deaconesses. Women provided the infrastructure of the church. They made up the support system. They taught and healed. They cleaned and cooked. They set up communion tables and changed the flowers. They arranged bazaars and church fairs, visited the elderly and developed many new aspects of ministry. Eventually women became employed by the church as secretaries, organists, and counselors. Yet their given status in the church—no matter how powerful and creative they were as individuals—remained subordinate to the all-male clergy and to the laymen.

The last two decades have experienced radical change in that women, although they continue to serve the church, no longer are willing to be subordinate to men, letting their will be done, their values go unchallenged, their theology be the standard for all theology worth the name. Women have declared themselves ready to serve as priests. They want to do theological research to test their theological views, and they want their share in the decision-making process of the church. And in many churches they have begun to do so.[1]

It is by no means unique for women who enter the professional world to experience resistance before they are accepted. But it is uniquely difficult for many churches to accept women in the priesthood precisely because the church for centuries has formulated, preached, and practiced the subjugation of women. For this reason it is of paramount importance not only for the church but for the well-being of the society in which the church dwells and holds sway over the conscience of the people that the issue of the subjugation and equality of women be illuminated. The tradition holds power over the consciousness of men and women influencing their actions at home and at

1

work: traditionally men have expected women to keep house; traditionally women have not claimed partnership with men in the public world.

For people who have experienced increased equality it is painful to discover how inequality has persisted and prevailed through the ages. It becomes a necessity to expose the past in order to start a "consciousness-raising" process to make the problem felt by others. People who formerly were marginalized undertake this task with some risk. With only one foot on the hierarchical ladder of power they have much to lose. The powerful consider them "one issue" people and their cause as peripheral and divisive. But for marginalized people—whomever they may be, blacks, women, the native Americans, small nations, the very poor—this issue is the key.

As Jean Baker Miller has pointed out, in our modern world inequality inevitably creates conflict. It is not the marginalized people who are trouble-makers. It is the situation of inequality that creates the conflict.[2] Those in power are usually slow to detect the value of the efforts on the part of the subordinates who raise the issue with them. One formidable obstacle is that the powerful seldom admit to having power. They just claim to do what "is done," that is, stick with the tradition. When those in power focus on a conflict they want a quick solution on their terms. This mechanism of wanting a settlement without taking the underlying problem of inequality into account has almost become an automatic reflex in order to preserve the status quo. The subordinates, however, resent having their fate decided for them. To have less, to be treated as lesser beings, to be repressed and con-sidered to be of less worth is the root of disappointment, discouragement, anger, and hatred.

The rising tide of conflicts over inequality has inundated the West during the past decades. Among the many conflicts the one surrounding the status of women has attracted wide attention. When women were admitted to the graduate schools of prestigious, white male universities they soon discovered their marginality and raised the demand for special Women's Studies. As this term has become clarified by usage I offer a specific definition. "Women's Studies" does not mean studies with women as objects, neither does it mean women studying women. It means a study where gender is a recognized analytical category with a potential for making a difference. Such demands were not popular either with the administrations or with the teachers. But whether or not such specialized centers were created, books about women written by women eventually began to fall like meteors on the fields of history, art, literature, psychology, and religion, where they lie like foreign objects shunned by the established power that in the beginning looked upon this singular approach with amusement and disdain.[3] These books are now so numerous and such a familiar part of the landscape that they can hardly be ignored. The discovery that one-half of humankind has been shunted and stereotyped or plain forgotten has given scholarship a new angle. The feminist approach has begun to be incorporated into the main body of literature, and a feminist line has begun to be argued by both women and men scholars.

This did not happen overnight. The process took time and perseverance, but eventually people are coming to see that there has been a blind spot, and in consequence a huge white field on the map lies open for exploration.

My special study deals with a small segment of life in a small country in the ever shrinking Western world. It is a case study of how the Church of Sweden has received women into the priesthood. I believe that the forces I have studied at work in that small place among the clergy (about 4,000 in a population of 8.3 million) are of more general significance. Actually Sweden with its homogeneous culture and the church with its doctrinal conscious-ness, each and together make for a laboratory situation with a considerable number of controls for an investigation of what can happen when women enter the power structure of the central workforce. I perceive the study to radiate signals both to other churches that ordain women and to women who seek ordination in churches that do not ordain women. I believe furthermore that male supremacist sentiment in society at large can be better understood by analogy through the looking glass of the conflict in the Church of Sweden that this study presents.

In Sweden the ordination of women aroused an unequalled controversy among the clergy. Swedes know about the conflict, but only if they are clergy can they tell how serious it has been. The majority of the Swedes are amused or annoyed that the clergy can be so rude and nasty to each other. They see the conflict entirely as the concern of the clergy. That here we are dealing with a problem surfacing also in many other institutions is seldom adequately understood.[4]

I myself, frankly, never thought of the issue as earthshaking. Being born in Sweden, educated and socialized in a society that put high premium on equality, I took for granted that after the church had argued the case and decided in favor of ordaining women to the priesthood—as it did in 1958—the struggle would be over. Sweden would soon have women as priests just as it had women as doctors, lawyers, politicians, journalists, and so forth. And that would be that.

This is not what happened. There were leaders in the church who bitterly opposed the decision, and there were ministers who closed their churches to women priests. When I visited Sweden or received visitors from Sweden, the talk when the church was the subject always reverted to this issue.[5] From my horizon it seemed ridiculous that so much energy should be lost and so much animosity generated on what seemed a peripheral question.

I now realize that I had come to think of equality as something that is given from the top down and not something that has to be fought for from the bottom up against hierarchy and tradition. I will tell how my eyes were opened, how it happened that many seemingly disparate signals came together leading to the insight that the highest threshold for women to step over in their struggle to gain recognition as authentic human beings is indeed to obtain entrance to the priesthood.

I had pursued literary and theological studies which among other things brought me to write a book on the works of Søren Kierkegaard. This in turn led me to study the life and works of Fredrika Bremer (1801–65), Sweden's first major novelist. My interest in her was kindled when I read in Kierkegaard's *Journals and Papers* how upset he was with her reference to him as a "ladies' author." It was as if she had destroyed his career. Why, I asked myself, did he get so upset about that? The rest of what she writes about him shows perceptivity and positive appreciation of his works.[6] Of course, to be a "ladies' author" was in Bremer's mind high praise, while Kierkegaard thought it diminished his efforts and made his books less desirable for men readers, who were the audience he wanted to reach.

It was when I studied Fredrika Bremer that I got on the inside of why the women's question is so sensitive particularly in the field of religion. Bremer wrestled with what seemed to her a most horrendous problem: perhaps she opposed the will of God when she wanted something other in her life than to marry, have children, and serve a husband and family. When a theologian and friend, Per Böklin, told her that she had the right and freedom to pursue her own calling, she experienced an enormous relief.[7] Liberated she went her own way. She studied philosophy and religion and had a burning wish to serve humankind. She might have become a priest had women at that time been permitted, but since they were not, she remained a novelist and essayist molding her views and visions into plots.

By looking at her problems with the family structure, her struggle with Bible texts, her despondency with her career, and her elation with the advice of Per Böklin, I began to see how deeply our gender-related thoughts and feeling are rooted in religion.

Scholars have pointed out how in both Jewish and Christian traditions women have been defined by their relationship to men.[8] Their role has been understood as dependent. As daughters they belonged to the father who had the right to give them away to a husband whom in turn they would serve and obey. Through the centuries theologians have poured over the meanings of the creation story, and of Adam and Eve as a paradigm for the relation between women and men. The fact that Eve is said to have been created after Adam and out of his rib, thus being derivative of him, has been seen as proof of women's lesser status. This order of creation did not necessarily mean that women were of lesser worth in the eyes of God *(coram deo)*. But here on earth among "men" (coram hominibus) women should know their place as subordinate and second to men.[9] This understanding of the relationship between men and women has been the mainline tradition. Both men and women came to take for granted that this is how it is supposed to be.

Overagainst this mainline view of the relationship between the sexes stands another view that preachers and teachers, for example, Böklin, have explicated. They have lifted up the astonishing words in the other creation story in Genesis 1 where it says that men and women both are created in the image of God (vv. 26–27). They have pointed to the words of St. Paul in the Epistle to the Galatians saying that "in Christ there are no longer Jew or Greek, slave or free, nor is there male and female" (Gal. 3:28). In Christ subservience has given way to freedom.

These two strands of tradition have existed side by side within the church. Although the one embracing the subordination of women has been the stronger, the prophetic vision of equivalence has always been present to mitigate and inspire. The women who have been described in the footnotes of history books of the church have usually been those who were uncommonly pious, outdoing themselves in obedience and humility. The women who challenged tradition, questioned dogma, and even formed their own communities (like Anne Hutchinson and Mary Baker Eddy) have received short shrift. Equal treatment has been out of the question.[10]

But there is also a third trend. It is curious and instructive to visit art galleries and look at the way artists over the ages have pictured women. There is a mysterious quality behind all these wonderful eyes that see beyond the onlooker and the mouths that maybe or maybe not suggest a smile: Woman as an object of conjecture. The artists exhibited, who almost without exception have been men, must have perceived women as a wholly different kind of species. So also in theology. The dominant tradition has tried to read God's special wisdom in the biological differences between men and women, and these differences have been emphasized. Women are what men are not. The two complement each other. In modern times this polarity has been developed into a third model. Bremer was very attracted by the idea of complementarity. It avoids the harshness in the doctrine of the order of creation. By speaking for a special place for women in church and society it circumvents the question of equality: Separate yet equal, sort of. In the complementary model of thinking it is not the women who decide who they are as human beings, but the men who decide what women are not. This model is merely a more sophisticated argument against equality.

These three types of thinking about women have lived side by side in the church for centuries. First with the advent of the ordination of women the lines were drawn hard between them, and people were forced to take a position. And a struggle broke out in earnest because by then women themselves had started to reflect on the tradition and discover how they had been left out from decisions about what kind of human beings they were. They learned that they had been given a negative identity, being what men are not, men being the principal prototype. Naturally women could not see themselves that way. They too were individuals created by God in God's image, human beings, and authentic people. Jesus had followers both among men and women, and they felt called by him. With women speaking up, the lines were again redrawn.[11] Women emerged to challenge the stereotyped patterns of piety, poetry, and mystery with their authentic experiences.

In 1960 the first three women were ordained in the Church of Sweden. In 1982 there were approximately 400 ordained women, that is, over one-tenth of the clergy. A critical mass was obtained. It seemed an ideal time to investigate how these women have pioneered in a profession that so long has been dominated by male leaders, thinkers, and social reformers. How have the women been received, how do they fare, and what is on their agenda? Those were some of my motivating questions.

Obviously the topic for study was sensitive since the conflict over the ordination of women had nearly split the Church of Sweden. The long male tradition is mighty. The struggle to leave it behind blighted the spirits. But precisely for that reason the Swedish experience is valuable. It laid bare unresolved tensions that do exist, though more covered, in other churches and in Western society at large. What to the conservatives in the churches seemed as matters of faith and doctrine also exists in vaguer forms in the minds of many in a more secular setting. One of the advantages of doctrine is that it makes tangible those sentiments that otherwise lie submerged in a culture. It is the habit of theologians to see crucial issues of anthropology and theology where others just muddle through. It is the task of theologians to reexamine such issues in light of a dramatically changed situation.

In order to present a full picture of the conflict over the ordination of women, I have approached the subject from several angles. I begin with six interviews with people who played a part in the early debates and decisions, letting them tell about their views of the ordination of women. All six are ordained. Two of them are bishops. Three of them are women, and three are men. All remember vividly the times of the 1950s before the decision was made to ordain women. Six voices with different timbres tell the story from different perspectives. Together they witness the anguish. Each of the men represents a different theological outlook on the status of women in the church. Each of the women has gone through her personal struggle to gain clarity as to what God wants with her life. All six interviews lend scope to the investigation.

Chapter 2 backtracks. In sweeping brushstrokes it paints the Swedish society as it has developed from agrarian times, when priests were at the height of authority teaching people their place in creation, to the modern industrial society where the church has lost its self-evident authority. The modern Swedish church has become to a great extent a "service church," a place for baptisms, weddings, and funerals, services which people still demand and see as accompaniment to the life cycle. This chapter illustrates the difficulties the clergy have experienced in acknowledging the changes that have taken place all around them, and especially it takes note of how difficult it has been for the clergy to accept what the transformation of society has done to them in their status and function as priests. The conflict over the ordination of women has actually absorbed within itself many of these unsolved problems, insecurities, and hesitations—the fear of losing the tradition.

Chapter 3 brings to light how church and state in Sweden have been closely connected and how this establishment plays a role in modern times. The particular intensity in the conflict around the ordination of women in Sweden is perhaps best explained by the ways in which it was entwined with issues of church and state. The chapter centers around the arguments given for and against ordination of women. The intention is not so much to familiarize the reader with the arguments—though that is important—but to introduce the frontlines and illustrate the political nature of the argumentation. Although the minority that was against women's ordination lost in 1958, a so-called Conscience Clause was adopted. This clause enabled the opposition to carry on its resistance against the ordained women. It took twenty-four years before the Church Assembly debated whether or not to do away with the clause because it was unfair in that it considered the conscience of men only. That debate is highlighted in this chapter. Before 1960 men had discussed *about* women. Since 1960 the women are both part of the scene and of the discussants. This fact becomes an essential ingredient in the transformation of the conflict.

Through an assortment of documents, some important as background to the conflict and some speaking to the conflict itself, Chapter 4 reveals the ongoing debate on how to expand equality in society at large, as well as the difficulties of adjustment with which the church and its priests have had to cope. Those who vehemently opposed the ordination of women published in 1960 a statement of guidelines in seventeen points for how the resistance should be carried out in local parishes. These so-called *17 Points* became extremely influential. It took the Church of Sweden almost two decades to publish a counterdocument, a statement of guidelines for how men and women priests are to cooperate and coexist in the church. But then it proved to be too little too late. The government took initiative, and, after a study, produced the report that proposed to abolish the Conscience Clause and bring the priesthood under the umbrella of the already existing general equal rights law of 1945. This proposal was adopted by the Church Assembly in 1982.

Chapter 5 deals entirely with the present. It contains the results of a questionnaire sent to all the ordained women in active service in the Church of Sweden and to an equal number of men priests randomly chosen. (The questionnaire and the responses are accounted for in Appendix 1.) The situation of 1982 is presented with statistical numbers: What the priests do, how they live, where they work, where they studied, how they were called, where they get their support, how they evaluate their work, and how they look upon the ministry of their male, respectively female colleagues.

Finally, Constance F. Parvey has written an extensive history of the international and ecumenical situation concerning the ordination of women. This chapter is an invaluable part of the study project but due to its length and specific character it is placed as Appendix 2. Since ecumenical relations so often are referred to as either an obstacle to or a promoter of women's ordination this review documenting how the question has been dealt with in the World Council of Churches during the last fifty years provides actual continuous information on a history that never before has been illustrated.

The concluding chapter is called "The Force of Tradition and the Future of Women in the Church." The rich tradition of the church is not merely the possession of the clergy. It belongs to all Christian people. It has come into being through the intermingling with many different societies. In some the church is still dominant. In other places, like Sweden, where the process of secularization has gone far, the tradition of the church yet touches the minds and hearts of people. Unconsciously parents bring up children the way their parents brought them up. They tell children things they were told, and they do things their parents used to do. Tradition plays a great role. There is an ongoing dialectic between what is good for me and what is good for society. In that process the words, the commandments, and the rituals of the church are held valuable. Precisely for that reason it is also important to take care that the inner workings of tradition are not spoiled. To use an analogy from music: something which once was good and true can by repetition and routine become bad and false. The tradition is in need of reform and transformation, in order to regain vitality, or it will become contemptible.

When women became priests the conformity with an old patriarchal model was visibly broken. The traditional view of the priesthood was up for reevaluation. The tradition began its transformation. A new model for ecclesiology, more democratic, more demanding of the priests as well as of the laity went in search of its practitioners.

1

SIX INTERVIEWS

BO GIERTZ

Bo Giertz came early Friday morning through snow and ice on 5 February 1982 to be interviewed at the Institute of Sociology of Religion in Stockholm. He had been somewhat apprehensive and had asked to see the questions in advance. I, too, was a bit nervous when I looked out of the window while waiting for this man who had been the leader of the opposition to the ordination of women. In the 1930s he had influenced many people as a fiery lecturer and traveling secretary of the Student Christian Movement. Then for ten years he had his own country parish at Torpa in the diocese of Linköping. During that time he had written *The Church of Christ* (1939), *Church Piety* (1939), *The Rocky Ground* (1941), *The Foundation* (1942), *Sola Fide* (1943), *The Great Lie and the Great Truth* (1945), *The Struggle for the Human Being* (1947) and *With My Own Eyes* (1948).[1]

In 1949 he became Bishop of Göteborg and remained in that post until 1970 when he retired and returned to lecturing and writing. Giertz is often credited with having been responsible for *The 17 Points,* an action program for the opposition, recommending to priests and laypeople what to do in case they encountered a woman minister.[2] When I now saw him coming around the corner, tall and youthful in spite of his seventy-six years, with ruddy complexion and a forceful gait, I knew I would meet a strong personality, one accustomed to speaking with authority.

Q. You became the leader among those who opposed the ordination of women. Was that a role that you readily accepted because of your position as bishop, or was it a task that you only gradually came to see as yours?

Until 1957 the great majority within the Church of Sweden were against the ordination of women. According to a poll taken among the Swedish priests just before 1957, 85 percent of them rejected the idea.[3] Perhaps what distinguished me from the others in the majority was that I had somewhat more insight into the exegetical part of the question. I had been a pupil of Anton Fridrichsen, the professor of New Testament exegesis in Uppsala. Perhaps I also guessed that there would be a harsher political pressure than most of the other bishops imagined. I urged Archbishop Brilioth to call an extra meeting of the bishops sometime in the early summer of 1957 in order to plan for the Church Assembly. However, there was little time left for this question since Brilioth used the opportunity to get some other business out of the way. And our discussion showed that the others thought this question would be dealt with like any other item on the agenda. I don't think I had any position as a leader, in any case not in the beginning when I was merely on the side of Ernst Staxäng and of G.A. Danell from the diocese of Växjö.[4] In 1960, when I was elected to the chair of the Coordination Council for the Church Consolidating Around Bible and Confession *(Kyrklig Samling Kring Bibel och Bekännelse)* I did to a certain degree get a leading position. It was given to me, and it has cost me a great deal of suffering.

Q. What do you remember as the most decisive moment during the Church Assembly of 1957?

Clearly it was the storm the press whipped up after the Special Committee with a biblical motivation had rejected the new proposal to the law.[5] I have the impression that many that morning began to revise their stand. I will never forget the panic and pale terror on the faces of the people assembled in the reading room: We have the whole press against us.

Q. How did you interpret the decision to call a new Church Assembly so soon afterward?[6]

As a clear challenge on the part of the government. They wanted to put the church in its place and to show that the church cannot go against an almost unanimous Parliament. They wanted to exert political pressure. Those bishops who had formulated the decision of the Assembly (with a different formulation than that of the Committee) had asked for time to gain greater clarity and unity (I think that was their phrase). It was precisely this extra time that the government refused us.

Q. What in your view made the vote the next time around go in the opposite direction? Was there any decisive argument?

Hardly, because the people who came to the 1958 Assembly were those who had been elected according to their views of this one issue. Their stands were locked in from the beginning owing to the hefty polemics that had been going on throughout the winter. It was the first Church Assembly that I know of which had been elected under palpable agitation from the mass media.

Q. How did the Conscience Clause come into existence?

The secretary to the Special Committee of the Church Assembly, Jerker Victor, a lawyer, was surprised by the good spirit of objectivity and mutual respect during the deliberations of the Committee. It was in contrast to the picture of the "split" in the church given by the mass media. If I remember correctly, he had already proposed at the third or fourth meeting that the Committee should express the great unanimity that actually existed on a row of basic questions. So it was decided that we, in our stated opinion, should first give expression to some basic views from which to see the whole question. To these belonged the guidelines of cooperation for the future and a demand for respect (without time limit) toward those who continued to hold the beliefs that the whole church up to this point in time had always held. There was no disagreement on that point. Neither was there any in the Assembly. Victor's introduction had made it clear.

Q. When you sat down to formulate *The 17 Points* at that time what were your hopes for the future?

I did not formulate *The 17 Points*. They came into existence during a rather long and thorough work period by a committee. For my part, I wrote only the first draft of the introduction. The points themselves were worked out by two different groups, one consisting of priests and one of laypeople. The laypeople had formulated points 10 through 17 on their own. They were not exclusively men; there were several women among them. We priests worked out points 1 through 9, and there were different opinions among us, to which point 5 bears witness. *The 17 Points* were then released for publication when the first women were ordained. The newspapers printed them. The introduction was never published.[7]

My hopes were—as the introduction spells out—that these points were going to help those for whom women priests represent a deviation from biblical Christianity. They would now meet them in praxis. Above all it was important to avert desperate measures that could split the church. Such were urged from some corners, yet we succeeded. The church has not split. The harsh feelings are the fault of the press and of the hurt feelings of the politicians whose sense of power is wounded. Also the women priests are at fault who will not let people live with another kind of faith. This is a sign of their lack of faith, in my opinion. We can live with Baptists and with teetotalers who have a different opinion from ours, and we respect their beliefs although we do not share them. At bottom this is a matter of faith. We stand on the biblical, the apostolic faith that cannot be manipulated.

Q. When you look to the Swedish church of today, do you think that the women priests are its greatest weakness?

No. The greatest weakness is—as also the introduction to *The 17 Points* declares—that the church has become so insecure about its creed. The introduction reads: "Parts that are central to the Christian message have been suppressed or denied. There prevails great uncertainty about what the authority of the Word of God means and to what it obliges us. These are the consequences of long-lasting maladies within the church that we experience today."

What is special to precisely this conflict is that the different beliefs lead to different ways of *acting them out* that cannot be unified. As long as we act in the same manner (concerning the office of priesthood and sacraments), it is not noticed whether the underlying beliefs differ, and it is easy to work side by side. Now for the first time in our church we act differently. Two incompatible ways. Therefore this question ought to have been handled with greater caution than was the case.

Then too, one cannot look away from another fact, the concession that the church gave the state in 1958 has given many the idea that everything in the church's teaching is relative and negotiable and that we in the church will finally have to conform to public opinion. We have since 1958 really experienced a downward slide within the church concerning both Christian faith and Christian life that nobody believed was possible at the beginning of the fifties. However, that cannot be blamed on this question alone but on the general insecurity and submissiveness that stamps the church and its leadership.

Q. Do you look upon the diocese of Göteborg as a purer diocese, a witness to a truer church, a remnant that in the future will prove its power?

One cannot write a report card for a diocese in a spiritual way. The church of God is present where the Word is rightly preached and the sacraments rightly handled, and such parishes we find both here and there in our country. It is possible that there are more of them in the diocese of Göteborg. In that case, it is due to the Word of God and not to their opinion on the question of women priests.

But the Church of Sweden is so unsure of its foundation on the Bible and on its confession. The Roman Catholic Church and the Orthodox churches stand firmly on the Bible and on their tradition.

Q. How tied are we to the Bible and to the confessions?

In the question of the ordination of women we meet in concrete form what is heresy and denial. Another example of the same phenomenon happened in the Norwegian church when the theological faculty at the university got too liberal: Hallesby founded another theological faculty (*Menighetsfakultetet*) that kept close to the Word and the Lutheran confessions.[8]

Q. What do you consider to be a call to the priesthood?

There are two kinds of call: One inner and one outer. The inner call comes from God and the outer from the church; each is according to the will of God and in accordance with the Bible. When I was bishop and talked with a candidate for the priesthood, I never asked him about the inner call. I told the candidates that I trusted them.

Q. What do you think of the present educational preparation of priests for the ministry?

The Swedish theological preparation for the priesthood today suffers from two weaknesses. First, their theological education —which takes place at the state universities—is purely academic. The personal faith of the teacher or the students is regarded with complete indifference. To provide communal worship or some kind of counseling as part of the theological preparation is not thought as proper.

The other weakness is due to the crisis in our educational system which bears down on all studies at the university, namely, the cuts in requirements which among other things have as their consequence radically diminished language skills. At the theological faculties they have had to trim back rather drastically, for instance, on the knowledge of Greek. When I studied, it was obligatory that each student in theology knew how to read and translate the whole New Testament. Today only one sixth of the text is required.

Q. How do you look at the future?

God might remove his candle from Sweden. But this disagreement might also be a spur to free the church. I hope that new priests will be attracted to such a free-church. By their fruits we shall know their worth.

My fear is that the deepest currents will dry up, that groups such as the Renewal of the Church, Friends of the Bible, the Laestadian Revivalism, the Church Consolidation, etc. will all fall away if the Swedish Church Assembly accepts the new proposal that does away with the Conscience Clause thereby declaring the classic conviction of the church heretical.

Q. If you were a young priest today, where would you like to start your ministry? In the country? As a writer?

If I were young today, I would like with all my heart to become a priest again. The question is whether I would be accepted in the Church of Sweden. Some bishops would certainly not accept me today, but they are in the minority. Even if I were allowed to become a priest or perhaps already were one, then it is absolutely clear that I, like those who share my conviction, would not have any possibilities of upward mobility but would have to take whatever was left—which I would do gladly and gratefully. It would most probably be a one-man parish in the country, the only place where a priest still cannot be removed by militant opponents, who would insist on forcing us to celebrate with a woman priest.

I have been a writer only when God has directly called me to it. As a bishop I have not been able to find time. There is a twenty-one-year lacuna in my authorship. Now as retired, I am writing again. I am glad to have meaningful work—preaching, teaching and writing.

As a priest, the time in Torpa was the happiest. I was with people; I knew them; I followed them from baptism or confirmation; I sat at their deathbeds; I buried them. When I came into a home, I could jump up on the woodbox and sit and dangle my legs while we talked. In the country so much is preserved. In the city there are too many souls per priest. There is much isolation, and as a bishop one is further isolated.

Q. Is the old priest role gone?

In the city a priest is tied to his many tasks. But a new type of ministry is beginning to show up with modest success. A large group of laypeople are willing to help. The priest stays in the center, and they go out to the people. I have made some video cassettes where I speak to these people, telling them what Christianity is all about. Then they tell others. It is an invitation. It is much better than urging people from the pulpit to come to church, which they won't do anyway. It is a lay ministry, like Christ's outstretched hands.

Q. Do you know any young people, and what do you think of the young people of today? Do they impress you? What do you think of their different habits and styles of living?

Yes, on the whole, I am impressed by their eagerness to evangelize and by their openness. I think some are somewhat naive talking about world poverty and wearing expensive jeans with patches.

I am thrilled by their willingness to study the Bible. In the little town of Borås, for instance, we have a group of two hundred youngsters in Bible study. It is a nondenominational group that has grown very much by itself. They read and pray together, but they cannot go to church together. The poor kids have inherited our divisions.

(But the youth will turn away from the Church of Sweden if the Church Assembly approves the repeal of the Conscience Clause. This is a bleeding problem. It is a grotesque situation that Margit Sahlin and the politicians have forced upon us.)[9]

Q. How do you read and interpret Romans 14?

If you mean concerning the question of women priests, then the weak are *we* who oppose the ordination of women. The strong are those who accept it, those who eat all kinds of food. But the strong must accept the weak, it says, and not force the weak to go against their conscience. The weak in their turn should not judge the strong. This could mean something like letting the Conscience Clause remain. However, this chapter in Romans should be compared with the conclusion in 1 Corinthians 14. This is "a command of the Lord" (14:37). In this instance the text speaks about the women in Corinth directly, while in the Epistle to the Romans the issue is food. In 1 Cor. 14:33 it says: "As in all the churches of the saints, the women should keep silence in the churches. For they are not permitted to speak, but should be subordinate, as even the law says. If there is anything they desire to know, let them ask their husbands at home. For it is shameful for a woman to speak in church." St. Paul would not have recommended the solution that he gave to the people in Rome—where the question is whether or not to eat unclean food—to the people in Corinth, where the issue is the status of women.

But here in Sweden the church has accepted that solution, and we now must try to live with it. For us who have looked upon the Church of Sweden as part of the apostolic church, this is of course a disappointment. All we can say now is that the apostolic church still lives within the framework that the Swedish Church organization provides. We know that we never can get a pure and faultless church here on earth. Let us learn two things from Romans 14 in the situation we now are in: We shall not force anyone and we shall not judge anyone. That is what we have tried to do, to live together. We who oppose (the ordination of women) have not wanted to split the church, and we have done what we could to keep her together. The question is whether we will be forced to leave her.

INGMAR STRÖM

Five days later, on 10 February 1982 Ingmar Ström was interviewed at an old people's home where he was visiting that morning and where we first had coffee with the old folks. Ström was born in 1912. He is the former bishop of Stockholm, the diocese that holds the greatest number of ordained women. In the early fifties, Ström was the editor-in-chief of *Vår Kyrka* ("Our Church"), the semi-official weekly of the Church of Sweden. From 1959 to 1971, Ström was the director of the Central Council of the Church of Sweden and thus held a strategically vital post that gave him an overview of the status of the church in society. He became bishop of Stockholm in 1971, and for eight years he was the head of that diocese. Ström is completely unafraid. His outspokenness has won him many admirers and has made him a favorite personality on radio and television. The Swedish people know who he is and listen when he speaks about Christian faith. He speaks of what he knows and also tells people when he does not know. Typically, his last book is entitled *Vad tror du själv?* ("What Do You Think Yourself?"). His influence reaches far beyond those who attend church. But his talent for communication and his often acerbic comments about church behavior and its cryptic ordinances have also earned him some enemies.

A slight man of average height, his appearance is not immediately striking. He seldom smiles except when suddenly amused. His sense of humor is compelling. His spiritual comments are stamped by an understatement that is so typically Swedish, a leaning over backward in order not to seem hypocritical or pious.

Q. Why did you yourself become a priest?

I never thought of it. I studied for years and years and I had some vague ideas that I wanted to be a journalist or a cultural essayist to cut some figure in cultural work. After ten years of that, my father who was a minister said to me: What's the matter? Why are you dawdling? Why not become a priest? Then you can do whatever you want. You can teach, you can write. That's fine. The priesthood is so wide and varied a field. Well, that was when I went off to Uppsala to get my theology degree—the legitimation to get the job. Also, I wanted to get married.

Q. As editor and as director you carried out so-called specialized ministry. Do other young priests also want to specialize?

Almost every one of those who came to be ordained have said so. Both women and men want to do work with students, or in hospitals, with the elderly or some other kind of social work. They are afraid of the old patriarchal role. And they are convinced that things will change. After a while, however, they are sucked into it. There they are. It is not easy to find new patterns, especially not in our church where the positions are locked in regulated promotion with set salary scales. Young clergy get caught in a system where they have to take the positions that are available, and their time fills up with their prescribed tasks.

The women have done the same as the men. I had hoped that the women would bring about some renewal of the preaching language, but that has not happened.

Q. When the struggle over ordination began, did you have an inkling that it would be so divisive?

I thought it would be a phase that quickly would pass. In 1958, when I was editor of Vår Kyrka, we were going to refurbish and redirect the paper to make it more professional. We got a new editor, Margit Strömmerstedt, who had been editor-in-chief of a big national weekly. We succeeded. The subscriptions doubled in a year. It was spectacular. Until I wrote a little review of a tiny book about a woman who wanted to be a priest.[1] In the review I said that this opposition to women was ridiculous. At the paper we could not believe the response. Half of the clergy cancelled their subscriptions. An avalanche of letters to the editor protested my words.

From then on we have had to live with this struggle. I never thought it would be so. Everything seemed to me then to be in place and clear sailing ahead. The Committee had done a good job. Its exegetical expert, Erik Sjöberg, had written extensively and convincingly.[2] We had published a book, Women—Society—Church, to which Krister Stendahl had contributed a crystal clear piece of exegesis.[3] We thought it was just a matter of time before people had digested the facts. Fat chance. We are now locked in our adversary positions more than ever.

Q. How important was the reaction by the secular press?

The reaction of the press was astounding. Daily, city or country editions, weeklies and monthlies, you name them, every one of them was for the ordination of women. One has never seen such unity on an issue. And the priests have been severely tested by this fact. Those that were against the ordination—and that was about half of the clergy—were bewildered and some of them angered. I believe this to be the reason why they have created the myth that it was the state that forced the church to accept women priests. As you know, the Church Assembly of 1957 voted *no* to women priests, while the 1958 Church Assembly voted *yes*. They say that this switch happened because there was so much pressure from the state. The church had said its *no*. But that is plain untrue. There was just as much politicking in the election to the 1957 Assembly. At that time there were also some laity who voted against. People were not yet informed and knowledgeable concerning this question. But at the '58 Assembly you could no longer find any laypeople who were against ordination because then the debate had started among them. And the Assembly had been called together expressly to solve this question.

Q. What did you think when you opened the paper and read *The 17 Points*?

As I said, I was editor then, I knew the time had come to fight. But it was almost too easy. The press was on my side. Everything I wrote about this was picked up in editorials of the big papers.

I hold Bo Giertz responsible. The threads lead back to him. At a private lunch I said to him: You must understand that it is thanks to the Bible that we too have reached our position. We also get our arguments from the Bible. We too are speaking *for* the Bible, *not* against it. At the moment we were so near an agreement. He said: If only I could see it your way that would be wonderful, but I can't. Then he added. There are so many who expect something different from me.

I will not try to sidetrack, but the following had to do with what happened during that period. At the Central Council we had developed a program in social ethics that we carried in *Vår Kyrka*. It was a very exciting program with about 2,000 study circles all over the country which dealt with social ethics from a Christian point of view.[4] We were on our way to building up a consciousness for ethical problems in our society. There was great enthusiasm and lots of people of all kinds were involved. Bo Giertz was the chairman.

Then came this question of ordination of women. It killed this initiative and every other new program. Suspicion of motives crept in.[5] Take, for instance, the church and state issue. We had just begun to form a new awareness of membership in the church. Had we succeeded, our Folk-Church would have looked very different today.[6] But that went by the board, and now it is too late. I have been very positive toward our special kind of Folk-Church, but now I have changed my mind. We should no longer have an established church in this country. That good old idea should be flushed down the drain. And it will be. It is only a question of time. The last proposition which warranted full support by the state to this church in its present condition makes our church the most established church since the days of Constantine. That just cannot be.

But we could have had a free Folk-Church were it not for this issue that pushed aside all other important questions.

Q. Margit Sahlin worked also at the Central Council as your colleague. She was highly merited, but she said she had a hard time. Do you consider what happened to her as typical of what happens to women priests collaborating with men?

Margit Sahlin's book published in the early fifties, *Man and Woman in the Church of Christ*, advocated a kind of theology of complementarity.[7] She was not for women priests at that time. What she wanted was not an ordinary ministry, but a special office for women. We did not like that. But that has nothing to do with her being a woman.

Q. What was done to help and support the newly ordained women priests?

This is kind of ironic, because in fact there was a power struggle about who would care for the new women priests. Margit Sahlin said: It is I; I am the mother hen. Under my wings they should gather. But knowing Margit's iron will, few of them were willing to creep in under those wings.

When I was bishop, I tried to do something for the women who studied for the priesthood, because they really had a hard time when they went to Uppsala for their practical course. They had studied theology down here in Stockholm and now they had only this one required semester left which had to be done in Uppsala.[8] There they met male theologians who ridiculed them, questioned their call, and so on. When they came to our home, they told me all about this. I tried to give them arguments and encourage them to fight back.

In the beginning they also had a hard time here in Stockholm. My predecessor, Helge Ljungberg, who—although he was not in principle against the ordination of women—was in practice not much for it either and he dug in his heels—until the very end of his term, when he suddenly began to ordain whoever came along, for example, seventy-year-old women, and so forth. That was strategically not very good, because it gave women priests a bad reputation of being peculiar.

Q. What kind of influence does the Bishops' Council have?

Very little. The Council of Bishops has on its agenda items that are referred to it, and these rule the course of the meetings because they must get an answer. But in my opinion the members of the Council were solo players with no team spirit. During coffee breaks the conversation turned again and again to the higher taxes imposed on the official parsonages the ministers occupy and if they would be able to afford them in the long run. Nobody invited the others to share his feelings of anxiety and uncertainty for the future of the church. There were never any books discussed or recommended for reading, and never, as far as I can remember, was an expert invited as guest speaker.

Bishop Brattgård sometimes reported from the Lutheran World Federation and its ecumenical work, and that stirred up some theological comments, but it seemed as if they thought that this was Brattgård's turf. It happened now and then that someone said: We must say a word, but, in fact, the last time they did so was when they issued the so-called Bishops' letter on the question of sexual mores.[9] They got the press so against them, that it scared them to silence. And I always advocated that line: Why must we say something? If we do, we will probably be proven wrong, since we are not informed enough. A much better line to take was the one we took regarding homosexuality. The question came up, and we asked an expert on Christian ethics, Holsten Fagerberg in Uppsala, to write on it. His little book initiated debate.[10] We could refer questions to that book. That seemed to me the right way to tackle the problem. The Bishops' Council has no political power. It is not a decision-making body.

Q. How important is the opinion of the Parish Councils?

In the parish, cooperation between the priests and the Parish Council is crucial. The Council has the responsibility for the finances; a minister cannot begin any activity without the consent of the Council. With our program in social ethics we had especially wanted to recruit Council members, and they were terribly interested. These people are politicians who do not make it in the general elections; they are so to say the B-team that is set to govern the church. If a priest is able to cooperate well with them, then any program can be accepted. This means that through the Council the minister has contact with the leaders in the community. Thus, for instance, if the parish is in the country and most parishioners are farmers, then the leaders probably belong to the Center party—the former Farmer's party—which has the majority in that community; or if the parish is in a suburb where there is a Social Democratic majority, then the church gets access to their leaders; or in the inner Stockholm where the majority belongs to the Moderates (formerly the right, *Högern*), then the moderate leaders dominate the Parish Council. The minister gets this contact for free, that is without extra effort on his/her part. A program could easily be sold to these community leaders if the priests took this opportunity seriously. This they, in my opinion, do not do, because they are not prepared for that kind of collaboration. Often they make up a program all by themselves and present it to the Council who then says: What is that? We have no budget for this. Therefore, for instance, since the Parish Councils are very interested in buildings, each municipality has the bigger, more beautiful church than the next. There they want the best. But when it comes to adding a deaconess to the parish, they balk. If the social ethics program had continued, this would not have been the case.

Q. What has happened with the deaconesses in relation to the women priests?

The majority of the Ersta deaconesses here in Stockholm, for instance, are against women priests. That is a legacy from their former director, Sven Åke Rosenberg, a High Church man. His successor was a good, careful administrator but did not understand how important this question was. He gave no theological leadership. The church has four expensive institutions for the training of deaconesses: Ersta, Bräckö, Vårsta and Samariterhemmet in Uppsala. And then there is Stora Sköndal for deacons.[11]
For many years they had the hardest time recruiting young people. There were years when only two or three began their training, but now I think they get about eight or ten though they are of a different type than they used to be. They are older, often married women who want to get a meaningful job. I think the economic situation has a great deal to do with this.
The parishes would prefer to get a woman priest rather than a deaconess, because a priest is paid for by the state, while the parish must shoulder the expense of a deaconess.
We have got a parallel phenomenon in these "parish secretaries" that were a countermove to ordaining women during the fifties. They have longer training and lower salaries, and there are now no positions available to them. Crazy. Women were fooled to go into that line. It still exists. They are trained in Sigtuna.[12]

Q. What about the situation now, and how do you look to the future of the church?

It is true that this question for or against women priests has paralyzed our work, and that must come to an end. The discussions among theologians and the theological conversations among people must start up again. And now the grip is not so tight any more. My conviction is that peace could be brought about if the leaders of the church declared, loud and clear, that after a certain date no other persons would be ordained than those who collaborate with women priests. After all, the Bishops' Council has published a decree that "according to the confession and order of the Church of Sweden, the priest-hood is open to women."[13] It was signed by all the bishops except Gärtner in Göteborg. This must be respected. Those who don't think so are those who deviate from the confession of the Church of Sweden. If they don't respect the order of the Church of Sweden, they ought to join some other church or form their own.

I say this, because the great differences within Christianity today are not those between denominations; today differences cut right through denomina-tional lines. Instead, they go between the fundamentalists and the rest. By the way, that is true also in Judaism and Islam. The Church of Sweden cannot be fundamentalistic. Sure we can live with those who oppose women priests. But if they say that they cannot stand before an altar together with a woman priest, that we cannot have. They have in the past and do today stand before the altar together with me, for instance, whom they consider the worst of heretics. If they can do that but cannot do the same together with a woman, that shows it for what it is: pure sex discrimination.

OLOV HARTMAN

Half an hour's drive (twenty miles) north of Stockholm in the Mälar Valley lies Sigtuna, which a thousand years ago was the Christian stronghold against the heathen Uppsala. Now a small idyllic dreaming town with winding streets edged by eighteenth-century houses beautifully preserved, a tiny city hall, lovely gardens, old ruins of churches in contrast to the Gothic Maria Church with its thin steeple juxtaposing the expansive view over the lake, Sigtuna, long a refuge for artists, is today a place where the rich get away from the hubbub of the city to house themselves in peace and beauty.

Up the hill, hidden by stately firs and pines, lies Sigtunastiftelsen, a pioneer-ing Evangelical academy founded in 1917 by a powerful soul, Manfred Björkquist; at that time he became its first director. He left Sigtuna for a short interlude of twelve years to be the first bishop of the diocese of Stockholm—short, because Björkquist was born in 1884 and has just celebrated his one hundredth birthday. Sigtuna has been his home since 1913. The very interest-ing fact that he who was a layman nevertheless became the one who was elected to the post of bishop when Stockholm finally became an independent diocese in 1942 shows that in the 1940s the church was not adverse to bold innovations. When Björkquist retired, he returned to Sigtuna to keep an eye on the dream he had built into brick and mortar in the era of national romanticism. The building looks like a cloister. "Stiftelsen"—as it was called—was intended to stimulate contacts between church and society, to be a place where people could withdraw from the world for rest, study, and contemplation. To that end, it houses a chapel where daily prayers are held.

There is a good library and the finest archive of newpaper clippings in the country. People may walk in the "cloister quadrangle," read in their "cells," meet for meals in "the refectory" and gather at night for dialogue, if they so choose. In other words, Sigtunastiftelsen is a retreat house of unusual proportions—a creation of the Folk-Church leaders who around the turn of the century enthusiastically called the movement "The Young Church." In 1948, when Olov Hartman became its director it was no longer a vision but a monument.

For twenty-two years Hartman was its director, and he poured new life into this complex. He was a lively conference leader, a counselor and confessor to many, an excellent preacher, a dramatist and poet, the author of more than thirty books, four of which contain his autobiography, and many of which are translated into other languages.[1] He also had wide contacts outside the country.

He was one of God's grandchildren. His parents were officers in the Salvation Army. Hartman too began working for the Salvation Army but soon went to study in Uppsala. He was ordained in 1932 and for sixteen years served in the Växjö diocese where he was immediately attracted by the "Old Church" piety and tradition. This contrasted wonderfully with the liberal theology he had studied in Uppsala. Hartman is not easily pegged, because he was a Christian who read his Bible and changed his mind. He gladly involved himself in the High Church liturgical movement. He absorbed and transformed whatever he encountered into a personal vision. His contribution to Swedish cultural life is of no small measure. His wholehearted input for the future of the church was attested by the many and highly diverse people who flocked around him. He was once given a church that could be dismounted and transported wherever he wanted to have it put up for the experimental church services and masses he wrote. The drama that was performed at the Fourth Assembly of the World Council of Churches in Uppsala in 1968 was written by him.

When I went to interview him on 18 January 1982 I had to search for his home among the crisscrossing streets in a newly built part of Sigtuna where one-family ranch houses snuggled up against each other. Neat, economically designed, they seemed to keep each other warm.

His wife Ingrid opened the door to the narrow hallway. While I removed coat and boots, she told me about Olov's severe respiratory ailment. Then she brought me quickly into the spacious living room lined from floor to ceiling with tightly packed bookcases. There on the sofa sat Olov, now seventy-five years old, his face puffy and his breathing irregular. Yet his eyes shone with kindness, and soon he seemed to have forgotten his troubles. We talked for half an hour and then had lunch with Ingrid. When we said goodbye, I think he knew it was for the last time. Three months later he was dead.

Q. When you were on the Royal Commission to prepare a statement on
whether or not women should be ordained in the Church of Sweden, you
joined the minority who stated that the time was not yet ripe for such a
drastic step. You even wrote the exegetical motivation for the minority's
stance. How did that come about?

The exegetical motivation for the majority's decision that there were no
biblical hindrances for the ordination of women had been written by Erik
Sjöberg, an expert in exegesis. But we all knew from the outset what Erik
thought. We thought there should also be room for a second opinion. We
asked for it, but since that wish was not granted, I thought I had better load
my own cannon. I read, and I sent for more material, and I asked advice of
Anton Fridrichsen. Thus, the minority's exegetical opinion came into being,
and it is included in the statement of the Commission.[2]

Q. There you argue for the polarity of the sexes. Men and women are not
meant to be the same; they should complement each other. How did you
think that would work out in practice?

We thought that a special ministry for women had to be created. It was also
my idea that the polarity should be illustrated liturgically with women
participating in the liturgy. I thought of something along the line of the
Anglican deaconesses. These deaconesses should also have special theological
training.[3]

Q. What happened to this suggestion?

Nothing. Nothing at all. It disappeared. In the debate there was not a single
person who picked it up. I was alone and nobody understood my idea. I am a
person who likes to debate. I knew there were other trends in exegesis than
those Sjöberg had advocated. I knew that the complementary idea was
biblical, but this view disappeared.

Q. When did you yourself change your mind?

At the end of the fifties when the new international exegesis of the Bible
began to have its impact on me. But permit me to go back in time. When I
studied in Uppsala, the so-called liberal theology was prevalent. The liberal
view of the church was identical with the view of the free churches. That was
difficult for us within the Church of Sweden. Then in 1932 came Linton's *Das
Problem der Urkirche.*[4] We could get rid of the liberal yoke but instead we
almost got into the fundamentalist fold. I did not notice it. I had almost a

personal awe of the apostle Paul. In that situation both Bo Giertz and I, with our roots in the Old Church tradition, proclaimed a wedding between biblical revelation and the order of grace. When we began to sing the hours in the church, then the people in Småland said: That is how my mother used to sing. They had a feel that reached back before the time of Pietism. It was this combination of a High Church liturgical trend and the old biblical piety that brought us close to fundamentalism. What changed my outlook was the new exegesis in the fifties that made it clear that the authors of the New Testament never had meant to write a catechism. How did I get this idea? Slowly I began to see that there are different visions in the Bible, and that they live side by side. Earlier I had never wanted to speak against St. Paul. Now I saw that he speaks against himself.

The author Kerstin Anér opened my eyes to how close I had come to fundamentalism.[5]

Q. How important are the stories of creation? How normative are they for the man-woman relationship?

How one works with myths is always delicate. Jung's depth psychology and Neumann's *Die grosse Mutter* can still teach us much. I would not say "normative"; I would use the word "inspired." The polarity that has been so important for me is revealed in the stories of creation. I am influenced by Chesterton. The world is not boring and not one-dimensional. That which is different and odd and that which shapes the contrast must be preserved.[6]

Q. Is this now lost and gone?

No, but almost. Not because we have women priests—some of them are brilliant—but because the church—due to the influence of the state—is getting a new type of priesthood, a civil servant, a full-timer who is supposed to do everything in the parish between nine and five. In many places there is a fine collaboration between men and women priests. In practice what I wished for is now happening. Back then in the early fifties we feared otherwise. A woman I knew converted to Catholicism because she believed the church would get a type of manly woman priest. And it is true that when something new appears, it attracts all kinds of persons. Some neurotic people are immediately drawn to it. So we have some of that type, but they are few.

I have many other examples. For instance, one woman priest I know has married the pastor of the Mission Covenant Church in her town. They have a wonderful home and work situation. The motherly polarity to the fatherly priesthood is an asset. The great mistake in today's priesthood is that the priest comes first and then comes nothing and only then comes the laity.

Q. You are consistently positive in your appreciation of women. Why do you always mention only the positive passages in the biblical texts and never those which are negative toward women?

Because I have never noticed it. I have one theologian in this house you should not forget, and that is Ingrid. We two have had a lifelong debate about these things. We read the Bible every night together. She has not noticed it either. What has been a very important experience for me personally is how the virgin Mary enters the scene. An almost shocking experience. One day there she was. I cannot pull her from my heart. I have got a Mariological filter. I see her everywhere, typologically foreboded. But when the Bible wants to be positive, it can be diabolic. For instance, when it is said in the Song of Deborah: "Blessed are you among women" and then continues to tell the terrible story of Jael and Sisera (Judges 5), the tradition has gone awry.

But I don't think there are a lot of negative things, Maybe I have suppressed them. You must remember that my mother preached as much as my father. The times were different. Then even liberal leaders often ran their own store in a patriarchal fashion with absolute power. That was the pattern. That was the way to success.

Q. If you were to write today about the relation between society and the church, what would you write?

In everything I write you find a connection. The church, as I see it, is meant to be a model for society. Therefore, the church should not imitate society. It should work with equality and polarity both. I have had the freedom to work out this pattern liturgically in my experimental church. I have not yet written a mass that does not work with the ideas you find in my "motivation" written for the minority report. The polarity model is both more catholic and more evangelical. And more natural. We have experimented with this for such a long time. First I worked for ten years together with artists and architects. Then we had to call on the help of writers and all kinds of people. It became a teamwork that was truly ecumenical. For example, Gunnel Vallquist and Arne Rask were two Catholics who helped me a lot. We crisscrossed the traditions and crossed the lines between priests and laity. We wanted to portray society as it is today and put it before the altar. We introduced free prayer, conversations, discussions in the middle of our services. What happened in these discussions, however, was that the world became so black, so full of sin and guilt. Suddenly I understood what the priest was there for, why the priest's role was vital. There must be someone to pronounce the forgiveness of sin. Someone must give out the gospel, let it be said. The gospel is so bold that not many understand it. A wonderful novel by Graham Greene illustrates what I mean. There you have the poor priest in *The Power and the Glory* who—though he endangers himself and others—must give communion.

Q. What do you see as the most hopeful sign for the church in the future?

The new people she attracts. But I feel we are in a crisis. The people who are most serious—and those we need the most—are on the side of *The 17 Points*. Their courage is paralyzed. The drain on the church is terrible. If the church does not manage this crisis, then it suffers a moral defeat. It is unfortunate that the question of ordination which deals with the relationship between men and women has dominated the discussion for so long, because it stirs up such an unreasonable hatred. A man can die from misogyny. And the reverse: women can come to hate men passionately. The new people are bewildered to encounter hatred in the church.

MARGIT SAHLIN

Margit Sahlin looks like a benign owl with her white tufty hair, her head tilted forward, the big goggles on a sharp nose and a mild, reluctant smile. She was interviewed on 27 January 1982. She brought me into a large first-floor apartment's tastefully furnished living room with French windows overlooking a park in the fashionable Östermalm part of Stockholm. The apartment has been converted into a place where small, as well as large, groups of people can meet for teas and suppers. The basement is redone into a brick-walled beautiful chapel and a lecture hall. As we look around, Sahlin can say proudly: This, with the help of God, is my creation. This is finally the city home of St. Katharinastiftelsen, the third incarnation of a vision that Margit Sahlin has kept alive for more than thirty years.

In a way, one could say that this is a younger sister of the Sigtunastiftelsen. Just as the aim of that institution was and is to bring the Swedish church and the Swedish cultural elite closer to each other in dialogue, so it is the goal of Katharinastiftelsen to bring in the intellectual personalities of Sweden today and to pump them on their views and beliefs and have them confront the Christian message. Just as Manfred Björkquist went out fundraising for his vision that became the Sigtunastiftelsen, so Sahlin raised every penny for Katharina. Its first incarnation was hosted in an aristocratic mansion far out in the country, situated in a diocese that was more or less hostile to women as leaders in the church. Sahlin, who at that time was not ordained, had little support from the surrounding neighborhood. Since her dream was larger than merely running a guest house with a Christian accent, she collected enough money to build a Katharina in the Stockholm diocese. Her hopes were that women would come—especially those who were leaders in the women's movement—and that Katharina would build bridges between them and the church. This second incarnation was situated north of Stockholm in the archipelago, a lovely place and a pleasing sight with the chapel at its center, shimmering in colors reflected from the stained glass windows. It was here that Margit Sahlin was ordained. Here she conducted innumerable courses, some of which were particularly aimed at women and their problems in contemporary life.

In 1970 Sahlin became the first woman rector of a large inner-city church where she served until her retirement in 1979. Then the Katharina house was resurrected in its third cast. The stained glass windows have been moved and are now glowing from the indirect lighting in the basement's chapel entrance.

Sahlin is the most visible of all the women priests. She is often referred to as the first ordained woman, although she was one of three who were ordained on Palm Sunday of 1960. But Sahlin was at that time already well known as a lecturer and preacher. The work she had done at Katharina house was widely recognized and admired. Born in 1914 into a family devoted to education, she obtained her Ph.D. in 1940. From 1950 to 1970 she was the director of Katharina foundation. She has written widely; three of her books concern the problems of women in the church and specifically the question of ordination. Due to her visible position, she has not only attracted admiration but has stirred up a great deal of conflict, suspicion, and intrigue. (See above, p. 15.) The interview was not free flowing, because time and again she asked that something be "off the record." She has many stories to tell about what may seem to be petty deeds of persecution where she has been the target.

Q. Would you tell something that you remember from your ordination?

I remember that I was immensely happy. A step had now been taken by the church that just had to be taken, and I was chosen to carry out that call. That certainly was liberating. It gave room for something that I had worked intensely toward—something that was bigger than my personal call.

Q. Do you, however, remember something personal from that time?

The ordination took place at Katharina in its small chapel. Naturally it was a tense time. But since Katharina then was situated in the country and its chapel could not hold many people, this service was warm and intimate. A religious service throughout. The crowds were not there, nor were the television cameras. They were in the cathedrals of Stockholm and Härnösand.

Q. You have been in the service of the church almost your whole working life. How and when did you decide that this was to be your way?

Don't forget that I changed careers completely. I had my doctorate in romance languages and literature. I worked many years toward that goal. But I was very much aware of the situation in the women's world. Women of influence, of education and drive, were almost all strangers in the church. They and the church were on a collision course. They got the message that the church was not interested in collaboration with women like them. The conference that this group of women arranged in 1945 after the war, *Planning for a New World,* did not list a single contribution from the church. It was not counted on. I had thought a lot about that fact. Already in 1938 I had been asked by Manfred Björkquist to write an essay about "A New Ministry for Women in the Church"; it was then published in *Vår Lösen.*[1] The church was unable to tap resources that were at its disposal. For instance, what could I do?

When I met the director for the City Mission, J. W. Johnsson, in the summer of 1943 and he promised me a position in the City Mission if I should go ahead and study theology, his encouragement meant an awful lot to me.[2] My bicycle flew up the hills of Dalekarlia—so happy was I after our conversation. That same summer I also met Professor Anton Fridrichsen, the New Testament exegete in Uppsala.[3] He too encouraged me to go ahead. I decided to begin a new career. I went to Uppsala and got a B.D. Then I returned to Stockholm and got a position as a counselor at the City Mission, with special intent to establish contacts with the women's movement. That was the beginning.

Q. Your first idea as developed in your book, *Man och Kvinna i Kristi Kyrka* was not the ordination to the priesthood for women but some special office as pastoral deaconesses.[4] You thought women should get another kind of ministry. When and why did you abandon that idea?

The idea was picked up from the English deaconesses. "Pastoral deaconesses" we called it. The leaders in the women's movement loathed it and thought it treason to their ideal of equality. And those on the opposing side thought it was coming too close to the priesthood. Nobody really understood what I was driving at. Nobody picked up the thought and carried it further. It died.

Especially the deaconesses were against the idea of pastoral deaconesses. They did not care for some form of "upper class" within their ranks. If they would not cooperate, it could not work.

It is true that Olov Hartman thought somewhat along these lines as well.

Unwittingly he was the one who convinced me that it would be better to seek ordination. He gave a lecture where he spoke about women in the church and defined the Eve role, the Mary role, the Martha role, and so forth. These seemed to be compromises, while ordination would be a new creation.

Q. You are the only woman who has been senior pastor and rector of a large Stockholm parish. Was it difficult for you as a woman to become "boss" for many people and other priests and to shoulder so much responsibility?

Afterwards they now say that it was a very good time in the parish because today so much that was built up then has fallen to pieces. Perhaps I had a better hand with personnel. One thing I know is that the tone in the Church Council changed during my time. First we dispensed with all titles and spoke informally without the stilted Mr. and Mrs. so and so. We began to laugh sometimes during our deliberations. This would not be considered unusual or strange at secular board meetings. A less formal style was in tune with the times. But the church had not been living in tune with the times.

The beginning was a hard time for me. Nobody welcomed me. They did not quite know what to do with a woman priest. For instance, nobody came to the sacristy to help me with the chasuble.[5] But all that quickly changed. I had one great advantage. I was used to being an organizer and a hostess. I had done it hundreds of times at conferences at Katharina. It was easy for me to preside at meals and to introduce people, to get people feeling at ease together in a more open milieu.

Q. You wrote *Man and Woman in the Church of Christ* in 1950 and *Time for Reappraisal* in 1980.[6] What is the decisive difference between these two books? Where, if at all in the later book, do you draw on your own experience?

There is not much difference between the two. When I wrote the later one, I knew who my opponents were and tried to present and address their arguments. My experience during these thirty years is precisely that this form of dialogue can be very useful. Dialogue is used in all our work here at Katharina. But, of course, on this question of the ordination of women I could not be absolutely objective, not letting my preference show.

Q. In retrospect, how important do you think *The 17 Points* were? Did they really make a difference?

I think they played an enormously important role. They told not only the priests but also all others employed by the church what to do. So, for instance, an organist can refuse to play when a woman priest officiates. This happened recently in Borås. *The 17 Points* released a hatred which otherwise might have been diffused. Now it was channeled into acts.

Q. Have you directed your work mostly toward women or toward men?

Toward both, in like measure, I think. We are anxious to see both men and women come to Katharina. Sometimes men prefer to speak to a woman and have a woman confessor, and vice versa. It is very individual how they feel about it. What has been difficult in my work is the lack of a team spirit among the women priests. We have had little opportunity to pool our experiences.

Q. How do you visualize the church of the future? How will the role of the priest change?

The world is so hungry for spirituality. All around us are people who are seeking and searching. In Stockholm we have all sorts of sects and cults. People are willing to try everything except the church. There is New Age, Hare Krishna, Zen, and other Buddhist movements. We invite these people to Katharina for dialogue. We have a kind of motto to go "radically inward and radically outward." Our program is firmly anchored in the Christian faith.[7] We practice prayer and Bible study. We have our services in the chapel; this is our center. Then we invite people from these groups to talk to us, and we try to understand their point of view. Is there something in it that could enrich our faith, and have we something that speaks to them? I think it is important that the church reaches people who are seeking a way for themselves in all these new ideologies but who never learn anything about the church. Otherwise they do not even begin to consider the church. They have so many prejudices about it as being moralistic and judging them. Modern people also often associate the church with a strange world view that locates God up in the sky, etc.

The Catholics have an easier time of it. In other countries a great many scientists are Catholic, while here it is almost doctrine that science and religion are mutually exclusive. We are about to have a program here called Modern Physics—Classical Mysticism. That program will discuss the new scientific world view that has arisen during the last decades.

Nowadays people do not come to church since preaching is at an all time low. It does not add to people's thinking nor stretch their imagination. The fault lies in the pitiful training of ministers. It is a catastrophe. The new priests are in no way prepared to lead people into Christian thinking. Many times they (the priests) are even unfamiliar with our own Christian heritage. They are without answers. That is what we at Katharina try to supply.

A change of priest role will come about with more experience. So far there is still much insecurity abroad. But experience will by necessity change the role.

ELISABETH OLANDER

A majority of Swedish ministers live in the old parsonages. In the country these are often large farmhouses, sometimes centuries old, and in the city they are huge bourgeois apartments. During my three weeks in Sweden in the summer of 1982, I stayed in one of these stately apartments with twelve-foot ceilings tastefully decorated in stucco. Four elegant rooms made a total length of fifty yards. A grand piano was easily tucked into a corner. There were two big bedrooms, a kitchen, a butler's pantry, and a spacious entrance hall with an open fireplace that served as a family room. It was the home of an associate minister in the Kungsholm parish who had generously lent it to me while he and the family were on vacation.

It was here that, in the blue dusk of a Swedish August night, I interviewed a then associate minister in one of the suburbs of Stockholm. Elisabeth Djurle-Olander, a softspoken, thoughtful woman, was also one of the first three women to be ordained in Sweden, but her career had had very different turns from that of Margit Sahlin.[1]

Q. From where did you get the idea of becoming a priest?

I grew up in a milieu where the church was a natural ingredient. Although my parents were not especially engaged in the life of the church, it was part of our life. As a teenager I brooded and had a vague foreboding.

I pondered the notion of salvation, and I was in a group that read and discussed the books by Bo Giertz. We went together to visit him at Torpa, and once I went there alone. It meant a lot to me, but I had planned to become a pharmacist.

Then one summer I took part in the hiking trips that *Frivilligkåren* ("the Volunteer Corps") from Lund did in our corner of the country. Young students organized these trips where they spoke and sang in the churches and visited with the priests and the people. They asked me to preach. I had never before opened my mouth in public. I was scared and shy. Nevertheless, the following summer I repeated it, and I felt that this was for me. I shelved the plans to become a pharmacist and went to Lund to study theology.

Q. You had to supplement your baccalaureate exam a great deal to make up for your pre-med concentration in high school. How did that feel?

Yes. I had none of the classical languages. I had to begin with Latin, Greek, and Hebrew before I could start in theology. Hard for me, especially since I was unsure of what I was doing and whether I could do it at all. And as soon as I began New Testament exegesis courses for Professor Hugo Odeberg, the boys in the class started asking me questions.[2] Another woman and I were the only ones among the men, and they asked me precisely what I asked myself: Is this right? Because for me those years of study were most of all a personal test. From 1952 to 1958 I worked the question over and over. Then came the decision of the Church Assembly in 1958 as an answer. It was the right time for me. I began the practical course. They asked me with fear and trembling all the time: You are not going to become a priest, are you? But by then I knew.

Q. Why were you three women not ordained together?

Strategically Archbishop Hultgren planned it very well. He personally asked Ingrid Persson of Samariterhemmet to take the practical course so that we would be three instead of two ordained at the same time, but not at the same place. Ingrid in Härnösand, Margit at Katharina, and I in Stockholm.

Q. Why did you choose Stockholm?

Because I knew that I was not welcome in my home diocese, Växjö. Bishop Malmeström did not approve. Neither did Bishop Bolander in Lund. He had given me permission (venia) to preach once but not to go before the altar.[3] But I had sisters and brothers living in Stockholm and there Bishop Ljungberg was positive toward my coming.

Q. Where have you served since?

Mostly in the suburbs. First in Nacka, in Vällingby, and in Spånga. It was Bishop Ljungberg's policy not to place women in a parish where there was any opposition. So wherever I went I was welcome and had good and helpful colleagues.

Q. When you began to have more women colleagues, did you then get together with them?

Not in the beginning. I think Margit Sahlin was disappointed with me that I did not come to her. She called many times and wanted me to come out to Katharina. But the service in the parish tied me down. And Margit has such authority. I think she resented the fact that I did not rally. And I am sorry that I did not, because we could have had a fine time together. But really, where I was, I had no problems; I got a lot of response from people. In my parishes there was such good will. Margit probably became the target for the ill will of the opposition. We women priests have only now begun to meet together, and only now do I understand why it is urgent.

Q. Did you have a model for your priesthood?

Ludvig Jönsson supported me and meant a lot to me.[4] I often went to hear him preach and wanted to preach as he did. But there were also many others of my colleagues. One who belonged to an ecumenical brotherhood told me after each meeting about everything they had discussed. But, of course, since it was a brotherhood, I could not go with him to the meetings. On the whole, though, I got a fine start, and people came to me with everything.

Q. You were not married those first years. After you got married and had children, how did the dual career work?

Now the thoughts of the family are always present in the back of my mind. At first when the children were small, I took a leave. We have three children: a girl and twin boys. One of them is as normal as can be, but the other is mongoloid and demands of lot of care. When the twins were six years old, I went back to work two-thirds or three-fourths time. Now I work half-time. My husband, who is an engineer, has to leave for work very early every morning. Two children go to school and one to day-care. This last one has to be picked up at four in the afternoon. I like to be home when the children arrive from school. I work at night and of course on weekends. My husband takes over when he comes home. His free time is eaten up this way—and mine too—and I experience the conflict. Both he and I are tired. But home and family have also given us a lot. I preach better now. I am a better counselor. On the whole I function better.

At the same time I'm glad that I had that time when I was single and could observe others. I have colleagues now who do not have families. It is important that I do not transfer my duties to them. It could happen so easily.

To have half-time work, however, has its problems. We half-timers are not quite counted on as being in the same league as the full-timers. Our work is difficult to evaluate when we seek other positions. When areas of responsibility are distributed in the parish, I am not given tasks such as taking charge of the confirmands or the work among the elderly. I now work with families and with children.

Q. How do you evaluate the economic security of your profession?

The safety net is quite sturdy. From time to time when lists of jobs that give a reliable income, a good pension, and so forth, are published, the clergy is always among those with high rating. We get priests who probably are attracted by that factor. Some people change their profession, take a few courses, and get dispensation to be ordained. Both men and women may arrive at the priesthood with motives that perhaps are not always thought through.

Q. Do people come to your church on their own initiative?

We must work very hard. In the parish where I am now there has not been continuity. The priests who have come are gone within a few years. Therefore we do not have a solid youth program and consequently no fresh growth. But it has been good for the church to discover that it has to work. As no other profession, the priesthood has been shielded from thinking about itself as "in the world." It has had no competition. Now we do have it, and there has been a decline in attendance.

Q. How much has the opposition to women priests had to do with the decline?

This is difficult to say. In fairness it should be admitted that the opponents are dedicated to the church and work ardently in their parishes. There is so much practical work and so little time for discussions both among the priests and with parishioners. For instance, we had recently this very important Church Assembly meeting where the future relationship between church and state was decided, but we had not discussed the issues beforehand in our suburb or even among us clergy.[5] Now with the women priests meeting each other I can share my anxiety for the future with some women colleagues.

Q. Don't you meet to plan your work in the parish?

Yes, we meet every Thursday morning when we have Morning Prayer and then plan the week's work over a cup of coffee. Also, once a year we spend two days out at Graninge, the retreat center of the Stockholm diocese. One day together with the Church Council and one day for ourselves. It is lovely to have that retreat together, but it is not easy to arrange. Some might have funeral services that day, or some other engagement. We study the Bible, or we discuss a book. We discussed Martin Lönnebo's *The Return of Christianity (Kristendomens återkomst).*[6] I like very much what he writes. But then again I become uncertain. Bishop Lönnebo has said that he welcomes also the opponents in his diocese. He has expressed himself to be against abortion. It is difficult to judge from such pronouncements what view he has of women. He should come clear. In my opinion there are only two bishops now who are clear-cut pro on this issue, the bishop of Lund and the bishop of Stockholm. The rest are opaque. People have ceased to talk about the ordination of women. Instead the prevalent issue is said to be the church's "slavery" under the state, but I do not believe that the ordination issue is dead.

Q. You said that you belong to an informal group of women priests. Have you ever thought of including women from other professions?

Perhaps we should, but for the present we must meet each other. There is a psychological warfare going on, a shadow that grows and darkens our work. Nothing in the practical course at the university prepares the young women for this, and they must know where to turn when they encounter it.

Q. What do you see as a solution to the present dilemma?

I wonder if it really would be so dangerous if the church split up. I also think we must roll away the safety net. The present situation is unsound. If the church splits, then perhaps we could begin to work without being suspicious of each other. The opponents now do not come out in the open, but there are tendencies to create "pure" churches, i.e., churches without women priests. At elections they are organized. They vote alike and thus their candidates win. There are now about 50 percent of the clergy against women priests and more are coming. Both in Uppsala and Lund there are student houses like St. Laurentiusstiftelsen in Lund and St. Ansgar in Uppsala. These are highly influenced by the High Church movement which is against ordination of women. Without noticing it the students who live there become biased and soon begin to think that the Bible is only on one side.[7] They have excellent speakers. For instance, Gustaf-Adolf Danell and Bertil Gärtner (see above) have been chaplains at Laurentiusstiftelsen. When these students become clergy, they are of one mold. Their friendships from student days develop into a network to protect the church and keep her "pure." Therefore women are "forgotten" when it comes to call together a conference, or to get speakers, or to select people for highly influential posts like those on the Central Council of the national church, or in elections for positions at certain city churches.

When I talk with priests of this persuasion, they are often very charming and yet authoritative in their pronouncements. They make me feel as if I lived in a fantasy world, something I have made up by myself. What they hope to achieve with their policy is that women as priests will eventually fall away, disappear from the horizon, drop out.

This will not end if we do not make a clean break of it.

Q. How do people in general look upon the question of equality?

People in general do not understand what we clergy are talking about. They have a much easier time because for them equality is self-evident. Without reflection they are closer to the gospel. When I became ordained I had many reasons for becoming a priest. Equality was then the law of the land. But now I know it is also the gospel.

ELSE ORSTADIUS

The third woman ordained on that memorable Palm Sunday of 1960 was a deaconess, Ingrid Persson. She had come from the north of Sweden, and she returned to Härnösand to be ordained in that diocese. She has been retired since 1979. I chose to interview another former deaconess, Else Orstadius, an associate pastor in an Uppsala parish. She was interviewed at her home on 13 August 1982. Since 1983 she is on leave from her parish to direct the retreat center at the Sigtuna Foundation.

I found her house at the edge of a forest, beautifully placed in a landscape with mossy rocks and high pines right up to the walls structuring the steps and windows so that indoors and outdoors complemented each other. This house was built in 1975 by Else and the builder, Anders Diös, in close cooperation to make it an inviting place to congregate for church groups of all kinds and ages, including easy access for the handicapped. Although the house functions as a parsonage, she owns it. The last five years Else has been married to a teacher who is also an organist in the church. The atmosphere of their house is filled with light and music. The day I arrived, Else stood outside picking blueberries while she waited for me.

Q. Before you were ordained, you were a deaconess with Samariterhemmet in Uppsala as your mother house. Were there any complications in the transfer?

Yes. As you perhaps know, there is a considerable number of deaconesses who do not approve of women priests. These were my friends. For many years we had lived together in the shared life that is characteristic for the community of deaconesses. Ingrid Persson was the Rector of Studies at Samariterhemmet.[1] She already had a B.D. degree when she was asked in 1959 by Archbishop Hultgren to take the practical course in order to be ordained. I think it was a shock for her, as it was later for me, to be asked to return the cross we had received at our deaconess ordination, and thus to realize that we were no longer *personae gratae*. I was no longer one of them. The sisterhood was considered broken.

The situation at Samariterhemmet has not yet changed. However, at Ersta in Stockholm, where my former colleague in this parish, Bengt Wadensjö, is now the director, there are indications that something is stirring. They have, for instance, hired a woman priest as hospital chaplain.

Q. Would you tell me about some significant things from your personal history? For example, your call to the ministry?

Even as a teenager I knew I wanted to work full-time for the church. I felt funny about it, as if somehow I had gotten the wrong chromosomes. Had I been a boy, there would have been no question about my future. Self-evidently I could have become a priest. But since I was a girl, this was not possible.

I wanted to be a priest. Not because I come from a family with a long line of clergymen. My father was a priest on the west coast. I noticed early that his work lay heavily on him. He was often depressed. I understood the cause to be that he did not get enough stimulation out in the country. He told about a recurring nightmare in which he got stuck in a wall between the sacristy and the pulpit. Only his head got through. Nevertheless I wanted to do what he was doing. Of course I had a father fixation. He had two churches where he preached every Sunday, and I went with him to both services. The family (my mother, my four brothers and a sister) went to one service and sat there very correctly. But I was the only one who accompanied him to the second service. I sneaked into a pew that of old had been designed for the "churching of women."[2] There I hid and enjoyed myself in the house of God. Thirty years later I suddenly realized what my favorite pew had stood for and why it had always been empty. I smiled because "churched" was just what I had been since my early years.

Our family was poor, as were ministers' families in those days. None of my siblings wanted to be priests. I was the only one; I often read Ezekiel 34; this "shepherd chapter" became my favorite, and my wish was to care for the "sheep." Since the priesthood was out, I decided to be a social worker, getting my education at Samariterhemmet. There were no career counselors at the high schools in those days. So I had to do my own thinking. I wanted to care for the sick—which meant that I would have to get experience in nursing and in hospitals. I was afraid too, because it would involve eye operations. I had a phobia where eyes were concerned. Yet I went to Uppsala and Samariterhemmet—I was willing to go through with it whatever it would involve. To be ordained as a deaconess was the closest to becoming a priest.

I arrived in 1946, just at the time when Samariterhemmet opened a new line of theological studies. I got all excited. What was the purpose? I did not want to be a teacher. Some sort of "pastoral deaconesses or secretaries" had not been sufficiently worked out or thought through, although it was talked about. The director of Samariterhemmet, Samuel Palm, could not really explain to what this new line of study would lead. But I took this chance to study. My father had enough trouble in supporting his four boys. Here I could study at no expense to the family.[3]

To take one's studies seriously is more difficult when it is uncertain where they will lead. I broke off twice. In 1948 I went to Katharinastiftelsen and took a course with Margit Sahlin which I must say was just as good, if not better, than the practical course given at the university for theological students.

Two years later Sam Palm called me in and ordered me to get ready to go to the south of France as an assistant in a poor Lutheran parish in the stark, coal-mining town of Sainte-Etienne.[4] My duties were to help the old and the sick, to be responsible for Sunday school, to arrange day-care for young mothers, and generally to visit people and give all I had to give. I had two weeks to get there, and I was to stay for a year. And a long year it was. I had only my school French and no training in nursing, as had the deaconess whom Sweden had sent to this post to help immediately following the war. I felt I was a most inadequate replacement. I worked hard, but the isolation was tough to take. It turned out to be very good training for my later ten years in Africa, but I did not know that then.

In 1952 I finished my B.D. degree and right away became traveling secretary for the Swedish Women's Missionary Society. They were going to celebrate their fiftieth anniversary. I did a lot of reading and a lot of imagining of what it would be like out there on the mission field. My task was to give lectures and stimulate interest for foreign mission. Especially in the diocese of Göteborg people had high demands on the knowledge and the experience of their speakers. When they realized that I had never been a missionary myself, they asked me rather to lecture on the diaconate.

I held that post for three years, knowing that this was not it. I asked God what I should do, and there was no apparent answer. Until one day I attended a meeting of the Central Board of Mission in the Church of Sweden. That day they discussed the deteriorating situation in Tanzania and the immediate need for teachers.[5] Before the sun had set I knew that I was going to Tanzania. And there I stayed for ten years.

Now my theological training could be used in the most wonderful way. My task was to train future African ministers in the knowledge of the Bible, how to preach and conduct services. First, of course, I quickly had to learn Swahili. I taught in English but I needed Swahili in order to check whether or not they had understood. After a year, I was given the responsibility of building up a Bible school. I had one African colleague and twenty-four students. We started literally from scratch by building a school house and a chapel. I had to plan the curriculum and teach it, now in Swahili. The students themselves were already teaching other people, and I had to supervise them. They were all men, and I felt the handicap of being a woman. In particular, perhaps, because I had to instruct them in liturgics. It became of utmost importance that our new church should not have an altar rail, because in that case I could not approach the altar inside the rail. Although I was the rector of the school and had the power of decision, I was also a woman; it would be totally wrong for me to walk on holy ground. This sentiment is very strong in the African Synod and is not a feeling that Europeans have fostered. It is a sociological fact there that a woman cannot approach that corner of a home where the head of the family does his daily sacrifices and libations. It has no connection to Christianity. I was fully accepted as a teacher, but I could have nothing to do with the sacred.

Out there I had 150 miles to the nearest store, the post office or a telephone. There was not a single European around. The isolation from the West was rather complete. But I was not lonely.

Q. In that situation did you find that the Bible texts opened up in new ways? Did you see things you never thought of before?

The first thing I noticed was that the Old Testament was so much more alive and real to them. The East African Revival movement became a problem because many of them came from this fundamentalist background. They were born-again Christians. In their piety they felt sorry for me: There she stands talking about salvation without knowing what it is all about. Texts were never seen in the light of what we can do for others, but always: Please, Christ, come and take care of me! For example, in the parable of the Good Samaritan or the story of the foot washing, the admonition to "go and do likewise" was not heard by them.

Q. You translated the New Testament into Luhaya, the local language. How did you accomplish that?

Yes, when I came out for my second period in Tanzania, I started the translation. We were three who worked on it daily. When we finished a chapter, we sent it out to be "washed" by twelve other teachers who sent back their changes and suggestions which we worked over. Every quarter of the year we all got together for a week and combed the text again before I typed out the final version.

You can imagine how—with all the material I then had at my disposal—I was filled to the point of bursting. But I was not allowed to preach. Philippo who had no theological training could, however, preach as often as he wanted.

In 1965 I returned home. It was then possible for women to be ordained in Sweden. But then I had a crisis. It came about because a young American priest seriously questioned me on precisely what you asked me earlier: Did I have a call? So I postponed eventual ordination and began another avenue. I started to study psychology and go through analysis at St. Lukasstiftelsen.[6] I began to pay attention to my dreams. I dreamt wildly during that year, since it took me a year to reach some clarity about myself. But then I knew wholly and from the core of my being that I should seek ordination. Yet up to the very last moment there were people who tried to get me to refrain from taking that step.

Q. You have spoken generously of the time up to your ordination in 1967. How was it afterwards?

As the very first woman priest in the city of Uppsala, I was in a kind of vacuum. I became an embarrassment to some of my former friends who did not now know how to treat me. They looked away when we met on the street, and they did not come to church on the Sunday when it was my turn to preach. But those years were useful as a testing ground. Then I had the chance to make use of my training at Lukasstiftelsen, because I got the position of chaplain at Ulleråker, a hospital for the mentally disturbed here in Uppsala. We then had over thirteen-hundred patients there. It was a very challenging, specialized ministry that I held for five years. Just enough for me. The last year I was constantly anxious when I prepared my sermons: Can they take this text, or is it too strong a medicine? I began to long for a normal parish. So in 1974 I came out here to the suburbs.

Q. Do you have any complications here?

My only problem is the church itself, and by that I mean the actual building. We have a new church building that had not been decorated when I came. Then the artwork began to appear on the walls, and this made me physically ill. There is nothing Christian in these paintings, and what is worse, they are anti-Christian. What was first meant to be God the Father looked like a little blue gnome with his feet on a cloud. He has now been changed to what is said to be Christ sitting as a little blue gnome on a cloud. A tree, a man in a suit, and a barefooted woman with a babushka on her head are frenetically gathering supplies in what is supposed to be heaven. Around the walls are pictures from Swedish history—great events within the borders of our diocese: Erik XIV murdering the Sture brothers, Queen Christina shooting a hare on a hunt, Gustavus Vasa with his sword, etc. And behind the altar you see the biggest chunk of gold mosaic glittering. Both the altar and the baptismal font are made for giants. I cannot reconcile myself to this milieu. I almost resigned, but after having taken counsel from my brothers, I had to admit that people are the main thing, not the building. The Parish Council is responsible for the church building and its decor. Its members got themselves an art critic who certified that this was fine art, and they were thus convinced that the pastors were not competent in judging aesthetic matters. This sorry story has badly hurt our collaboration. (Cf. interview with Ström, p. 16.)

Q. If that is the bad part, what is the good part of your work?

To meet people at their homes. Every Sunday we have four or five baptisms, and I try to visit the parents beforehand. I like that the most, for this way I meet young people. Of course, I call on sick people and the families of those who have died, but it is different with those who recently have had babies. I also arrange gatherings for the parents of the confirmands. And once I took all sorts of people, from teenagers to the eighty-year-olds, with me for a visit to Taizé in France.[7] That was a great experience. But what is most wonderful is to handle the sacred. To say mass on Sundays and Wednesdays. Not very many come—about thirty people—but they are fine. I appreciate our deacons especially.

Q. What do you think of the liturgical language? Don't you find it very masculine?

We have worked with the liturgy from a feminist point of view. As a rule I say "God" and do not use "He" excessively. But when I function, I do not think about it. Sometimes in a prayer I will pray to God, our Father and Mother. Sometimes I bring up the question in my sermon. And I try to avoid the worst sexist hymns.

Q. Do you get together with other women and discuss these matters?

Yes, we do in this diocese. We did not in the beginning when we were few. We have recently used the World Council of Churches' *Study on the Community of Women and Men in the Church* which has been translated into Swedish.[8] But there is the problem of time. My own continuing education tends toward pastoral psychology. I read Jung: everything about him and his ideas. I read Lönnebo and Wingren, and I forced my dear deacons *(kyrkvärdar)* to study Küng, the German Catholic theologian, which perhaps was too much to ask for.[9] We have also made experiments with "active imagination," to project personal problems on others the way authors do it. Like Dante, or like John Bunyan.

Q. Finally, one question: Did you have someone in mind on whom you wanted to model your ministry?

No. For that reason I am glad I was not young when I was ordained. When it happened, I dared trust myself.

To begin this case study with oral history was a means of obtaining close-up pictures of some of those individuals heavily involved and to hear what they remembered and what they are now saying in hindsight. Here are honest people with strong commitments to their vocation as priests. All the priests interviewed tell how deeply the pain of the conflict over the ordination of women has affected them.

Two bishops are strongly profiled on this debate. Bishop Giertz believes that women priests represent a deviation from biblical Christianity. The church's decision to ordain women was, in his opinion, a concession to the state. It has given many people "the idea that everything in the church's teaching is relative and negotiable and that we in the church will finally have to conform to public opinion." Neither Bishop Giertz nor his successor in the Göteborg diocese can for the sake of conscience ordain women.

Bishop Ström has ordained many women. According to him the clergy was unprepared for the crisis that the ordination caused, and they were ignorant of its causes. Ström wants to root out sexism in the church and is convinced that peace could be brought about if the leaders of the church declared loud and clear that after a certain date no other persons would be ordained than those who cooperate with women priests. Love it or leave it!

Giertz and Ström stand at the opposite ends of this issue, yet both declare that the Bible has led them to their respective views. Many spectators believe this means that there are "these two kinds of faith" in the church battling each other. But that is clearly false. There is a common faith. What the interviews indicate is that there are many shades of interpretation. The interviews with the three women illustrate how long their road stretched to ordination because they in themselves had to trust the victory of the gospel over a strong tradition.

2

THE CHANGING ROLE OF
CLERGY

The place of the church and the role of the minister have undergone drastic changes during the last centuries. In order to understand the crisis over the ordination of women it is necessary to have some background knowledge of history, sociology, and theology. To illustrate how different ages have formed their ministers, this chapter offers three scenarios: the picture of a priest in the agrarian society of the eighteenth century; the life of a minister's family in the early twentieth century at the time of the growing industrial society; and finally the professional struggles of two women priests in the present days of the full-grown industrial and pluralistic Sweden. The key word is authority.

Sweden remained an agrarian society until the middle of the nineteenth century. People lived off the farm, and the society was organized in a quasi-feudal manner. The government had even at times been in the hands of an absolute king. The emerging industrial society eventually necessitated a change toward a more flexible government and a more diversified bureaucracy. The development toward a full-fledged industrial society then proceeded rapidly during the twentieth century without interruptions by wars and violent upheavals.

In the old agrarian culture most people knew and understood what other people were doing. There was little division of labor. In the new industrial culture a multitude of jobs have been created and many of them with high demand of special knowledge and competencies. In these days of professional specialization people have only vague ideas about what their neighbors are doing. Even less do they know what they are thinking and believing about life and death, good and evil, right and wrong.

In the old culture people turned to the priests with their sufferings and questions and wrestled with the church's answers. In these modern times of specialization and expertise, new experts have emerged to care for people's frustrations and sufferings. The new culture harbors a pluralism of ideas of what life is all about, of what is good and what is right. Among these waves of ideas inundating through the media it is hard for people to discern currents in the church which they commonly identify as being something of the past. And it is hard for the priests to know how best to help and advise people. Their once self-evident authority on life and death questions, on creation and eschatology, is lost. Their task is to win back the confidence of people in a fierce competition of voices. The interviews with the two women priests at the end of this chapter reveal how difficult it can be for modern priests to achieve such confidence.

A recent sociological survey of the people who are active in the Church of Sweden revealed that only 7% of the whole population are regular church attendants. Another 18% confessed to strong affinity with the church although they did not attend regularly. Forty-eight percent said that they believed in God, and 29% answered that they prayed to God at least once in a while.[1] Hence only a minority of the Swedish people is professing interest in religious matters. Yet more than 90% of the population belong to the Church of Sweden.

This paradox has its historical explanation. Two hundred years ago the Church of Sweden was the only church. The territorial parish covered the Christian congregation. All children born were baptized and registered as parishioners in the local church. God was part of reality, not something to believe or not to believe in, and the priest was God's messenger. The authority of the priests had its anchor in his close connection with God. But, furthermore, the people had reverence for his learning and respect for his status as an emissary of the government. With the rapid secularization in the twentieth century, the priests have lost their position as God's special messengers in the eyes of the people. Older people searching for religious response come to church, but younger people, families, and the majority would rather read, listen to music on the radio, putter around their country home, play golf, drive their motorboats, or go to a sports event than go to church on Sundays. The allure to all the competing activities has created intimidation. People do not speak to each other about religious matters. They do not give one another insight in their religious experiences. Religious life as shared experience in the church has become impoverished. "Christianity in Sweden seems to have fallen into a spiral of silence," writes Hans L. Zetterberg. "Thereby the process of secularization feeds on itself and spreads wider and wider."[2]

THE OLD AGRARIAN CULTURE

Life as it once was organized and established in parishes revolved around the church. The calendar's holidays were holy days which brought people to the church. There were Christmas, Good Friday, Easter, and Pentecost. Fall came with the day for thanksgiving for the harvest, and then there was All Saints' Day followed by the "small" fasting period between Advent and Christmas and the long fast in Lent before Easter. The church bells were

ringing for weddings, baptisms, and funerals. The church stood in the middle of the village, with its graveyard right around.

The Lutheran minister became above all a teacher.[3] It was his duty to preach and to educate the people about the Word and the way to salvation. A minimum requirement was that the confirmands learn Luther's *Small Catechism*. Nobody could be confirmed and considered a full member of the parish without having been instructed and knowing the catechism by heart. Confirmation became a rite of passage to adulthood.

The priest also called together house meetings where the head of each farm assembled everyone on his homestead to be examined for their knowledge of the Bible.[4] These meetings gave the priest an opportunity to get to know the problems of his parishioners and to give advice when the crop had failed, when a sickness festered, when the animals died, and so forth. He was often the only educated person in the village, the only one who had been outside the parish and had "seen the world." He knew how to dig a well, plant an orchard, use a fork and knife, and so on. The ministers were themselves farmers.

A minister had authority in the community, due not only to his administering of the holy Word and Sacraments but also due to his general knowledge of people and the ways of the world, and, of course, to his status as an arm of the government. He was the king's man. Together with the judge, the doctor, and the sheriff, he constituted the elite.

I have come to cherish the mid-eighteenth century painting of the Hjortberg family. Here is a Protestant family in its prime and pride.[5] The Reverend Hjortberg is sitting at the left in his ministerial garb, wearing the Order of Vasa that had been given to him by the king of Sweden. His hand points to the center of the painting where a drapery has been drawn aside to show a crucifix beyond which the sky opens heavenward. The sheet of paper he proudly displays is inscribed with his name and his merits in life and a reference to Isa. 8:18: "Behold, here I am and the children that the Lord has given me." Hjortberg is surrounded by his seven sons on the left side of the picture. On the right side, sitting just as proudly, is his wife surrounded by their seven daughters, one baby still in the cradle and one baby, who already had died, is pictured in her coffin. The children look like small adults and are dressed as adults in the very finest bourgeois fashion. There is a neat division of roles defined by place in the picture. Although the crucifix is the center of the painting and of their life, it also gives a clear hint of how religion seats the men on one side and the women on the other, as was done in church.

Behind Hjortberg is his library. The titles of his books connote his scientific interests in chemistry and biology. The flasks and bottles tell us about his experiments, as do the measuring tools. The most prominent objects are the globe and the monkey-cat that one of the boys is holding on to by hand and by foot.

As a young minister, Hjortberg had been a ship's pastor. He had made three journeys to China, holding morning and evening prayers, preaching to the crew, and burying the dead shipmates. At the university he had become an ardent admirer of the great botanist, Carolus Linnaeus. Eventually Hjortberg himself became a member of the Academy of Science in consequence of the observations and finds from his journeys. When Hjortberg finally settled down at home, he became the vicar of Släp's parish where he remained to his death. He turned his mind to farming and taught his parishioners how to care for their cows and dig ditches, what to grow in their gardens, and how to build better houses. He built an organ for his church; we can see the pipes in the picture. His fame as a doctor spread far and wide, especially when he came up with a cure for the lame and those handicapped by arthritis. He had brought a little electricity machine from London and administered shocks to the ailing.

This picture explains better than a thousand words the role a minister could play in a Swedish rural community. He possessed a natural dignity and authority. He had curiosity in God's marvelous creation. The division of labor was self-evident between husband and wife. The center that held the world together was the mystery of redemption, the love of God "as it was in the beginning, is now, and ever shall be."

We do not know much about Hjortberg's wife, except that she outlived him by many, many years. There is a poem by Anna Maria Lenngren, a Swedish poet of the same epoch, which depicts a visit by a countess to a vicar's home.[6] Although the poem satirizes the hustle and bustle and the subservience to a person of higher estate, it nevertheless speaks to the kind of family life, the chores, the staff of servants and the standard of living that Mrs. Hjortberg presided over. If the vicar was busy with numerous projects, visits, readings, healings, preparations of sermons, and so forth, she was busy with children, servants, visits, parishioners' complaints, and the like. The priest was not alone in caring for the parish; his wife stood at his side shouldering her share of the pastoral work.

The pastor's family was a model family. Every member was aware of this responsibility. But since the yoke of faith was not a heavy burden, the boys looked forward to following in their father's footsteps and the girls to marrying a minister. It is not until much later that this picture becomes quaint. The children begin to feel uncomfortable and the wife to ask questions.

It is significant that the public libraries in many communities have their origin in parsonages like the Hjortbergs'. The priest lent his books to the parishioners who came to him with their questions. When this activity became too popular and burdensome for the ministers, they began to buy books for the parish and established parish libraries (sockenbibliotek).

In the eighteenth-century world, the Bible was taken for granted as literal truth, and God was thought of and talked of in androcentric terms as "he." God was mysterious and wonderful. In the Words, God revealed how he could even change his mind. Prayer in those days was a means to impress on God to change his mind, to restore what was lost, to help the helpless, and to perform miracles. People saw miracles in the heavens and in the tiniest blade of grass. They felt the tension between Creation and Redemption, and they proudly pointed to their Redeemer. In the agrarian society God was as real as the trees, wells, winds, and seasons.

THE ADVANCE OF SCIENCE

In the nineteenth century such an outlook on the world was jolted and received some deadly blows. Natural science challenged the literal reading of the Bible's story about creation, and biblical criticism challenged the view of redemption and the divinity of Christ. The foundation was shaking. A scientific world view was forming in opposition to the biblical view. The picture fell apart. Faith and knowledge were no longer "siblings."[7] The matter of faith now became the yes answer to the questions: Do you believe that it happened exactly as it is written? Do you believe in the virgin birth? That the creation happened in a week? That Jesus flew up in the sky? The Bible was scrutinized for answers to questions it never intended to raise. The theologians waged a rather hapless and hopeless fight against such questions, because to these crude questions people wanted plain, crude answers. Faith now depended on knowledge but knowledge in a new key, that is, certainty about life's mysteries. That this simplified type of discourse became prevalent was caused by crude teaching to begin with.

When the scientists set out on the exciting expeditions of discovery, the theologians were thrown back on the defensive road of apology. And the students who arrived at the theological faculties were of a new kind.[8] The majority were no longer the sons of priests who self-evidently followed their fathers' footsteps but bright boys in the parishes whom the ministers had detected and encouraged, boys for whom an academic career meant a rise above their allotted estate. Some of them became skeptical scholars, some heroes of faith, some able stewards. Some priests embraced the warm faith of Pietism, holding out the promises that cannot betray.[9] In other words, the priests became less secure in tradition and more introspective, and many people became rattled. The authority of the priest buttressed by the Word of God was no longer self-evident but ambiguous.

THE FOLK MOVEMENTS

The major causes for the priest's loss of authority over the people were not just theological—not even primarily so—but also sociological, demographic, and economic. The emergence of new industrial communities made the difference.

During the early nineteenth century, Sweden was poor and getting poorer. Farms could no longer feed the people even in good years, let alone in bad ones. Necessity forced young people, especially men, out on the road. The church instituted poorhouses for young and old who could not care for themselves. However, it was seen as a disgrace to end up in the poorhouse. Better to move away and make a living somewhere else. Solutions were to be found "elsewhere": in emigration, in working on the railroad, in becoming a sailor, miner, or logger. Suffice it to say that people began to disappear from the villages and turn up in newly constituted communities growing around the factories that for obvious reasons often were built close to the railroads in order to ship their product. Conditions in these new communities were often dreadful: crowded housing, no organized life, long working hours, little pay, lots of liquor, many illegitimate children—in other words slums, often considered the Sodom and Gomorrah by right-thinking folks back in the villages.

In these newly constituted communities the folk movements took hold. These folk movements were of immense importance for Sweden's development. The first was the free-church movement. Preachers often trained in the Anglo-Saxon world preached penitence and deliverance from "sloth, drinking, and whoring." In so-called mission houses, they preached repentance and a second birth in a cleansing baptism. People found a new life, support, and joy. The language the preachers used was familiar from the old house-meetings. "To cleanse oneself in the blood of the Lamb" was pietistic Bible language, language people had learned in church and school. The pietistic movement within the church thereby, so to say, became a godparent to the free-church movement. The language and piety that had entered the church through Pietism was now popularized by the evangelical free-church pastors. The mission congregations grew rapidly. The question, "Are you saved?" was answered with the "Allelujah, Praise be to God!" No problem with hermeneutical intricacies. There arose a class barrier between those who were better off and attended the old town or village churches and the free-church congregations at first peopled by those who were considered uncouth and uneducated, but who learned ways in which it was possible to survive in wretched surroundings and rise above them.

The second folk movement that found fertile ground in the new communities was the temperance movement with its zeal to turn people away from destroying themselves with hard liquor. An educational campaign accompanied the preaching against the "Devil Gin."[10] Ordinary people read pamphlets and books that told them about their bodies and told stories of how people had been lured into drinking by their employers, even by the priest himself. In order to better themselves, they had to abstain completely from the devil of drinking. Only through hard work and abstinence could they become healthy and wealthy. The free-church movement and the temperance movement worked well together.[11] The combination eventually came to produce the core of a new merchant class. A life style suitable to cope with the new industrial situation was fostered within these folk movements.

The third folk movement was the labor movement, finally the most successful. The union organizers with their training in Marxist critique of religion told people that there was no "pie in the sky." If they were to have a better world, they should not expect it in heaven. Unite and work for it here! Many who had neither been challenged by the preacher nor convinced by the temperance movement heard from the union organizer a message that answered their bitterness about their living and working conditions. The labor movement distributed its pamphlets, which contained much that was hostile to the church, viewing the ministers as lackeys of the establishment and at times even ridiculing the Bible. For the first time, people studied educational material in the books published by the ABF (The Workers' Educational Association). The ABF became a great popularizer of science. Many read the new truth as carefully as if it were a new Bible.

These three folk movements rescued the communities and organized the people, who until then had been—to use a clerical term—"like sheep without a shepherd." Since the local church was still to be found in the rural village or in the middle of the old town, the priests were carrying on their ministry there and were rarely seen in those places that had invited the competition. The clergy had mixed feelings about the "mission-house" of the free churches, the lodges of the temperance movement, and the "people's house" of the labor movement.

Meanwhile, the priests were busy at their own location. The government had introduced a school reform in 1842 that would enable all children to receive basic schooling. With the help of the priests it had been carried out. Typically these schools had been placed in the villages. The local pastor was, in the beginning, the self-evident chairman of the school board, just as he was of the Parish Council, of the poorhouse, and then of almost every social service institution that came along. Together with the district police and the sheriff, the priest was authorized by the government to look after law and order. Many people in the early folk movements were anticlerical, but they were not anti-Christian. It is of paramount importance to understand this mesh.

THE TRADITIONAL PARISH MINISTRY
OF THE EMERGING
INDUSTRIAL SOCIETY

In the rural communities, well into this century, the priest had "status," and the church had "class." Personally, I remember well when in the early 1940s I visited a minister's family in a rural community in the southern part of Sweden. The family lived in a spacious parsonage surrounded by a lovely garden with old cherry trees, apple trees, and raspberry bushes. There were long raked gravel paths and a flagpole that flew the Swedish flag every Sunday. The farm that belonged to the parish was now run by a tenant farmer.

Every Sunday the seven children in this family walked neatly dressed and watercombed to church with their parents. The minister, Reverend Thorén, knew everyone he met, and they all greeted him with reverence. But only a small flock reached the church to worship in the huge edifice. It was not from worship that the minister knew them, but from his office where the parish records were kept. His parishioners had come there to ask him for papers to be able to move, to apply for passports, marriage licenses, and birth or death certificates.

The minister was a learned man. People respected his learning, but they did not understand it and were not curious about it. His garden flourished, the house was filled with activity, and his wife was forever entertaining people with coffee and homemade buns and cookies. Her office was in the kitchen where she taught young girls to cook, sew, put up preserves, and take care of children. He visited the sick and the dying, instructed the confirmands, spoke at commencement at the local school, performed marriages, baptisms, and burials. Where he went the church was present but the church building became more and more empty and stale; it was frightening in its dignity and official formality that so clashed with the tiny group of congregated people who spoke with hushed voices. Those who did attend church never dared to approach the front pews but sat far apart from one another and sang with lonely voices the five chosen hymns. The contrast between the lively, even turbulent, home with its enormously varied activities and the church with its rigidity and—despite the splendor of the architecture, color, and music—poverty of church life was heartbreaking. The minister prepared his sermons meticulously, yet I hardly remember a single one. But I remember well the relief of returning home to "church coffee." Around that table there was communication, celebration, and happiness, and the minister was the center of our discussions—whatever they were about. He knew things, and if he did not, he looked them up in his voluminous library. He displayed humor and taught us compassion and reverence. He was a marvelous teacher, and each summer the parsonage was filled with summer confirmands, young people who came from the cities to spend a few weeks in the country to be instructed in the Christian faith. There must have been hundreds of such parsonages and hundreds of priests like him who carried out a tradition in church and at home. But they did not change it.

There were, of course, individual ministers who looked beyond the boundaries of the parish to the changing world. There were those who identified with the poor, and there were those who in spite of the labor party's stated object to abolish the established church joined that party because of its claims and its achievements for justice and equality. But the more significant stirring for renewal within the church went politically to the right where the support for the institution was solid.

THE FOLK-CHURCH

In the beginning of the twentieth century the church got its own folk movement to which the young ministers and the theological students could enthusiastically adhere. It called itself the Folk-Church movement. Its purpose was to enliven the activities in the local churches all over the country. It differentiated itself from the congregational free-churches where one became a member by personal confession of faith in Jesus Christ as one's Savior, and through being baptized. Membership in the Folk-Church was automatic from birth. It was not built on people joining the church but on God's grace that manifested itself in the baptism of little children.[12] The slogan went: "The people of Sweden—a people of God." The Folk-Church was thought of as a huge fisherman's net sunk into the sea of the people of Sweden. Christianity was present in the nation. The Word and the Sacraments were at work. This presence has had its impact on life and culture. The church is conceived as responsible for the nation's spiritual welfare. Thus, it is not merely the individual of a particular congregation who is the object for redemption but the whole nation.

This vision originated from and had become extremely popular in Denmark where the established name of the established church today still is The Danish Folk Church. In Sweden the nationalistic trend of this vision proved to be inspiring for young people. Manfred Björkquist (see above, pp. 22–23), the founder of Sigtunastiftelsen, the first Evangelical Academy in Europe, became the leader of a group that called themselves the Young Church. However, this was not a grassroots movement, a genuine "folk" movement. It was not "participatory" in practice, but operated "from above." Students from the universities, often dressed in student caps, went out in the country on "crusades." They formed so-called Voluntary Corps who wanted to bring about a revival in the Church of Sweden and to bring people to a new awareness of what the church of old had brought to Swedish life and culture. Several of the most brilliant theologians like Einar Billing, J. A. Eklund, Nathan Söderblom, and Gustaf Aulén were inspired by this vision and worked tirelessly to form its theology.[13] The folk-church ideal therefore influenced the thinking of young ministers during the first part of this century. In order to understand why the Church of Sweden still today is not willing to disestablish, this view must be kept in mind.[14] It has been deeply ingrained.

Ironically, "folk-church" actually came to mean a priest-church. Since the majority of the people were leaving the life of the church behind them, finding jobs and new life styles in the cities, the Church of Sweden actually became a priest-church where the clergy were the only visible members. "The invisible church" which was such a beautiful thought—God at work in mysterious ways amongst the people, "the net still in the sea" (Matt. 13:47–50)—became in the minds of the people a church synonymous with the clergy.

If the church were to be defined not by the community of members but by the activities of preaching and sacraments, then it seems inevitable that the minds of the clergy gravitated toward seeking clarity and inspiration from a right understanding of their priestly office. That is precisely what happened within the Swedish clergy. And since liturgy is less vulnerable to small numbers in attendance than the sermons from the pulpit, the nonpulpit centered activities gained in attention.

THE ALTAR, THE PULPIT, AND THE HIGH CHURCH MOVEMENT

When we enter a church or a temple we instinctively lower our voices. We look up to see what can be found as the center: an altar, a shrine, a table, a book, a crucifix, a painting or flowers. Sweden has many and marvelous churches from nine centuries. Although they vary widely in style, the altar is what immediately catches the viewer. Adorned or unadorned, the altar is located so as to draw attention. Partially surrounded by an altar rail, it stands separated on holier ground. Dressed in alb and chasuble, the priest opens each Sunday service *(högmässa)* standing before the altar and speaking the words: "The Lord is in his holy Temple. His throne is in heaven. The Lord is nigh unto those who have a humble and contrite heart. . . ." From the altar, the texts of the epistle and the gospel are read, and at the altar the eucharist is celebrated with the communicants kneeling at the altar rail.

The custom of the Church of Sweden is that in the middle of the service the priest leaves the altar, goes out to the sacristy, and then opens a little door, climbs a few steps, and stands in the pulpit looking out over the congregation that awaits the sermon.

Preaching has a special legacy in the Lutheran tradition.[15] Luther excelled as a preacher. His sermons witness to his inspiration and power with words. His two Swedish pupils, the brothers Olaus and Laurentius Petri, introduced Luther's reformation to Sweden. Not least owing to their mighty preaching which did not shrink from upbraiding even the king Gustavus Vasa, the reformation caught the ear and the fancy of both high and low. History has since seen a long row of excellent preachers, movers, and shakers who have stirred their listeners. There are Svedberg, Schartau, Wallin, and Rosenius to mention a few and to stop significantly in the middle of the last century. Not that there have not been wonderful preachers since, but the relationship between the people and the person in the pulpit has changed.

The strong tradition of mighty preaching made the pulpit more important than the altar. Some city churches from the Baroque era harbor fanciful pulpits that are beautifully equipped with baldachin heavens held up by herald angels over the wooden captain's bridge protruding from a wall or resting on a pillar of sculptured Old Testament prophets. Other churches have more modest basket pulpits. What they all have in common is that they hang high in order for the preacher to be heard and seen. The pulpit gives the speaker a platform for the message. It must give an exhilarating feeling to open that door, climb those stairs, and then to look out on the expectant congregation. Remember the opening line in Selma Lagerlöf's famous *Saga of Gösta Berling,* "Finally now the priest had entered the pulpit."[16]

Few things so enhanced the status and aura of the priests in the past and nothing so overwhelms the priests in the present as those pulpits. The ministers stand up there "to comfort, teach, exhort, and admonish" the people with the Word of God.[17] The tradition is heavy. The burden of having something to say that is worthy of the splendid surrounding rests with the priests. And they remember of course, the word in Rom. 10:17: "Faith comes from what is heard, and what is heard comes by the preaching of Christ" (RSV). People come to faith from listening to the sermon.

With the opening of ecumenical channels in the beginning of this century came increased awareness of traditions other than German Lutheran, which formerly had heavily influenced both theology and praxis in Sweden. Now its hegemony broke up. Nathan Söderblom was pastor in the Swedish church of Paris around the turn of the century. He became an important link to other churches. He traveled widely in Europe and in the U.S. He became archbishop in 1914. Through his influence the ecumenical movement held its first great ecumenical meeting on Life and Work in Stockholm in 1925.

To look at pictures from the two ecumenical meetings that have taken place in Sweden, Stockholm 1925, and Uppsala 1968, is interesting and very instructive. The laity dominates the scene in 1968; all kinds of people of different races, many women and young people mill about. In 1925 the clergy are prominent in official garb and garment. They are the representatives of their churches, Lutheran, Anglican, Orthodox, and so forth. In 1925 a growing High Church movement was mainly a clergy movement that was given a boost at the time from the ecumenical meeting, which demonstrated for all to see that the church did not just have a history behind it but that history was a living tradition.[18] It justified the veritable inventory the High Church movement had begun. The church buildings were searched; the walls were examined; the sacristies, the attics, and the cellars yielded old treasures that had not been in use for centuries. The church year calendar with all the fasts and feasts and saints' days was revived; the symbolism in colors and the magic in symbols became the object of research and subject of practice.

The altar regained its sovereignty. It was the duty of a priest to preach the Word of God and to administer the Sacraments. When the preaching became problematic some priests warmly welcomed the return to the altar that the High Church movement marshalled. Customarily, communion services had been rare and solemn occasions, four times a year or even only once a year in certain places. The emphasis had then fallen on the forgiveness of sins and on the mournful remembrance of Christ's death. Now weekly and even daily eucharist services returned. Mass was often said without a sermon. The communion service became a eucharist rather than a service of remembrance. The Gregorian chant was reintroduced.[19] The hours were kept. The church became a haven, a beautiful world of worship. Those who took delight in this retreat to the church could soon be recognized because they distinguished themselves by wearing special garments, hats, and medals. They formed societies with distinct differences between clergy and laity and between men and women. The High Church movement flourished during the thirties and forties. It contributed richly to the fullness of the liturgy. But the glories of the past seemed somewhat to blind these worshipers to the reality of the present. Little credit was given to the actual pluralism within the church universal. Only ecumenism to the right was acknowledged and the left was disowned.

The word used in Swedish for office or ministry is *ämbete,* a word with specific weight. It belongs to a social stratification where there are various such *ämbeten* instituted by divine right (kings-judges-priests). While the use of the word has practically died in common language, it lingers in connection with the church. The word *ämbete* is derived from the German *Amt.* During the forties and the fifties a flow of books and dissertations on the subject of the priestly *Amt* appeared.[20] The thing itself, which ever since Luther had been a rather self-evident matter of order in a church that hailed the doctrine of the priesthood of all believers, now became elevated, mysterious, a separate office once or even twice removed from the laity. The High Church movement thrived upon the new theology of the *Amt.* It moved the Swedish clergy nearer the Roman Catholic church, the Anglican church, and the Orthodox churches. The fluke that Sweden had preserved *successio apostolica*—the unbroken chain of laying on of hands claimed to reach back to the apostles—also after the Reformation, since a Catholic bishop had been present at the first installation of a Protestant bishop, now took on great significance. To be ordained came to mean to enter into a sacred order of the *Una Sancta.* A very special sacred authority was bestowed on the ordinand.[21]

The liturgical renewal within the Church of Sweden that the High Church movement brought about enriched the life within the church walls. The people who had the time to steep themselves in the knowledge and the sheer exercise it takes to worship, meditate, sing, and pray in the beautiful old manner were naturally priests and theologians. Only a small elite of the laity could afford the time. The services at the altar and the many rituals surrounding them became intensely precious to these people. The altar was not a place for a woman. The role of the priest was not her role. The vestments were not for her. For some just to imagine a woman in alb and chasuble was like transvestism and blasphemy. The mixture of religious and sexual images deepened the challenge.

WOMEN AND THE *AMT*

Just when the *Amt* itself stood as the focal point for much theological thinking, then women began to press for admittance to the priesthood. Women too had come to conferences and begun to study theology. They too had savored the message of the glory of ministry. For them also to become "real" Christians was seen as synonymous with becoming a priest and serving at the altar. (See interviews above with Sahlin, Olander, and Orstadius.)

In the old church law of 1686 there is no dictum against a woman becoming a priest. It was simply taken for granted that this could not be. Now, however, the situation was different. Women were independent. In every other profession they had equal access by 1945. Why could they not also take the priestly vows and serve the Lord? Of course, that should mean eventually a change in how the priestly role would be worked out. The patriarchal authority figure would disappear, but that did not concern the women because it had already started to happen. They were eager to begin in the set role-patterns just as women doctors, women lawyers, women professors, women members of parliament, and so forth, had done. The main thing for them was to obtain this legitimation to become "real Christians" and to serve the Lord full-time in the *Amt*. What they did not count on was the strength of the patriarchal biblical tradition, "the order of creation," that considered women subordinate to men, especially bolstered lately by a host of theological inquiry into the history of the *Amt* and by the praxis of the adherers to the High Church movement. Two factions, the evangelical fundamentalists and the High Church movement, joined forces to fight off any move toward ordination of women.[22]

The women who became priests had, of course, thorough knowledge of the Bible and of the tradition, and like their male colleagues they had great affection for it. They took for granted that it was a tradition of liberation. They thought they could adapt to the *Amt* and bring to it what people in a contemporary society were looking and searching for. The women were ready to shoulder a new role, but how could they know what it would look like? It had to evolve with time.

And there were many among the regular churchgoers who felt a sort of liberation, as if they were getting rid of something forbidden, when they saw women move into the holy space behind the altar rail. Instead of a father or a judge they experienced the presence of a mother who encouraged, pleaded, and understood. People in general had no problem with welcoming women in the priestly role.

The patriarchal tradition of old had asked for grave, public responsibility from the priests. They had to answer for the welfare of their parishes. People's eyes were upon them and their families. They had to exercise self-discipline and live up to the norms they represented. Now the patriarchal system was dissolving in society. The norms for living patterns were no longer taken from or identified with the priesthood at all. The private life of the priests has almost become anonymous. They have gotten rid of exigencies on their behavior. New demands, however, have not been defined.

Ingmar Ström mentioned that neither the women nor the men who today enter the priesthood want to shoulder a fixed authority role. Priests want to exercise spiritual leadership. The new crew is looking forward to doing ministry in a personalized mode, somewhat different from how it used to be. They look for more collegial models. But, he added, "they get caught up in the system." A system shaped by centuries is hard to break.

TWO INTERVIEWS WITH
WOMEN PRIESTS

In order to fetch a random look at "the system" and gain an idea of how women accept it and function within it, I had the privilege of interviewing two women, both of them priests in the Stockholm diocese. One is working in an inner-city parish, and the other is serving a country congregation. They both invited me to conduct the interviews at their homes. These interviews, held in August 1982, were not taped but taken down as notes. They strike me as illustrative in the context of our discussion of priesthood and authority.

In the City

In the city I walked up three flights in a typical apartment house and entered a one-room rented apartment. The room seemed filled with furniture, and there was something bachelorean and temporary about the place. Lillemor Hogendal, a young, tall, ashblond woman with a wonderful smile greeted me and began to tell me about herself.

She did not come from a Christian home but had been drawn into the local church's youthwork program since she was a good athlete and liked to play Ping-Pong. She had become a member of the Student Christian Movement at her high school. She had continued to study theology at the University of

Lund. When she was ordained she began to serve as student-chaplain in Stockholm but understood rather soon that she was too young and too inexperienced for that sensitive post.

After three years as student-chaplain she became an assistant priest in the Engelbrekt parish where Margit Sahlin was the senior pastor. There her responsibility was to take charge of the program the parish had set up for children. It included a special preschool, which is like any ordinary school except for its special emphasis on Christian education.

She had been called by Sahlin, and she very much appreciated the attention Sahlin had given her and her work. The years with Sahlin had meant great development. When Sahlin retired, the new senior pastor who was elected happened to be an opponent to women priests. The new situation brought a lot of stress. Although there was no open hostility, there was no cooperation either, and that deadened her spirit from taking initiative. It was not long before matters that perhaps were not intended as ill will could be interpreted as opposition and intrigue. The trust level and mutual support were gone.

When Hogendal studied in Lund she had observed how many of her male student colleagues who came to study theology roomed at Laurentiusstiftelsen, a housing complex supported by the High Church movement. There they ate together and also went to church together since the building has a built-in chapel. And, she said, there the students were somehow self-contained. They found their friends there, and together they formed their opinions. Although they had their discussions, they did not need to get in touch with nor comprehend the surrounding world. Gustaf-Adolf Danell had been the chaplain at the Laurentiusstiftelsen and after him Bishop Gärtner, both of them fine, persuasive preachers, she said, and both of them strong opponents to women in the ordained ministry. She held the opinion that the network that has developed to form a separate synod within the Church of Sweden had its origin among these male theologians at Laurentiusstiftelsen together with its counterpart in Uppsala, the Ansgarsstiftelsen. These people, she said, consider themselves the real Christians and true defenders of the faith in the country. In their opinion women priests pollute the holy places and the holy word. In Stockholm this group of opponents to women priests is small, but in Växjö, from where she comes, the work of the opposition threatens and undermines all the work being done by the women. Smiling, she readily admitted that she was stereotyping the opponents, but she was troubled by the amount of time and energy this controversy had taken. It had put a big stick in the wheel.

Her main concern was whether people would ever return to the church and how the message of Christianity could be heard in this "postchurch" situation. She saw it as a disaster that the priests spent so much time on trying to get people back into the church buildings when people now were definitely unchurched. She asked: Should not the priests rather develop other work-forms, other ways of reaching people? This was the kind of question she wrestled with as she moved in her community.

She also observed that the opposition through its network somehow had managed to take hold of many central governing positions in the church. Hogendal regretted that the Church Assembly of 1982 had tied itself more closely to the state. She feared that elections in the future would be politically engineered.

Women priests, in her opinion, had not even begun to confront the many complex problems that emerge with women practicing ordained ministry. She saw it as a good sign that there was an awakening to the issues raised by the stated need for inclusive language. In Stockholm continuing education programs for the priests are compulsory, and in these courses where men and women work together she expected some positive results. However, it had been a great shock for the women like herself to find out that they were feared and hated by some of their male colleagues. It made it hard for them to introduce changes. She thought that neither men nor women had much stake in the traditional priestly role and that this shared recognition could be a starting point for something new. Concerning salaries she did not think that priests were either overpaid or underpaid in comparison with other academically trained people.

In the Country

The other interview was with an associate pastor, Marianne Sautermeister, in charge of a parish with about 4,000 inhabitants. Earlier that same day I had attended the Sunday service which she conducted well. There was, however, no hint of her awareness of the need for inclusive language. The God/He language appeared as prevalent as it always has in the past.

The parsonage was a yellow wooden building on a hill with a pathway to the idyllic church. It was airy and light with big rooms, high ceilings, lovely wallpaper, and a large garden with a flagpole. Next door stood a rather humble, red log cabin that once belonged to the poet, theologian, and biologist Samuel Ödmann (1750–1829). I was greeted by the roundfaced, middle-aged woman who lives here with her two teenage children.

Early on in life Sautermeister had wished to do something in the church, but since the ministry then was not open to women she considered becoming a missionary. She had married, had a family, and was later divorced. She began to study theology in Stockholm, where the director of The Theological Institute, Gösta Höök, had encouraged her to enter the priesthood.

She had belonged to the Student Christian Movement and had been in touch with the High Church liturgical movement. There she learned that being a woman excluded her from the *Amt*. During her studies, however, she understood that her long wish to become a missionary overseas really could be understood as a call to the priesthood here at home.

During her first two years after her ordination Sautermeister had served as a hospital chaplain. She had chosen this line of work because she knew it would be a test to overcome her shyness by forcing her to witness to her faith in a person-to-person situation.

The task that took most of her time in her present position was counseling, not necessarily only with parishioners but also with others since the reputation of her willingness and her ability had spread by word of mouth over the parish boundaries. Her main interest outside of counseling concerned the conditions in developing countries. She regretted that her education, though it had been thorough in theology proper, had been so void of any knowledge from the fields of economics and sociology.

When asked whether she had any model for her ministry, Sautermeister said that she often thought of the wise women of Russia in olden times. Her ideal was to become a wise woman to whom people could turn for counsel. One problem she had, however, was to find a confessor for herself for her own spiritual direction.

On the whole, she was content with her work. She felt the salary to be adequate and was grateful to have a job with security for the future. As a mother with children at home Sautermeister found it difficult that she had no regular working hours and no compensatory free time for all the evenings when she was occupied with meetings.

She did not think of the parsonage as a personal advantage but considered it a definite asset for the parishioners since they gathered there for meetings of all kinds. At earlier times when a man had lived there, his wife had served Christmas breakfasts and coffee between services, and so forth. She as the priest, obviously, could not do so, and she thought that probably, at least in the beginning, some people had resented the break in the tradition.

To be a minister in the country was a great privilege. She enjoyed the beautiful nature around her, the fresh air, and the long walks in the woods. Her heavy-duty time fell during the summers since her parish was a "summer-people" place. Then the population swelled to 20,000 and the little church filled up. She never took vacation during summertime. I asked her if she got in touch with the "summer people," and she said that she counted them as her parishioners. She led a Bible-study group, and while the core consisted of only ten people, many came "now and then."

I made a few observations after these two random interviews. These two women have grown up in an egalitarian society. They are products of egalitarian legislation and modern professionalism. They speak matter-of-factly about salaries, and they are concerned about overwork. But it seems to me that their ideas about their roles as priest illustrate how much they still are dominated by the old clergy role.

Consider the woman in the city parish, a professional single woman in her own easy-to-care-for flat. She has several years of varied experience. She has worked happily with Margit Sahlin and has chosen to specialize in the kind of work where women excel: teaching children. She stressed that she liked her work. When Margit Sahlin retired she expected the new senior pastor to run the parish, to give the orders, and set the tone. She expects positive leadership. When she does not get it, she becomes uneasy. The hierarchical system seems to stifle her confidence in what she is doing as a priest.

She asks very good questions: How can the Christian message be heard in this postchurch era? What kind of workforms can be developed? How do we reach people? She is occupied by these problems but does not see any solutions coming. Where would they come from? She seems to expect some kind of leader just to appear. She is stretching toward a future, but the future has no distinct shape. Many men priests have the same problem, she said. She knew it from the continuing education courses which are compulsory in Stockholm. Men and women wrestle with the same problems. If they do, then is there not a collegial model of ministry being worked out?

The country priest seemed to have adapted well to her country parish. At first it seemed to me as though she had just slipped into the old clergy role. There was not a trace of change in the service she conducted, and although she said she did not think of the parsonage as an advantage she clearly enjoyed the space. She pointed out that the parishioners were disappointed that she did not serve coffee the way the old minister's wife used to do. That tradition was discontinued. She did not appear to have made the laity do things for themselves. She seemed to be the one who ran things, who led meetings, conducted Bible studies, called on people, and thereby had precious little private time.

But then she had a surprising and original model for her ministry: to become a wise woman with experience and healing power, like in old Russia, a counselor trusted by people who in the name of Christ could free people from burdened consciences.

This chapter has briefly sketched the transformation of the authority role of the priesthood over the last centuries up to the present confusing stage. It should be stressed that this confusion concerning authority is not a phenomenon limited to the institution of the church. It touches all kinds of establishments: education, medicine, law, business, journalism, and, to take a drastic example, the monarchy. Less than a hundred years ago the monarch was crowned and installed as "God's anointed," invested with divine power—a true *Ämbete*. What people today expect from royalty and what royalty themselves think of their roles will probably show as much confusion and divergence as what people expect from the priests and what the priests themselves think is expected of them.

People accept authority when they perceive it as legitimate. Today when almost all women and men work outside of the home it seems that the institutions have lost their luster of authority. Modern autonomous people are a law unto themselves. They are suspicious of authority and refuse to be manipulated. The loss of legitimate authority on the part of institutions has, however, also left the individuals totally to their private judgment as to what they make out of their life situation. They are on the one hand liberated from the restraints that the institutions as collectives once put them under. But on the other hand they are put under private strain concerning the worth of their work, and they are bewildered about life and where to turn for advice. There is a lot of anguished searching going on concerning the changing roles of the professions. And there is a lot of professional expertise giving conflicting answers.

The past centuries have seen the priesthood change from an inner-directed authority during the eighteenth century, taking interest in and giving leadership to whatever happened in a parish, to a more other-directed authoritarian role, getting its clout from social status and its connections with the state during the nineteenth century. In the twentieth century when the territorial parish remains but the congregation has almost vanished, the clergy has turned in several directions: outward in nationalistic crusades and inward in search of tradition and the meaning of the *Amt*. When the women entered, neither they nor the leaders of the church were in any way prepared for the second half of the century with the strain it has caused for institutions as well as for individuals in the society as a whole.

At this present time there is an authority crisis in the church. And the way I sort it out is to see two trends. One is the way in which people in general see the church and its priests. For them it is a cultic place where the priests perform services. This is what is expected for them, and this is the work they should do. It is both significant and ironic how the High Church movement gives the clergy theological dignity and motivation for functioning in such a "service church." The preoccupation with *Amt, ämbetet,* is a kind of clergy response to the popular expectation of the priestly role from the vast majority of Swedes.

The other is the way that the majority of the priests understand their priesthood. They perform the services faithfully, but their calling is to bring Christianity to the people through their personal gifts. The two interviews confirm that standpoint, as do the answers to the questionnaire.[23] The priests have a personal agenda, something that they through their total personality must give to people. That they "get caught in the system" means that the services and the regulated work in the office take a lot of their time and energy which they rather would have wished to spend on developing contacts and more meaningful activities for the spreading of the gospel. This "personal agenda" has not yet coalesced into a program or a platform for the priesthood in the future.

In this overview of the changing roles of the priesthood it is clear and should be stressed that the issue of women's ordination played no integral part. Yet that became the issue by which the clergy in the Church of Sweden was forced to come to grips with the change in church and society.

3

ARGUMENTS AND
DECISIONS

Although Lutheran theology has been forcefully taught and mightily preached by the clergy, a liturgical priestly tradition from earlier Catholic days has remained characteristic for the Church of Sweden. This combination of Lutheran orthodoxy with a high liturgical function is unique. The word for pastor or minister in Swedish, when used for the clergy of the Church of Sweden, is *präst* ("priest") and that is why this study uses the word "priest" although it might sound strange to Protestant ears. The decision to keep the use was made so as to remind the reader of this combination which has given the question of the ordination of women a dimension that does not exist in most other Protestant churches. In fact, when the Church of Sweden introduced women as priests some members of the High Church converted to the Roman Catholic church in order to remain in a church that retained the priestly tradition from earlier times.

Another factor which has had its impact on the arguments and the decisions concerning the ordination of women and on the status of ordained women is the involvement of the government. The Church of Sweden is an established church with close ties to the state. The roots of this coalition are deep and entwined. The history can only be traced in its contours here but the state-church relation has played a decisive role in moving the ordination of women to the vote. This ingredient in the conflict and in its resolution, therefore, needs a short background sketch.

The christianizing of Sweden began in the ninth century, but it took three centuries before the country could be considered a Christian country, and the Roman church had established itself in all parts with a center in the archdiocese of Uppsala.[1] The people paid a tax to Rome (Peters penning).[2] In the thirteenth century monasteries were flourishing, and pilgrims fared the roads and waterways.

In the fourteenth century the remarkable woman, St. Birgitta (1303–1373), the only Swedish saint who was properly canonized, went to Rome to have the order that she had conceived through vision and revelations sanctioned and legalized by the pope.[3] Her rule had the unusual, though not

65

unique, feature of including both nuns and monks within the same cloister under the leadership of an abbess, the Mother Superior. Birgitta had to wait a long time before her request was granted, not because her request was strange, but because the pope at that time lived in Avignon, and Birgitta demanded that he return to Rome, a proper place for St. Peter's successor. She died in Rome, but her daughter Katharina carried out her plans and established a Birgitta cloister in Vadstena. The cloister church is still standing, a beautiful edifice called the Blue Church. In modern times it became a central meeting place for the people of the High Church movement in Sweden.[4]

In the sixteenth century, at the time of Luther, the Roman church was strong, rich, and well established while the Swedish state was weak and divided. It was with the aid of the church that the usurper liberator Gustavus Vasa gained control of the country. Together with the two brothers, Olaus and Laurentius Petri, who were followers of Luther, he rebelled against Rome and began the work of the Reformation. With the severance from Rome, the king became the head of the church in 1527.[5] He strengthened the national state by closing the cloisters, enriching the coffers of the state with their treasures, and by confiscating their lands, sending the church leaders into exile. In the brothers Petri, the king had found excellent new leaders who carried out the reformation of the church constructively. In Laurentius Petri *Church Order* (of 1571) the liturgy, the teaching, and the church's governing were outlined. In 1593 the Church of Sweden formally adopted the Augsburg Confession, "the pure evangelical confession," and claimed partial independence from the crown.

Almost a hundred years later King Charles XI took away the partial self-government the church had enjoyed. The church became subject to the crown. In 1686 the church was given by the state a new authorized church law; in 1689 the Catechism; in 1693 the Service Book; and in 1695 the Hymnbook. A new Bible translation was authorized by Charles XII in 1703. The Church of Sweden was wholly incorporated into the state of Sweden. Together they constituted a unified whole. As one of the four estates—the nobles, the clergy, the burghers and the farmers—the clergy kept its voice and its vote in Parliament. Out in the parishes the priests served the government. The priests looked after the secular affairs as well as the sacred. All Swedes born were registered as members of the Church of Sweden. The priests were seen by the people not only as servants of God but also as agents of the crown. Church and state depended upon each other. Together they built up a unified Swedish culture.

During the nineteenth century this unity began to change. There were three significant steps. First, in 1809, a new paragraph was written into the constitution: "The King . . . ought not to force or let cause to force anyone's conscience but should protect each person's practice of his religion as long as he does not thereby disturb the peace of society bringing about general dismay."[6] This paragraph meant a first step toward freedom of religion in the country. Earlier the unity of religon had been considered the self-evident pillar of strength for the preservation of society, and the state religion had been seen not only as the right faith but also as the sturdiest support for a successful government. During the time of the pietistic awakening, the government with the support of the clergy estate forbade by law any gatherings for the purpose of worship in private homes without the leadership of ordained clergy (konventikelplakatet, the Decree against Conventicles, see above). To participate in such gatherings was punishable first by fine, then by imprisonment, and finally by exile up to two years. Instigated in 1713 the law was not abolished until 1858. Its purpose was to keep the religious unity of the Swedish people intact. With the Constitution of 1809, however, came the idea that people should have the right and the protection of the crown to practice the religion of their choice. The king himself, of course, and the cabinet ministers, the judges, and other state officials should, however, belong to the "pure, evangelical faith."[7]

Second, in 1862, it was decided that the communal parish meetings (sockenstämma), which up to that point had handled all local concerns under the chairmanship of the priest, should split into two bodies: one secular (kommunalstämma) and one ecclesiastic (kyrkostämma). The priest was to keep the chairmanship of the church council while the communal council was to elect its own chairman.

Third, in 1863, the Riksdag, Parliament, was reconstructed. The four estates were abolished in favor of a two-chamber Riksdag. Since the presence of the clergy as one of the four estates was seen as being for the protection of the Church's interests and the privileges of the clergy, the parliamentary reorganization included the establishment of a Church Assembly (with about equal numbers of clergy and lay members) as a complement to the Riksdag in handling matters concerning the church. While the power of making church law remained in the hands of the Riksdag, the Church Assembly decided about internal church affairs and had veto power concerning church legislation. The Assembly should meet every fifth year under the chairmanship of the archbishop.[8]

This division of responsibility between Riksdag and Church Assembly was in operation until 1982, that is, during the years that our study covers. In 1982 a radical restructuring took place. Lay participation increased. After 1982 bishops are no longer self-evident members. They have voice but not vote. They have to be elected to become voting members of the Church Assembly.[9] Likewise, the Senior Pastor is no longer the self-evident chair of the church council.[10]

Since 1951 Sweden has a law stating that those who so wish can freely leave their membership in the Church of Sweden. Not many people have done so, although the conflict over the ordination of women caused some to leave the church. But approximately 90% of the population are still members. The past has created a kind of civil religion, a tipping of the hat to God and the flag. Not many Swedes think that this situation will change in the future.[11]

Why has the Church of Sweden not become a free church, divorced from the state and taking hold of its own affairs? One answer is, of course, this long historical involvement which, among other things, also has to do with money. The church is a landowner, and the clergy enjoy certain privileges. The state is the guardian of the church's money, and the state pays the salaries of the clergy. The local communities pay for the work in the parishes and the maintenance of the churches. A small percentage of the tax money goes to the church. Of all the denominations in Sweden, the Church of Sweden is the only one that enjoys such privileges.

But the answer is perhaps less a matter of money than a concern for the priestly tradition, the *Amt*. When the free-churches began to constitute themselves during the nineteenth and early twentieth centuries, there was a certain amount of condescension toward them among the clergy. The free-church pastors had not the academic training nor did they have the apostolic succession. Their mission houses were without style. Their celebrations lacked the dignity that age-old tradition availed. The conflict with the free-churches have some features similar to the conflict over the ordination of women. When in the 1970s the Church of Sweden was offered a proposal from the government to receive free status, the Church Assembly instead voted to tie itself more closely to the state. It is a very long tradition.[12]

This background knowledge of the priestly character of the Swedish clergy and of the close relationship between church and state of Sweden must be kept in mind in order to understand the arguments and to follow the decision-making procedure.

THE IMPORTANCE OF INFORMAL ARGUMENTS

Before presenting the formal arguments presented at different Church Assemblies, the fact must be stressed that formal arguments in documents also have informal ancestry. In the case of the conflict that arose over the issue of the ordination of women, it can be presumed that informal discussions between colleagues and private talks between husbands and wives on the subject had been lively and frequent. These talks cannot be wholly discounted, because they reflect how the priests actually felt about their relationship to women and how they understood what women felt. Obviously there is sexism involved. Sexism can be defined as "any attitude or action by individuals, groups, institutions, or cultures that treats individuals unjustly because of their gender and rationalizes that treatment on the basis of biological, psychological, social, or cultural characteristics."[13] How men priests talked about "women priests" and how they made jokes about the subject in private is not entirely unrelated to how they argued the case formally and officially. Men's dependence upon women has seldom been acknowledged to the same degree as women's dependence upon men, except in poetry. Also in the informal sphere there is a split between those who favor and those who oppose the emergence of women. In the interviews Bo Giertz blames Margit Sahlin, and Ingmar Ström holds Bo Giertz responsible for the rift. Arguments easily become *ad hominem*.

ARGUMENTS BEFORE THE DECISION
TO ORDAIN WOMEN

Already at the time when women won the right to vote there was a discussion abroad whether or not women should be allowed to enter the priesthood. The issue of women's status in the church and the possibility of ordination was raised in Parliament. In 1923 a formal proposal (SOU 1923:22) went before the Church Assembly for review and comment. This proposal favored ordination. For practical reasons and in order for the women to perform efficiently it suggested, however, that they remain unmarried. The proposal engendered lively discussions before it was tabled. It was never taken off the table.[14]

The question, however, did not go away, and in 1946 after the Equal Rights Law had been approved in 1945, Parliament voted to request a new study.[15] A commission was appointed and its report (SOU 1950:48) became the basis for the discussions and actions of the Church Assemblies of 1957 and 1958.

The majority of the commission favored the ordination of women. The minority registered and motivated their dissent. The exegetical part approved by the majority was written by the New Testament scholar, Erik Sjöberg. The minority's dissenting views also included an exegetical exposition, written by Olov Hartman (see above). Sjöberg's expertise was further undercut when the professor of New Testament studies in Uppsala, Anton Fridrichsen, issued a statement signed by all the teachers of the New Testament exegesis (save one) both in Uppsala and Lund:

> We the undersigned declare herewith as our definite opinion resting on careful research that to introduce to the Church a ministry of so called women priests would constitute a departure from faithful obedience to Holy Scripture. Both Jesus' choice of his apostles and Paul's words about the place of women in the congregation are built on principle and are independent of time-bound circumstances and views. The current proposal of allowing women to enter the priesthood of the Church of Sweden must therefore be said to entail serious exegetical obstacles.[16]

The commission's report went out to all the dioceses for comments, seeking their opinion, and twelve out of the thirteen diocesan Councils turned it down. The anxiety and the bewilderment in the church were increased by a sarcastic press or by calls for quick action by the women's movement. One woman, the author Märta Leijon, a member of the commission, had registered her dissent to the report because the new proposal did recommend that a woman priest may not get a position in any other parish than one where "at least one male priest occupy another position." She turned against this paragraph as being an insult to women theologians, to the parishioners, to the bishops, and the church authorities as well: "In spite of everything said in this great report, this paragraph after all puts the woman theologian in a separate position which gives her a kind of lower priestly rank than that of the man theologian. This can neither help the Church nor the joy of her co-workers in their vocation."[17]

A line up along two adverse positions formed. Books were published by both sides, and when the Church Assembly of 1957 finally debated the new law based on the proposal from 1950, the lines were drawn.

On the one side were those who loved the church as it was, loved its liturgy, its tradition, and who hoped that, if not in the present, in the future people would recognize this source of life again and turn to its rich reservoirs for renewal. They were joined by those who considered the Bible as norm in a literal manner. True to the letter of its orders and laws, they wished to be faithful to the commandments as expressed. As mentioned above, a new coalition came into being. The High Church people and the evangelicals found each other. They began to publish a magazine where the opposition to the ordination of women was repeatedly argued.[18]

Over against them stood those who deeply believed that the church now needed a re-formation in what they saw as the spirit of the New Testament. They never formed a formal coalition. Individuals wrote or spoke for reinterpretation of the Bible that would allow the Holy Spirit to speak through the church to the life situation of the contemporary world.

First and foremost the arguments concerned the Bible. What does it mean, according to the Bible, to be persons, male and female. On the one side it was stated that according to the creation story in Genesis 2 and 3, man was created before woman who is portrayed as the weaker vessel, the husband's helpmate to be ruled over by him. Women's subordination is built into creation, and this anthropological understanding is used by St. Paul in 1 Cor. 11:3–15.

On the other side, it was argued that such anthropology is a reflection of earlier societies, and in a modern society that model is impossible. Instead, the creation story of Genesis 1 was lifted up (esp. 1:26–27). Women and men are equally created in the image of God. They are coresponsible for the fate of creation. They have an equal origin and an equal destiny. This type of anthropology is intensified by St. Paul in Gal. 3:27–28, where he argues that in Christ there is not even "male and female." There his words are seen as overcoming specific cultural roles and envisioning a new prototype of humanity.

To some, the priest's role as representing Christ and the church was pressed as to require maleness of priests. Since Christ was male there is a symbolic meaning in the maleness of a priest. The priest is an icon of Christ, a new Adam, especially when he celebrates the Eucharist. For others the emphasis was on Luther's words about Christ's presence, "with, in and under" the elements of bread and wine. The church, i.e., the congregation, not the priest, is the locus of Christ's presence. The gender of the priest can be of no importance.

A persistent argument concerned the meaning of the different biological functions of men and women. They are created different for a purpose.[19] Through the centuries much speculation has focused on biological facts of reproduction, which until recently have been considered a mystery. In many cultures, it has been believed that only men were agents in the reproductive cycle. Women were mere vessels for the homunculus (the little human being contained in the seed which grew quietly in the woman's womb). Women have been considered unclean during menstruation and after childbirth. There have been cleansing rituals for women, and in the Swedish hymnbook of 1937 the liturgy for a "churching" (kyrktagning) of women after childbirth was still included. In 1923 when the first proposal had recommended ordination of women, it had typically suggested that if there were to be women priests they should remain unmarried.

That men and women contribute different biological gifts to the process of being human was also used as an argument in favor of including women in the priesthood in order that ministry might be more diversified. Men and women are interdependent, in need of each other—biologically as well as societally in terms of judgments, reactions, and experiences. Women who are mothers have special knowledge.

Today, male/female identity is explored by many in the context of new life styles. In the 1950s this new partnership had just begun to be glimpsed. Arguments against equal status for women on the principle of justice were based upon a deep distrust of secular thought. Equality was argued to be a product of the Enlightenment, an agnostic movement which had no claims on the church and which should have no power over its tradition, which is based in the superior power of love.

The arguments for equal status, on the other hand, saw it as a Christian principle of justice. To find justice established at the center of the Church—in its ministry—as a symbol that all barriers of race, class, and sex are erased in Christ and that through Christ a new humanity is being built, should be a priority item. That the principle of justice should become realized was understood as a renewal of the broken creation, one of several necessary ways to carry out the will and love of God.

Then there were also the arguments about women not being equipped with natural ability for leadership, voice, authority, and stamina to carry out the demanding physical as well as psychic tasks of an ordained priest. To this others pointed out how women already were used as missionaries, counselors, and the like. In the future, therefore, women should also serve at the Lord's table, baptize and confirm those whom they had taught. It seems compatible with the vocation they had already entered upon.[20]

Those who argued to exclude women from ordained ministry did so sometimes on the basis of tradition. Compared with the situation in many other churches, those who opposed ordination of women made less use of the argument from tradition. In a Lutheran climate tradition has a relativistic tinge one could not afford. For it was admitted that the tradition certainly has evolved over the centuries. Tradition is a flexible instrument. When the argument was used it was with a distinction between renewal within the tradition itself and an innovation. The ordination of women was considered as such a discontinuous innovation unless it could be established that women actually were ordained in the early church. In Sweden, especially with the coalition of the High Church people *and* the evangelicals, the arguments had constantly to be pushed back to the biblical level and to biblical times.

Those for the ordination of women argued that the tradition within the church depends on the Holy Spirit. The church is the place where the Holy Spirit renews the tradition and finds pathways to the future. Looking back over the history of the church, they claimed that revolutionaries such as Thomas Aquinas, Martin Luther, and John Calvin were once seen as disruptive people who had destabilized tradition. Today they are considered benchmark figures reflecting the tradition.

Finally, there was an argument that was brought up again and again. Women's ordination could lead to a break within the ecumenical movement. Churches would withdraw their participation from movements for Christian unity. Negotiations for uniting churches would be more difficult.

Those who argued for the ordination of women, however, pointed to the vast number of churches where women and men already were working together in ordained ministry. To acknowledge this fact and to further its implications would be to witness toward the unity of humankind. (Concerning the ecumenical movement, see Constance Parvey's appendix, pp. 139–74.)

ARGUMENTS AT THE 1957 AND 1958 CHURCH ASSEMBLIES

In his book *The Church Assembly Argues*, Dr. Tord Simonsson, now bishop of Strängnäs, has analyzed the debate as it was carried out both at the

1957 Church Assembly and then at the 1958 Church Assembly meeting that had been called together exclusively in order to resolve the question of the ordination of women.[21] He demonstrates how the arguments for and against were brought forward with force and specificity but not always with logic and insight. The debate was less a theological dialogue than a political battle where the quickness of attack and defense were the main strategies for most of the speakers who used their ingenuity in order to further their already made commitments. They aimed to seek out shortcomings in the positions of their opponents, thereby often being unconcerned with whether or not their own arguments were strictly logical and consistent with their stated principles.

Ethical decisions, particularly of a theological nature, are not easy to reach. To measure what is most fair and least damaging is a long and agonizing process of discernment. Simonsson's book opens with a quotation by Bishop Giertz in his appeal to the 1958 Church Assembly in its very closing hour: "Now the debate should actually begin. Now when all the speakers have said what they had been figuring out ahead of time that they must say because it was dear to them. Now we should really begin to scrutinize what has been said, and to try, if possible, to reach a little more unity between us."[22] Sadly, such appeal was neither heard nor heeded in the ensuing deliberations in the wake of the Assembly's decision. Simonsson's objective analysis demonstrates how the two convictions already were developed and how each side then accepted any argument that furthered its cause without giving full attention to their consequences and implications.

All parties agreed that "the Bible is the norm."[23] But right away their agreement fell apart because there were wide differences of interpretation. The first problem appeared: What did Jesus or Paul or Peter actually say or do in a specific situation? The second problem issued: What does this text mean for us today? For Lutherans, this posed the problem: What is Law and what is Gospel, and what is the relation between them? What is "the letter" and what is "the spirit," what is central and what is peripheral? What did St. Paul mean when he said that he had "a commandment of the Lord" and when he said "in Christ there is no longer man and woman"?

The same difference in interpretation occurred when the discussion turned to the "tradition as norm" and to the writings of the reformers as normgiving.[24] The two different views that had appeared concerning the interpretation of Bible texts split again over the meaning of tradition and confessions. They became irreconcilable when the issue of equality was brought up. Although everybody seemed to be for the equality of persons and many expressed their admiration for and agreement with the emancipation of women, the agreement withered when the discussion turned to the ordination of women. "According to the Bible," said one member, "a woman and a man are equal before God. But the Bible emphasizes also a difference between man and woman that is rooted in the order of creation and prevails in the world. This biblical view of equivalence *and* difference, is mirrored in the world of the Early Church."[25] "Before God" a woman has equivalence with a man, but what does this special equality mean? It was argued that this theological equality should not be confused with social equality in the world.[26] Therefore, women should not have equal access to positions open to men in the church. Some argued for the special ministry that Olov Hartman had proposed. Here was something that could be right for women, a position created to fit their special gifts; separate and complementary, yet equal.

Reading through the minutes from the two Assemblies 1957–58 it is almost moving to see how anxious many speakers were to put on record that their opposition to equal access to ordained ministry in no way meant any depreciation or disparaging view of women. One member contributed this memorable saying: "I would rather wish that today's debate in the Church Assembly could convince the women of Sweden that in the Assembly's decision—whatever it turns out to be—there lies no hidden contempt or lack of reverence for women."[27]

There were those, however, who fleetingly suggested that a "taboo conception" could lie behind the resistance to the ordination of women. The Dean of the Cathedral of Stockholm remarked: "I am not so sure that such an idea, however unconsciously, might not in some quarters be at the bottom of the question."[28]

Thus the debate thrashed back and forth through the arguments. The impending vote became viewed as a test between two different views of interpreting the Bible, but the debate revealed that there were many cultural and social elements involved as well.

When it did come down to a vote, the option of a special ministry for women fell away. As the debate developed over time this was not seen as a real option, but rather a diversion and an evasion of the question for or against equal access for men and women to ordained ministry. Olov Hartman himself had already abandoned this stance (see above).

In retrospect many people have come to believe that there was one aspect that contributed decisively to the negative vote of the 1957 Assembly—namely, a feeling among the clergy that the church should not be pushed into a decision by the state. The church should exercise authority over its own affairs without pressure from the state. Therefore, when shortly thereafter the second Assembly was called together by the government, the affirmative vote was looked upon by the opponents as giving in to the pressure from the state and the media (see above, the interview with Giertz). This defeat left a bitter aftertaste, which might explain to a certain degree the extreme measures the opposition proposed in *The 17 Points*.[29]

THE CONSCIENCE CLAUSE

As Bishop Giertz remarked in his interview, the state officials involved had been sensitive to what was happening, and partly owing to their cooperation the so-called Conscience Clause came into existence. As soon as Parliament had accepted the law of ordination for women and sent it back to the Church Assembly for ratification in 1958, a Special Committee was appointed to work out recommendations to ease the tensions. Jerker Victor from the Justice Department was instrumental in the formulation of the following paragraphs:

> Whether or not the proposal for a new law is accepted the fellowship within the church will be exposed to tension. But since it is vital for the work of the church in and among our people to avoid a churchsplitting separation the Committee views it necessary that these divisions not be exaggerated or sharpened and that neither side be pressed in such a way that it can be regarded as persecution of belief or breach of the freedom of conscience.

> Were the law proposal to be approved the Committee is anxious to point out that this may not bring to a bishop the duty to ordain a woman against his religiously founded conviction. Likewise the Committee wishes to express as its unanimous opinion that a priest shall not be forced to act in his ministry in a manner which obviously would violate his conscience because of the conviction he holds in this question. Neither may the priestly vows be so interpreted that a person who is opposed to women priests should not be able to give them.[30]

This Conscience Clause was intended to ease the pressure on those who could not accept the new order in the church, but it became instead a weapon in their hands. Although written as an opinion by the Special Committee in a preamble to the law, it soon was considered the law of the land by the opposition. Over the years that followed the Conscience Clause was taken as an excuse for harassing women priests and not letting them perform their priestly duties. One can speculate that had the minority not been given this olive branch by the Special Committee then the dialogue that Bishop Giertz had wished would come about might have got underway immediately. Instead the opposition froze in its stance. The ethical and theological questions were not discussed further between those of different convictions. The positions were not brought forward in dialogue. Instead a brotherhood was consolidated between those who rallied around Bible and Confession, and among the brethren a dialogue was unnecessary. They were not in the usual minority position where power must come from persuasion. Rather in this case the minority assumed power and exerted it under the umbrella of the Conscience Clause.

TWENTY YEARS LATER—THE 1982
CHURCH ASSEMBLY

When finally a new law proposal went before the Church Assembly in 1982 it was fitting that its title read *Reconsideration of the Conscience Clause* (SOU 1981:20). After more than twenty years of opposition, the time was ripe for reevaluation and change. A new study requested by the government resulted in this new proposal. The question was no longer whether or not to ordain women. That had already been declared law in 1958. It was in accordance with the order of the Church of Sweden that women were ordained, and almost 400 women were now serving as priests. Neither was the question to be debated this time the banishment of those whose conviction went against ordination of women. The Church of Sweden had already emphasized in 1958, and reiterated at the Church Assembly of 1979, that it did not wish to shut out those who believed differently on this issue. The issue in 1982 was whether the Church of Sweden would accept Sweden's general equality law of 1945 as a law governing her own life without qualifications; whether it would repeal the law of 1958 with its Conscience Clause preamble and take upon herself the responsibility for solving the problems of cooperation that might arise within the church. The matter came before the 1982 Church Assembly, the last with the old structure.

At this Church Assembly of 1982 there were 251 delegates, 64 of them were women and 7 of them were women priests. Ten of the 13 bishops were present.

On Tuesday 11 May 1982 the proposal to withdraw the Conscience Clause and make the law of 1945 valid also for the church was up for debate. Archbishop Olof Sundby began the day by saying that the goal for the future is "that all priests cooperate with each other in all priestly functions."[31] Bishop Bertil Gärtner in Göteborg, the stronghold of the opposition, took up the challenge and in his speech stressed "the responsibility for the minority" that the Conscience Clause had guarded would now be taken away. He urged the church to shoulder this responsibility for "a minority of a thousand priests" who want to remain in the old tradition of the church.[32]

Christina Odenberg, a priest in Stockholm, later spoke to the point that the Church of Sweden does not have two but only one official view of the priesthood. She stressed that a priest ought to be loyal to that view. As an analogy she mentioned that not all priests think that infant baptism is the right practice to continue in a secularized society. Out of loyalty to the Church of Sweden where infant baptism is common praxis, priests never refer to their hesitations [concerning tradition] and refuse to baptize children. She found it important to ask whose conscience needed extra protection.[33]

The dean of the cathedral of Strängnäs, Carl Strandberg, who opposes women priests mentioned "that we must get away from the idea that one can legislate in questions of belief." He wanted to view the question in an international and ecumenical perspective.[34] Dag Sandahl, a priest who had formed a resistance splinter group that aimed to create a synod, agreed: "Together we could ask for material that shows how they reason in other churches about the priesthood and women's ministry. Ecumenically people are not prepared to say to the opponents that their opinion cannot be accepted. On the contrary; it rests on factual ground."[35]

The argument of ecumenical relations was then taken up many times. Bishop Lönnebo in Linköping made a moving and irenic speech where he said: "For a long time now we have been lacking in respect for each other concerning the question of the priesthood in our church. Therefore the conflict has been more malignant in Sweden than in any other country. It is first during these last years, I think, that I have understood how hard it has hit our sisters. It must be the very worst experience to be perceived as having a nonexistence in one's identity as priest. The big ecumenicity between the churches is fast bringing the Christians of the world together. More difficult has been to accomplish ecumenicity within our church but we are not without means to succeed. A reconciliation within our church should be an exercise in miniature for how the union of churches should happen, and we in turn become a model on a small scale for the union of peoples."[36]

Anna Greta Erikson picked up the theme of togetherness: "We must work with ourselves and our attitudes, our theories and our consciences in order to reach a life-style in which we together take responsibility for everything in our Swedish Church. We need schooling for such things, teaching our youth to be open to those who think differently and to have respect for other people's calling and faith.. . . ."[37]

Bishop Brattgord, knowledgeable about the Lutheran World Federation, gave a survey of the situation in other Lutheran churches. He mentioned that 75% of these churches, with 56 million members, now have women priests. Eighteen percent of the churches, with 13 million members—mostly in Africa and Asia with very different cultural backgrounds—have not yet ordained women, but he said, "A process is in motion and progress is taking place."[38]

Bishop Werkström of Härnösand, now the archbishop of Sweden, analyzed the crisis he thought the church had gone through during the last decades. The first stage was shock, and the second had been reaction. The third stage, in which he thought the church now was involved, he characterized as the stage of reparation. The fourth stage, which he envisioned for the future, he called "the time for new orientation": "I cannot guarantee that the development will go in this direction but we can believe and hope that it will be so."[39]

The person who gave the most incisive analysis was Bishop Tord

Simonsson in Strängnäs. He noted with satisfaction that the present proposal for legislation left room for different views in the church concerning the interpretation of the Bible, and he expressed his hope that now when the different dioceses were to shoulder the responsibility for coexistence it also may work out. "Co-existence however, presupposes openness or co-existence has no future." He then mentioned a factor that had locked the positions in the past and made it impossible to coexist. It is a certain tendency built into religious dicta. Their implications, which at first are limited to one problem, then tend to spread out and widen over the whole field. The opposition to the ordination of women, a specific question, had become a general question about faithfulness to the Bible and then for some even a question of salvation. It seemed to him very important that when people spoke about faith and convictions they took into consideration how their own beliefs had been formed and how social and psychological factors like that of belonging to a group had influenced them. Then he said: "The present situation is that we really want to cooperate in the same church. Already that means a form of acceptance. The person who refuses to do it is in reality putting a stop to co-existence. This is a matter of sacrificing personal positions but not one's faith. Such sacrifices should be gratefully received. Thereby co-existence can come to signify the beginning of health and growth for the church."[40]

Bishop Lars Carlzon of the Stockholm diocese, where one-third of the ordained women now serve, was unable to be present at the debate, but in a written statement he pleaded with the Assembly to take into account also the views of the laity who find it natural with the present order which the Church of Sweden has established. "Let us serve together."[41]

The words most often highlighted were coexistence and cooperation. Many seemed anxiously aware of the bad image that the strife had dealt to the church and called for cooperation in repairing the damage. The credibility of the church craved that it solve the problem of cooperation. The church must learn to live with a pluralistic society and a nonstatic situation in a changing world.

Those who were on the side of opposition worried about what would happen to them. They pleaded for consideration and respect. This church was also their church, their "mother." They would not feel at home in any other church.

The last speaker, Per Blomquist, commented that the debate had been marked by openness and obvious will to understand each other. "May this good will be turned into action."[42]

All the speakers unanimously recommended the proposal, and the day ended with a vote in favor. Thereby a long struggle had ended. Church and state now stand united on this question. The law of equal access for women to all offices and positions needs no longer some special qualifications concerning the church.

This is remarkable. How remarkable will be completely clear when we compare the Swedish situation with the ecumenical discussions and arguments in Appendix 2. To come to clarity and to reach a decision in the question of women's ordination takes time and requires patience, stamina, and resolve. That the women have to raise their voices and claim full participation is a key element to progress. In many churches women have no institutional base from which to operate, and prove their care while men have the whole institutional staff holding to support their tradition.

Of the liturgical, priestly churches Sweden was actually the first to reach a decision to ordain women. There were no models. Sweden's clergy pioneered. They argued fiercely. In the end at the 1982 Assembly vote we can detect some fatigue and a common wish for fairness.

4

DOCUMENTS CONCERNING
EQUALITY

Sweden's development from an agrarian to an industrial and post-industrial state has changed people's lives in every way. The material living standard has risen to heights unimaginable in earlier days. Young people are brought up with a wide range of possibilities and choices. Not only have all institutions changed, but they are in constant transformation.

In this process two forces that once were allies now are often on a collision course: technology and equality. Technology has liberated people from heavy labor. Equality demands more job opportunities. Change has been a blessing, perhaps especially for women: less heavy tasks in the home, more opportunities for earnings outside. But the bright picture is fading. New machines are replacing people in their jobs. An advanced technological society craves more and more specialized knowledge. How to adapt to change is *the* problem for modern people. Once people were used to a stable world, and they could plan for the future. People yearn for stabilization. Individuals, families, and institutions all try to master change. Experts are called in and consultants are designing plans. Modern technology is scanned for new inventions that can make and keep a project profitable. Women's role in these long-range planning schemes concerns them very much. They do not want to be pawns any longer. They want to be players on equal terms. Modern technology has made equality possible. But ironically the blame for change is seldom on technology but often on equality: had not the women entered the work force, had not the immigrants taken the jobs, had not the pension and medical care for the elderly cost so much, and so on.

It has been said that the question of the ordination of women is not a matter of equality. In admitting that there are many other elements involved—the previous chapter displayed the arguments—the question of equality, however, can easily be brushed aside as less important. In fact, a commitment to equality is extremely important for how people interact with each other, in the church as well as in society. Equality has climbed down from a high philosophical pedestal to become a nagging everyday issue in Western societies.

The church is a part of society. Its priests cannot isolate themselves from the people. However much the priests would like to get back to an agrarian type of stable society where the church was the center of the village and Sunday was everybody's holy day, it cannot be done. The clock ticks forward and raises the anxiety for the future with more and more conflicting forces pressing upon each other. What is important for people, what causes their suffering, is also important for the church. How do people fare in a technological society?

There was a time not long ago when the priests lived in relative innocence about the question of equality, but the last decades have brought upon them its importance. The conflict has entered their own house. It struck on the most sensitive aspect of equality: the relationship between men and women, both public and very private in character. Here the clergy considered themselves to be experts. They had been used to mediate in family conflicts. Society needed them as marriage counselors. In cases of divorce the partners were obligated to meet with a priest. This rule was altered in the 1950s just at the time when the issue of women's ordination was heating up. Social workers often took over the role of mediators, a task that had taken much time and effort on the part of the priests. Government agencies provided policies that promoted equality. That fact put some clergy in an adversary position.

TOWARD EQUALITY

In 1971, the Social Democratic Party, together with the Swedish Federation of Trade Unions, published guidelines for the furthering of equal rights in Sweden. These guidelines were worked out by a committee under the leadership of Alva Myrdal, who from 1967 to 1973 was minister of church affairs in the Social Democratic cabinet. The report that the committee published in Sweden was titled *Jämlikhet*. An abridged version of the document was published in English under the title *Towards Equality*.[1] It begins by listing the many achievements toward an equalization of living conditions over the years. A look at that list makes us realize that through democratic procedure during the last fifty years, Sweden has undergone a peaceful revolution. Up to 1958, the critical year for the church, the following had been achieved, which both directly and indirectly affected the life of women:

In 1933, a comprehensive program to prohibit unemployment.
In 1935, a large-scale government aid program for improving housing, including housing subsidies for low-income families.
In 1935, −36, −37, a reform of the old-age pension system.
In 1938, two weeks' vacation with pay for all wage earners.
In 1939, a law that forbade the dismissal of a woman from employment because of marriage, pregnancy, or childbirth.
In 1946, −47, −48, substantial increase in old-age pensions and the introduction of a general childrens' allowance. Plus a more equitable distribution of the tax burden.
In 1950, a comprehensive school reform.

In 1953, the national health-insurance scheme to take effect from the beginning of 1955.

In 1956, the two weeks' vacation extended to three weeks with pay for all wage earners.

In 1958, the National Pension Fund was established increasing public influence over the capital market.[2]

During the 1960s the growth of the public sector continued. "The Social Democrats have worked for a democratization of education, improvement in the living conditions of families with children, increased services and higher living standards for old-age pensioners, equal rights for the handicapped, and greatly expanded labor-market policies."[3] A coordinated industrial relocation policy was begun which was aimed at geographical equality with respect to employment opportunities. In order to provide people living in sparsely populated areas with adequate public services, a comprehensive reform for local government tax equalization was implemented.

These accomplishments were achieved by the will and the vote of the Swedish people. General suffrage had been voted upon in 1919 and written into law in 1921, a time when the Social Democratic party was not yet in power, though on a strong advance. Then "all men" got the right to enter all schools and professions. The thought of equal rights for men—which just a few decades earlier had seemed impossible and unmanageable—was no longer a theory but a possibility for those who were strong and determined, healthy and lucky.

When the Social Democrats came into power in 1932, the opportunities were extended. During World War II, Sweden reinforced its defense and drafted a large percentage of its male population into military service. The experiences during the war both within the armed forces and in society at large, where women had to replace the men in the work force, broke down old class barriers and old-fashioned styles of behavior. The Social Democrats, who earlier had been in favor of women staying home and being freed from long and hard labor, changed policy and promoted women in the labor force. Society made great strides toward equalization both through legislation and through new living patterns. In 1945 the equal rights law was changed to remove the last vestiges of discrimination against women. The word "man" was stricken from the law and replaced with the word "citizen." Through §28 in the Swedish Constitution the doors of employment and promotion are open to "all citizens." The new law stated that *a woman should have equal access to all Government employment* and that she should be promoted according to ability and skill just like a man. Only the priesthood was explicitly excepted.

The decades of the fifties and sixties were years of expansion, prosperity, and progress. Legislation increased to extend the bounty to all citizens, and the progressive tax system contributed to an equalized living standard. During these decades the welfare state became reality. The question the report raises is: What comes next?

The underlying principle for equality is the equal value of all people. In the report it is stated in this manner: "All (people) have the same right to live a full and satisfying life."[4] The obvious goal is to bring those who are less favored by society into focus: the low income earners, the unemployed, the immigrants, the handicapped, the single person, the elderly, those who live in isolated communities—and women. The government has the responsibility to raise the standard of living for these categories and thus increase their opportunities to shape their own future. Women are seen as one of the categories among the disadvantaged.

Justice demands solidarity with those disadvantaged by the rest of society. The report states that democratic conditions mean that individuals should have the opportunity to influence their immediate life situation in cooperation with others. The prerequisites for better human relations between nations, as well as between individuals, are the rights to education and the freedom of choice to shape their own life, to have access to power and redress.

Thus, the report goes beyond a liberal view of equality which is being criticized for giving people merely formal and theoretical "equal opportunity," that is, the right to compete on equal terms. Those who are less aggressive are easily shoved aside in a competitive society. Instead they need to be heard. What the report recommends is "an active redistribution of power"—similar to what in the United States is called "affirmative action"—and it recommends that the programs already in place, such as the national health care, the pension insurance, day care, child allowances, and so forth, should be enlarged. Moreover, it enjoins that a less hierarchical organization of government be effectuated.

The report takes note of the fact that 90% of the unemployed—3% of the total work force—have only basic schooling. It points out that unemployment is regionally conditioned. Further, it notes how the poor inherit poverty, while the rich inherit—if not riches in terms of money—then easier access to power.

To achieve equality of the sort the report envisions means to give priority to measures that benefit the disadvantaged and harness the overt and covert privileges of the advantaged. Knowing that this is strong medicine to swallow, the report recommends "education for equality" in the schools.

It states in italics: "Questions of sex roles should be discussed in the school at all stages of the educational process." The school should actively intervene for equality of the sexes.[5]

Education is seen as the key. It should not just be reserved for the young in schools but should continue through life. Study leaves are recommended to alternate with gainful employment. To take a course should be considered something laudable. And it should be the right of every father as well as the mother to take paid leave to get to know their newborn child.

Some of the report's recommendations were soon implemented (e.g., paid leave from work shared between parents after the birth of a child). Most important, a law office was established to give special attention to the disadvantaged and to monitor their complaints, giving those who considered themselves discriminated against an opportunity for redress.[6]

The 1970s put Sweden to a severe test concerning its true conviction about equality. The test came in the response to the immigrants who had been arriving since World War II, and from the 1960s on in ever-increasing numbers. They come from poorer countries, drawn by the high wages and attracted by the social benefits offered in Sweden. During the sixties, Sweden suffered labor shortage, and these immigrants were most welcome to take the jobs that Swedes did not care to have. During the seventies, however, when the percentage of the unemployed began to creep up and the immigrant contingent did not diminish, the old maxim proved true that differences between individuals create divisions between peoples. Such differences lay the foundations for inequalities. The micro-world becomes the model for the macro-world. Swedes began to look askance at the immigrants, and suspicions took hold.

The conviction, for which the report speaks so clearly, that hierarchical systems should be democratized and people integrated with each other, is a conviction that must be understood and earned in struggle over and over again. The title, *Towards Equality,* is correct. "Towards" because a conviction is never gained once and for all. Its vision has to be recaptured.

In the international family, Sweden is well advanced when it comes to laws that care for the elderly, the handicapped, the young, and the immigrants.[7] Boys and girls get an equal start in coeducational schools. Women work side by side with men and get equal pay. The perspective of equality is everywhere in evidence. It is the law. But as with all systems of belief, it is also a matter of a decision: for or against. The reaction of the 1980s seems to be: We have gone far enough. Yet, the women in the women's movement say: We have not come far enough. We still live in a society that continues to be shaped and governed by men. Women still earn less. They still hold baseline jobs and do not advance at the same pace as men do. Formal discrimination is removed. Informal difficulties remain.[8]

ALVA MYRDAL—AN INTERVIEW

Alva Myrdal is now in her eighties. She was among the pioneers. She worked extremely hard in order to be heard among the men and win them over. She kept her figures straight and was sure she had them at her fingertips in order to convince her opposition. She joined the Social Democratic Party

early and became a spokeswoman for family related questions. She understood the importance of professional women organizing themselves to have
clout. For many years she held the chair of YK, a club of professional women.
She achieved not only the respect of her male colleagues but their vote and
approval of her policies. In succession she was appointed envoy to the United
Nations, Ambassador to India, Minister of Church Affairs, and finally a
member of the UN's Disarmament and Development Group in Geneva. Her
accomplishments are innumerable and her many honors well deserved, especially the Nobel Peace Prize in 1982. The Alva Myrdal Report reflects her
ceaseless concern for justice to all who are disadvantaged in the society.

In 1981 on one of her visits to Cambridge, Mass., I interviewed her about
her relation to the Church of Sweden. The first question put to her: Had she
been aware of the vote in 1958 to admit women also to the priesthood? Had it
made any impression? At the time she was Swedish Ambassador to India. Her
answer was that it had had practically no impact on her. "It made no
difference in my work, which was to serve the democracy of India." "I do not
recall any of the earlier debates and the stance of other leading women in
politics on that question. I remember Ester Lutteman leaving the church
because of its earlier decision not to admit women."[9]

When Myrdal became the minister of Church Affairs she received no
specific directives. Her goal was to accomplish a reform of church property,
to clarify the relations between church and state, and to get the free-
churches on a more equitable footing compared with the established Church
of Sweden. She had power to appoint bishops and, at some occasions, also
priests to certain major positions.[10] She was especially happy that she had
been able to appoint Margit Sahlin to the prestigious vicarage of the Engelbrekt parish. She mentioned that during her time the work on a new translation of the Bible, the work on a new Book of Worship, and on a new Hymnal
had been instigated. Her major efforts were concerned with the relationship
between church and state. They had resulted in the Myrdal-Gustafson proposal for restructure that to her disappointment had been rejected in 1979 by
the Church.[11] She admitted that she had not thought of the increasing number
of women priests as a problem but had only viewed the fact as a sign of
progress. "It was no problem then. It came later." She had never known any
women priests personally, nor had she made any special effort to get in touch
with them as a group. "I never spoke to them."[12] She had not considered them
as her allies in her work for equality of the disadvantaged or in her work for
disarmament. She had looked upon them as individuals and had not given
their specific problems with dual careers or with recalcitrant superiors any
attention. When asked what she would wish for the future of the church, she
made one suggestion fully in line with her expressed trust in education. She
hoped that the training of future priests would be strengthened, especially in
pastoral care. She believed that one day it would seem self-evident that

women enter the ministry. The resistance would disappear when the so-called Conscience Clause disappeared. She stressed that this clause had never been put into law, but over the years it had had an escalating effect and had become a cornerstone for the opposition.

THE CHURCH AND EQUALITY

When Ingmar Ström in the interview spoke about the church's social ethics program in the 1950s, which was quashed by the uproar around women priests, he pointed to something relevant. The people in the church had been on their way to discover that they had left ethics and social implementation to the state. Democracy at work for the welfare of the people took place outside the church. Social work became more and more a question of government programs. The input was up to the experts, the planners, and the statisticians, and they did an excellent job. But in the long run the complacency of the general public and the bureaucracy of the developing welfare system became a dangerous mixture. The average taxpayer began to complain about the heavy burden and about the cumbersome system that proved unable to catch all cases in its safety net.[13]

The social ethics program was designed to raise the social consciousness of the people and to help them see beyond their own needs to the needs of others, getting a better understanding of the social realities in society. Ström mentioned how in 1950 the bishops had issued a letter out of their concern for the change in sexual behavior, and the reaction to the letter had clearly taught him the necessity of being informed of social realities and public opinion.

THE BISHOPS' LETTER CONCERNING
SEXUAL MORES

The Christian advice that the church had been giving to people in the early twentieth century concerning marriage had habitually been traditional. The concern for the family was a major theme in their counseling. Eventually the changing sexual mores became the focus of much debate and lament among the priests. When the Kinsey report revealed wide differences in living patterns in the United States it released a storm of discussion in Sweden.[14] Sexual mores seemed to conform more with social class than with any other factor—religious faith included. Furthermore, Kinsey showed that the living pattern priests recommended was almost vanishing among the young. Was this true also in Sweden?

Both in the city and in the country the priests were appalled at the growing amount of advice on sexual mores that was now being given in the press and in the schools. Much of it went against the old ways. A new "mentality" was on the way to development. The church was losing ground as an authority on moral issues.

The Bishops' Council discussed their obligation to take a stand on the changing sexual mores of Sweden. With the church's traditional concern for the family, they felt that something was happening that threatened to loosen family ties and family responsibility. Some members of the Council felt pressed to show where they stood. For the first time in memory they published something like an encyclical, a word of guidance to priests regarding how to advise the people in the parishes. In 1950 Bishop Björkquist in Stockholm was instructed to draft A *Letter Concerning Sexual Questions.*[15] In the context of our study it is worth noting that although it did not aim at defining the role of women, it indirectly projected a view that rejected women's liberation and shows little understanding for society's growing demand on women's participation in the work force.

The letter declares that the aim of matrimony is the common welfare and fostering of spouses and children. The marriage vows are for life and unbreakable. Therefore, the church "is against the divorce mentality of the present, according to which marriage is a contract that binds the partners for as long as they agree. . . . Between spouses who both humbly submit to the will of God, the word divorce ought not even to be mentioned."[16]

Concerning sexual intercourse outside of marriage, the church holds the view, the letter states, that "it is a sin against both God and the neighbor. . . . The Church rejects all talk about trial marriages."[17] The letter continues by also rejecting the use of contraceptives within marriage, except under special conditions.

Concerning abortion the letter says: "Our Church does not share the opinion that abortion in all circumstances is reprehensible. But she looks in distress upon the abortion mentality that wants to give the pregnant woman free choice whether or not to give birth to her child. . . . The Church asserts vigorously the responsibility of the father-to-be toward the expected child and to its mother."[18]

Regarding sterilization, the letter cautions against its use, and regarding artificial insemination only "homologic insemination" as "by means of medicine to realize the purpose of marriage," can be accepted.[19]

The letter comes down most harshly when it speaks to the issue of homosexuality: "The person who practices homosexual acts is breaking God's commandments."[20] It expresses a fear that such persons may seduce the youth.

The uproar in the press caused by this letter was no doubt frightening to the bishops. It revealed a gulf between the opinions they had taken for granted that most people held and the shift in positions that the secular society had already accepted. The incident of the letter and the coincidence of a scandal concerning the truthfulness of one of the bishops undermined the credibility of the church and stifled new initiatives of frank and fearless debate on the relations between the sexes. The church, in spite of its ideology as a folk-church living in the midst of the people, discovered that it had isolated itself from the people. A clear policy concerning equal rights had never been worked out. Societal change had been ignored. For instance, in the case of women's rights where the introduction of birth-control devices is of decisive importance for the independence of women, there had not been a word that accepted and welcomed this fact. Instead the bishops had rejected the use of contraceptives even within marriage. No wonder that leading intellectual women in the women's movement had long since written off the church as being hopelessly behind the times with no vision for the future of women.

FOR OR AGAINST EQUALITY?

The discussion in the 1950s around the question of the ordination of women had to absorb these unresolved problems and much frustration. When the Church Assembly was mandated in 1957 by the government to debate and vote on the ordination of women, the recommendations from the Royal Commission of 1950 were clear and spoke for equal rights: "That a woman shall have equal right to ordination."[21] From the government's point of view the main agenda was to take a position on equal rights within the church, but since this meant access to the priesthood, there was general confusion. What might be all right in the secular world was perhaps wrong in the church.

The people who came to debate and to vote found no clear signals from the bishops. Rather, the bishops had warned against dangerous trends to loosen the family ties. The government's recommendation, however, was for ordination and equal rights. When it came to a vote, the Church Assembly of 1957 voted against the proposition for equal rights and ordination of women.

It is important to understand the climate. Here a whole professional group felt to be under siege from the government and from the press. Among the clergy and laity that assembled, there probably were many who never had had to take an official stand on principle. Here they were forced to do so. In school and university they had worked alongside women. Their mothers and wives were perhaps employed outside the home. They had seen women handle responsible jobs well. But then there were the obstacles in the Bible, there was the tradition, the church fathers, Luther. What finally led a person to decide for or against was in many cases hard to say. But a decision could not be postponed forever. Clergy and lay delegates alike encountered the question everywhere: For or against?[22]

As already reported above, the government did not accept the no vote. It sent the proposition for the change of the law without waiting for the consent of the Church Assembly on to the Parliament which debated promptly and voted yes. Then the government called the Church Assembly into an extra session. This time the vote was yes. The debates had been exhausted. The press was unrelenting. The stance of the minority had hardened. The outcome was therefore ambiguous. Women were no longer to be excluded from the priesthood and could not be refused ordination. It signalled a victory for women, and for equal rights, but a dangerous situation in the church, precarious for peace and cooperation because many priests were shocked.

The government understood that conditions had now been created which could involve a clash between the law of equal rights and the paragraph in the Swedish Constitution that says that nobody should be forced to act against his conscience. Therefore the Conscience Clause was provided. With the Conscience Clause behind them the opposition prepared for attack.

THE 17 POINTS

In 1960 it was announced that on Palm Sunday that year three women were to be ordained. On the very same day the opposition sent out a pamphlet that contained a guideline in 17 points for those ministers and lay people who could not accept women as priests, telling them how to behave should they encounter a woman priest. This manifesto, popularly called *The 17 Points,* can be summed up in one word: boycott. It was sent to all priests in the Church of Sweden. It was put together by a committee of priests and lay people—men and women—who had been working against the ordination of women. They called themselves the Association for Consolidation in the Church around Bible and Confession. Bishop Giertz was their leader. He wrote the introduction to the guideline:

Through its decision to open the priesthood to women the Church Assembly has introduced the Church of Sweden to an order that goes against the will of God and against Christ's instructions as given us in Scripture. The concern here is for such an important matter as the command to speak on Christ's behalf and to administer the sacraments in his name. If the church administers this task against the command of its Lord such an ordination cannot be valid. It does not mediate a mission from Christ. It signifies a misuse of the name of the Lord. The person ordained in such a manner is not *rite vocatus,* not rightly called to the office and not authorized to practice it on Christ's behalf. (The same is true were a woman to get *venia.*)

If one is to encounter such an office [holder] within one's own church, one cannot accept it but must keep one's distance. This disapproval concerns the matter itself. When it comes to the person one has to act with the tact that love itself demands. The responsibility for the present situation does not only hurt those closely associated with it. Our church has for a long time been insecure about its creed and confession. Vital and central parts of the Christian message have been mute and denied. There has been great unclarity concerning the authority of God's word and to what it obligates. What we experience today are the consequences of the long-lasting malformations within the church.

Hence it is important that on the one hand one clearly distances oneself from such things in the church which implicate deviation from the Word of God, and on the other hand that one always stays truly loving of the individual persons and in one's actions has their souls and the welfare of the church before one's eyes.

It is hardly possible to work out detailed guidelines before the fact. Nobody can foresee all the situations that may occur. The suggestions given here below are thus meant as advice, neither binding the conscience of any individuals, nor freeing them in each new situation from the duty to test their actions before God and their conscience tied to the Word.

Then the guidelines follow:[23]

1. Priests aware that the ordination of women goes against the command of the Lord obviously cannot assist at such an ordination and they ought to avoid being present. This last part of the advice is valid also for the laity.

2. Since a woman does not administer the office at the command of Christ, a priest cannot exercise his priestly service together with her, nor can he cooperate at the same service, nor go before the altar together with her, nor celebrate communion or any other church services, ordinations, etc.

3. If a senior pastor gets a woman as his assistant priest his position becomes untenable. He can hardly, owing to his conviction, ask her to perform tasks in his parish or open his church for a service that goes against the order of the New Testament. What route he should choose in such a situation will have to depend on consultations in each case. One ought to count on the leadership of the Church to avoid placements that will create such situations.

4. Other priests who according to the division of services within the parish must work side by side with a woman priest ought to remain in their positions but refuse to do any kind of priestly service together with her.

5. Concerning the task of the civil registry there is free choice between two stands. Which stand of the two one takes depends on how one understands the duty to do the civil registry regarding the church records. Since these things have hardly been thoroughly thought through and made clear by the Church a definite verdict is impossible. The decision is left to each priest's conscience.

a) The civil registry may be looked upon as a registry where the accountant as in all other registries has to use formal rules in classifying the data to be accounted for in accordance with the common nomenclature and other set rules. In such instances many descriptions are often used which, although they are not fully adequate, nevertheless are accepted since one has to make room for many different occurrences within a set number of rubrics. For example, Jewish weddings are listed under the heading of Church weddings although from a strictly Christian point of view this is false. Also when it comes to membership in the church or the birthplace of a person the rules now applied do not always give a true picture of reality. From a certain point of view such false notations can, of course, only be used with the presupposition that one knows that one is dealing here with a formal classification of data that does not connote any religious stance, either on the part of the church or on the part of the accountant.

From this view of the civil registry it ought to be possible to register acts performed by women priests according to actual statute. Obviously it does not mean that one thereby affirms that they have been performed in "right order."

b) On the other hand one can assert that the classification of data in the civil registry must also be correct from a religious point of view. It has been said that alternative a) could be looked upon as a concession and that even a relatively minor act in a tense situation can assume the character of a confession (*status confessionis*). From this point of view one cannot in certain cases register a service performed by a woman according to actual statute. It will become necessary then to investigate case by case as to how an act performed by a woman shall be judged. A marriage ceremony performed by a woman is valid by law. A burial service is a human custom which in certain cases can be transferred to the laity. A baptism performed by a woman should be considered as a lay-baptism which in itself is in keeping with the established church order but should be confirmed by the pastor. That a woman takes part in the education of confirmands is not in itself wrong but becomes so if she performs the confirmation and communion services.

6. Since every Swedish priest has the right to admit to the holy communion each person whom he considers having the necessary insights, he also may admit someone who is confirmed by a woman priest. In such cases a person should not suffer because of conditions for which the official church is to blame.

7. In other respects a priest ought to avoid participating in all church activities, legal or voluntary, where a woman participates in her capacity of priest. In certain cases he could continue to sit on a board even if a woman priest were to be elected to the same board. He ought to resign however, if the board employs a woman or takes responsibility in any way for her work as priest, unless by staying he can work for the confessional point of view and thus accomplish a better order. He may participate at pastors' conventions and meetings even if a woman priest is present and he should take part if important questions are on the agenda. He should not participate, however, in any parts of the program in which a woman performs some priestly function. Much must be decided case by case under the consideration that he does not withdraw from his priestly responsibility in the Church of Sweden, but he may not on the other hand give the impression that he silently accepts something that is and remains wrong according to the Word of God.

8. For the time being a priest whose bishop ordains a woman ought not for this reason seek another position in another diocese or withdraw from such cooperation with the bishop that according to the law and statute of the church is prescribed concerning conventions, visitations, installations, etc. He ought to show his bishop all the respect that belongs to his office. At the same time, however, it cannot be avoided that the deeper community and the full trust have been lost.

The same rule goes for behavior toward colleagues in the priesthood who, for example, have assisted at the ordination of woman and thereby demonstrated their stance against the biblical and apostolic order.

9. Owing to his conviction, a member of the Diocesan Council must oppose a woman's being accepted for examination and ordination. Further, he must refuse to examine her. He cannot be party to the employment of an ordained woman, or in any other way concede that she be treated as a person properly called to the priestly office.

The laity are under the following rules:

10. The laity ought to abstain from attending a service performed by a woman priest.

11. No children should be sent to a confirmation class conducted by a woman priest.

12. She ought not to be asked for counseling or for sickbed communion.

13. She ought not be asked to perform baptisms, weddings or funerals. If a Christian person, faithful to confession, were to be invited to be present at a service performed by a woman priest, he ought to confer with his confessor on what the considerations for the human community demand in this specific case.

14. The laity in a parish that has a woman priest must request access to another priest within the nearest neighborhood.

15. A layman who has a special commission within the parish ought to oppose all activities leading to the use of a woman priest in parish service. Deacon, organist and janitor should refuse to function at services where a woman priest celebrates. They could then ask for and expect the same consideration that according to the decision of the Church Assembly should be shown a priest, namely, that they "ought not to be asked to do such things that clearly would violate their conscience owing to their conviction in this case."

16. No person faithful to the confession ought to travel to meetings and conferences where a woman priest participates.

17. The laity ought to consider their responsibility for all those, priests and laity, who will suffer persecution and economical hardship for their faithfulness to the Word of God.

With this document the opposition to the women coalesced. They had a program for action. People on the other side felt a terrifying chill. The advent of the ordination was effectively undercut. In every way the acts of the future women priests were put in question. The document bewildered and enraged. Some people protested the opposition's behavior by announcing the termination of their membership in the Church of Sweden. Others became uncertain. Could it be true that communion services and baptisms performed by women ministers were not valid? The tradition of "the order of creation" had got the upper hand. It had been spelled out clearly. Equality had suffered a blow.

FROM CONFRONTATION TO COOPERATION

With all the signals from uncertainty to hostility, it is no wonder that the number of women who became ordained in the first decade increased slowly—from three to forty.

During the 1970s, however, the numbers rose rapidly. At the end of the decade, there were 371 women and 2,616 men serving the Swedish church. In 1982 there were women priests in all the 13 dioceses, and only one bishop,

Gärtner in Göteborg, refused to ordain women, referring to the Conscience Clause.[24] With such an increase it seems likely that almost all people, priests as well as laity, have on one occasion or another encountered women as priests. If not directly in situations of personal contact, they have seen them in action on television or heard them on Swedish radio.[25] An existential encounter usually brings with it some adjustment of judgment.

A change of attitude had also come about. The opposition no longer called for confrontation. Unhappy with the prospect of a future in a church with many women priests, it turned its energy into forming a separate Synod.[26] Other people in the church began strongly to emphasize cooperation. In 1978 the Bishops' Council took initiative to write their own guidelines stating that *The 17 Points* were to be looked upon as "a document of the past."[27] It could no longer be applied.

Thus, the Church of Sweden's official answer to the minority's challenge came almost twenty years after the publication of *The 17 Points;* twenty years during which the opposition took for granted that they were in the right, and for that reason women priests were not to be tolerated; twenty years during which they foisted their opinion on the whole Church of Sweden and maimed every effort to break out of the deadlock. With the new guidelines, the special situations that have occasioned their phrasing become vividly clear. Twenty years might not be a long time in the eyes of the Lord, but for the church a whole generation was lost owing to this internal strife. Still, the people who formulated the new guidelines are more concerned with men, with the conscience of men, and they express a wish to provide men with the possibility to "step aside," to excuse themselves from cooperation with women priests. The conscience of women and how women priests ought to act when they are discriminated against is not addressed.

On 1 December 1978 these rules were issued by Archbishop Olof Sundby: *"Rules for cooperation in the Church of Sweden between those who hold different opinions concerning the right of women to ordination."*[28]

Introduction

1. According to its confession the Church of Sweden sees the Bible as its guiding star and its highest norm.

Our different opinions have their origin in our different understandings of the message in the Bible concerning the form of ministry for our Church.

2. The confession of the Church is an expression of how the Church at different times has interpreted the message of the Bible. The advent of the law of 1958 meant that the Church Assembly had resolved that the ordination of women was in accord with the confession of the Church.

3. The Special Committee at the 1958 Church Assembly expressed it as its opinion that a priest ought not be asked to do such things as would manifestly go against his conscience owing to his conviction on the question of women priests, the so-called Conscience Clause. This rule wished to safeguard the right of free

speech and to protect the right of conviction for both sides. However, it has now become necessary to give further explanation to the import of this right of conviction. The following guidelines for coexistence and cooperation shall be valid both for those who are now priests and for those who in the future may become priests in the Church of Sweden.

Guidelines of Principle:

4. Nobody should be forced to act against their conscience. Nobody should try to obstruct those who want to follow the actual order of the church. Where different convictions confront each other, the official rule of the church must have precedence. He who holds another opinion has the right to step aside.

5. The question of women priests cannot be considered to be exclusively a question between priests. In concrete situations of decisions the consciences of other parishioners must be given great weight.

6. Those who hold another opinion concerning woman's right to ordination than that which the church's actual statute proclaims shall also in the future be able to be ordained and to obtain a position as a priest in the Church of Sweden. A prerequisite for ordination is that the priest-to-be is prepared to cooperate according to these guidelines.

7. The person who accepts becoming a bishop must be willing to be a bishop for both male and female priests in the diocese.

Guidelines of Practice:

8. Nobody should be denied ordination for reasons of gender.

If a bishop owing to his conviction cannot ordain a woman candidate she shall—after having been accepted by the Diocesan Council—be given access to ordination in another diocese for the purpose of serving in the diocese for which she has been accepted.

He who refuses ordination because he does not consider it possible to be ordained together with a woman candidate cannot count on a special ordination or on ordination in another diocese.

For those candidates for the priesthood who cannot participate in a common ordination service, the open possibility exists to seek ordination in a diocese where there is no woman candidate at the time and then at some later date, after having served that diocese, apply with the consent of the Diocesan Council for a post in another diocese.

9. The church records and the civil registration may not be made dependent on whether the priest is a man or a woman.

10. Every person is free to apply for any priestly position within the framework of actual statutes.

11. When a priest is sent to a parish position, the primary concern—excepting, of course, the needs of the congregations—must be that the conditions are made right for functional cooperation. No warranties should be promised that in any given position male and female priests will never have to cooperate with each other.

12. Cooperation in the workplace:

12.1 The services

12.1.1 A parish priest should on principle have the right to serve in all the churches within the pastorate. A division of work may not be made according to gender.

He who cannot do liturgical service together with a woman priest may not obstruct her service but may himself abstain from serving. If necessary, a substitute can be allowed to serve in his place.

12.1.2 It is important in coexistence that no priests take on a priestly task in another parish on any other occasion than through a call by, or in agreement with, the priest who has the responsibility for the pastoral care in that parish.

A parishioner always has the right of access to the parish church for a service according to the *rite* of the Church of Sweden. Further, the decision whether or not to open the church must not be made on the basis of the gender of the priest asked to perform the service.

Priests are to cooperate actively and to see to it that demonstrative acts are avoided in such cases.

When a priest visits another parish, called there to participate in some conference or other kind of meeting, the host parish is obliged ahead of time to prepare and set up for the services planned for the visit.

12.1.3 A suitable priest should be appointed to lead the services at diocesan or other kinds of conferences, without regard to gender.

12.2 Further instructions about cooperation in the ministrial work of pastors:

12.2.1 Coexistence presupposes that male and female priests in the same pastorate cooperate in their common tasks such as administration, planning, bookkeeping, etc., and that when they are off duty they greet each other in a manner that each Christian has the right to expect from a fellow Christian.

If a priest or a layperson responsible for a certain type of activity asks for occasional help, such help must not be denied because of different opinions concerning the ordination of women. Vice versa, it is obvious that nobody should give unsolicited help or try to influence the activity for which somebody else is responsible.

12.2.2 It is essential for coexistence that nobody refuses to sit on boards or committees or declines to take on tasks in the diocese or in the national church for the reason that it would involve cooperation with persons who hold a different view concerning the question of the ordination of women.

12.2.3 Different views concerning the ordination of women may not be given as an excuse for nonparticipation in consultations, continuing education courses, etc., that are arranged for the priests in the dioceses.

How to Proceed When Disagreement Occurs:

13. Problems that arise are to be solved locally in the first instance, through communication between those involved, with the help of these guidelines.

14. If the discord is not solved, the problem is to be referred to the bishop or to a person appointed by the bishop.

The bishop is supported by a consulting committee of the diocese, a referral group that should be called together either in order to solve questions of principle, or when conflicts have erupted, or when some of its members have asked for a special meeting.

A consulting committee consists of four to eight members.

15. A consulting committee on the national level should be instituted to support and coordinate the activities (in all the dioceses).

RECONSIDERATION OF THE
CONSCIENCE CLAUSE

The 1979 Church Assembly was held in a tumultuous and angry time. A new national survey had shown that 42% of the male clergy were against the ordination of women. The press reported cases of discrimination. The general public was shocked. Again there was a drop in the membership. People left the Church of Sweden disgusted with the long drawn-out process. Something had to be done to clarify the legal situation.

Hence these guidelines, which were on the agenda, were gratefully voted for adoption by the Church Assembly. They were then immediately sent for implementation to the dioceses. They were also recommended to the Parliament to be written into the law. The government—now in the hands of the bourgeois parties, a coalition that governed from 1976–83—could not, however, accept this recommendation. These rules were not for the general public but concerned only the clergy. The minister of Church Affairs, Bertil Hansson, appointed one person, the lawyer and state secretary, Elisabeth Palm, to conduct an investigation of the status of the women priests. She gathered at her side a contact group consisting of one representative from each political party. She was to confer with them and have them be her spokespeople when the respective political parties had to take a position with reference to what she would submit. She started her work in the summer of 1979 and submitted her report on 30 April 1981.

The document she produced, *Reconsideration of the Conscience Clause: Men and Women as Priests in the Church of Sweden* (SOU 1981:20), is a lucid, brisk yet compassionate, piece of writing that also brings out the historical background to the question of ordination of women and concentrates on its legal aspects and how these had been dealt with in Parliament and Church Assemblies.

During her investigation she naturally paid special attention to how the new guidelines for cooperation had been received and carried out in the different dioceses. She notes that, on the whole, the people both in Diocesan and Parish Councils "loyally have followed the decision of the Church Assembly and have demonstrated a marked will to work for cooperation in the spirit of the rules."[29] Although she pinpoints situations where the rules have been interpreted differently in different places and have brought about incidents of disagreement especially about the right "to step aside," she nevertheless stresses the positive factor "that only a few cases have needed to be treated by the consulting committees." And then she adds: "Irrespective of how to judge the value and effect of the Guidelines for Cooperation, it is perfectly clear . . . that the attention and the measures that the question of women priests have caused during the last years have had significant impact within the Church of Sweden. Today a clear sign of progress can be noticed."[30]

She sums up this development by saying that the first stage was marked by active resistance in the form of protest actions and harassment. This was followed by silent resistance no less harmful for the work of the church. She observes how often quite obviously women priests and their supporters have not been willing to pursue the conflicts when they have risen. But this state of affairs is now changing thanks to the effect of the guidelines.

The Conscience Clause had served as protection for the opposition. With that insight she came to the conclusion that her task was to delineate at the outset four points as a departure for a reconsideration of the legal situation:[31]

1. It must build on what the Church of Sweden itself has decided concerning its profession: It is in accordance with the confession of the Church of Sweden that a woman can be ordained.
2. Also the faith and the view of the Bible that the opposition maintains has a right to remain within the Church of Sweden in accordance with the Church's own decision.
3. The State wishes to avoid as much as possible to interfere with the inner life of the Church but can not abdicate its responsibility for the respect of the law.
4. The State can not exempt the Church of Sweden from the general principles of equality between women and men that are valid in society at large.

With these four points clearly stated she proposed as a first and favored alternative to a solution that the law of 1958 be annulled and with it the Conscience Clause. No new law would have to be made. The general rule and regulations concerning equality between the sexes that were stated in the law of 1945 would be valid also for the Church of Sweden.

As already reported this alternative was accepted at the Church Assembly of 1982. With the 1982 vote a fifty-year-long history of special treatment by the government concerning the question of women and the priesthood came to an end. Now the Church must take responsibility for its own future actions, abiding by the law of the land.

ELISABETH PALM—AN INTERVIEW

Elisabeth Palm is a woman in her forties. When she studied law in Uppsala many women were going into the professions. The new roles were already being institutionalized. She learned the ropes and played by the rules and was good at it. When special tasks came her way she accepted the challenge. More and more she was called in as an expert.[32]

Elisabeth Palm was sitting in her sunny but noisy office at the Civil Department (*Kommumdepartementet*) at Tegelbacken in the middle of Stockholm when she was interviewed in the summer of 1982 about her work as investigator.[33] She said that she had three qualifications for the task which in combination had helped greatly. First, she had been a delegate at the 1979 Church Assembly and was thus familiar with the issues as seen from the church's point of view; second, she was a lawyer, a judge in Göteborg, now on leave to the department; and third, she was a woman.

She began her investigation by traveling around to all 13 dioceses and speaking to all kinds of people and all kinds of boards, associations, and the like. She heard them out whether for or against. She said that the rumor went ahead of her that she was willing to listen. People gained confidence in her. After having assembled a mountain of material concerning special cases, mixed with "some unsubstantiated rumors and plain gossip," she made the decision to make her report on the dioceses short and factual. She, on her part, made it clear to the people she spoke to that she was a representative of the government: "There had to be a change and the Conscience Clause could not be written into law."

When her report then was published, people in the church had already understood the principle. She did not think that in the future there would be a split of the church. "People in general," she said, "do not understand the conflict over this question. To 90% it is a question that concerns the clergy alone. Those who now speak of a break with the state and want to form a Synod do so for other reasons, e.g., the new rules of electing delegates to the Church Assembly along political party lines. The objection is no longer on the grounds of the ordination of women but on the question of state-church relations."

It is striking that two of the people who have been genuinely instrumental in the change for equality in the church and thus are extremely important in the modern church history of Sweden are women.

Both these women are highly competent. They speak with confidence, ease, and precision. Alva Myrdal's record is phenomenal. She is "super woman" who made it in the men's world. The difference between them came to the fore when they were asked about the women's movement in today's Sweden. Alva Myrdal stood in favor of the newly instituted position of an "ombudsman" for equal rights to prohibit discrimination in hiring and promotion. As noted above, an ombudsman's duty is to hear cases of complaint and give opinion whether these cases should be considered for redress. But Myrdal was definitely not at ease with the idea that women are in some way different and should therefore be treated differently. Instead, she thought that "nowadays everything is much easier for women." She did not like what she recently had heard from the women's movement. The burden of proof of competence was on the women. Their complaints were mainly nuisance questions.

Elisabeth Palm, on the other hand, readily admitted that the complaints, innuendos, and rumors she had heard while traveling around to the different dioceses, were familiar to her from listening to women in other professions. "There is not a specific or formal policy abroad against women but there is an attitude that is difficult to pin down. Men do not usually like changes within the professions. The inclusion of women seems to signify change. If women do not conform a hundred percent they are not promoted or hired or given the same responsibilities as men. Women seldom want to stir up controversy. They therefore often seek shelter in specially women-centered areas of the professions where they do not have to compete with men."

Both Myrdal and Palm see the conflict now as the church's own business. They do not perceive it as an underlying conflict in society at large. They do not acknowledge that there might be a relation between the difficulties the women's movement has encountered in promoting equal rights and certain attitudes that emanate from the church. The idea that the church has fostered views of women that are still prevalent in society and that therefore it is important for society as well as for the church that this conflict over ordination is solved has not been contemplated by them; that the controversy in church is a test case for the whole of society is not understood.

In a society that experiences rapid technological change, the issue of equality is large and complex. With its strong emphasis on the family structure, the church has held to the view that the man has the greater responsibility. He is the head of the household, and in the public sphere he is the one to decide. A development from the Bishops' Letter and The 17 Points to the Guidelines is not a clear-cut, action-reaction-synthesis progression. These documents signify, however, that a new consciousness has slowly and painfully grown among the male clergy. What is necessary for further progress is that the women themselves speak up, take initiative, and work for increased integration. Women in the Church of Sweden today have access to institutional power. Myrdal and Palm are models for how to use institutional power for increasing the opportunities for equality and justice.

5

STRIKING SIMILARITIES AND SIGNIFICANT DIFFERENCES

The previous chapters have dealt with events, arguments, and decisions of the distant and near past. How does the present situation look? In order to test how women and men operate and cooperate in the priesthood a questionnaire was put together. (See Appendix 1.)

At the time the questionnaire was worked out, one of the concerns was that its subject—the conditions for women priests—to some would be so tiresome, to others so odious, and still to others so unimportant that they would not bother to fill it in and return it. This did not happen. People participated generously, and we can therefore speak to the present conditions with some precision.

The most obvious result is the striking similarity between men and women priests. The majority felt the impulse to become priests at an early age. Their personal call was seldom a sudden revelation but a decision that slowly matured over a period of time. Many of them have worked in some other capacity before they entered the priesthood. The main motivation for the choice was their wish to preach the gospel of Jesus Christ. The majority work full time. Their major tasks are preaching, teaching, and counseling. They bury, marry, and baptize, and in connection with these services they visit people in their homes. And they spend a great deal of their time on administration.

They live spaciously, are married, have children, and find the best support for their work from their spouses. They experience no friction in working together with colleagues of the opposite sex. They rarely think of the fact that the priesthood was shaped historically by men, and even more seldom do they talk about that. In their opinion the press has focused one-sidedly on this specific issue. They wish the press rather would inform the public about other aspects of the priesthood. They have little time for political and social activities outside of the church. The vast majority of them seem to enjoy their work and report that the priesthood has lived up to the expectations they had when they entered. Theological studies are generally seen as a necessary prerequisite for being able to do the work, and the priests express a strong need for continuing education.

These similarities are striking at first glance, and they should not be forgotten when the percentages are scrutinized and significant differences between men and women as priests appear. The majority of the priests seem to feel that they have a wonderful vocation, and they are not weighed down with thoughts of the future of the church or preoccupied by questions of the relationship between women and men priests.

LOCATION IN PRIESTHOOD

First, it is important to know how many women priests there are in relation to the men priests; where they work; whether they have reached prestigious positions; what size parish they have and how many colleagues; where they studied and what their views on theological studies are.

Percentage

According to Sven Håkan Ohlsson, *Statistical Yearbook of the Clergy in the Church of Sweden (Statistisk matrikel över Svenska Kyrkans Prästerskap,* 1982) there were as of 1 January 1982, 3,033 active priests in the Church of Sweden. In May of that year our questionnaire was sent to the 383 women listed in active duty, and to 383 men, approximately a tenth of the whole, randomly selected from the same yearbook. Three hundred nine men and 313 women completed and returned the questionnaire. Nineteen returned it blank with a note that in a few cases was hostile, but some were signed and informed us in a friendly manner that they on principle did not fill out questionnaires, especially not if these included information of a personal nature. Some were worried about anonymity. We were overjoyed to have an 82% response.

Age

Sweden has on the whole a young corps of priests in active ministry. The Ohlsson Yearbook reports that over 40% are younger than 40 years of age, and three-fourths of them are below the age of 55.

In our sample the women priests were in the majority among those priests who are younger than 34 with 9 years or less in the priesthood.

Geography

When looking at where women are placed and how they are distributed between the 13 dioceses over the map of Sweden, the majority of them work

in cities and thickly settled communities in large parishes. Particularly striking is how the women have gravitated toward Stockholm and Lund. These
two dioceses have and have had bishops who welcomed women, supported
their cause, and expressed opinions favorable to the work that women priests
perform. Göteborg, however, although it holds Sweden's second largest city
has only two women priests working in the diocese. Since the bishops there
have refused to ordain women, these two priests have been ordained
elsewhere and have later applied for positions in Göteborg.[1]

Promotion

Women have not as of yet advanced to the highest posts. Our sample
caught one bishop in its net. He, however, declined to complete the questionnaire. "On principle" he always declines participation, he kindly informed
us. Neither did it happen to include any deans of cathedrals (domprost). Only
8% of the women are vicars (kyrkoherde), while 42% of the men hold that
post. Women stand at the associate level (komminister) or are assistants
(adjunkt). This may be a reflection of their younger age, or it might be that
women do not apply for the post of vicar since it implies greater visibility and
responsibility. Maybe it is also that women are less interested in positions of
power? To what extent women have asked for part-time work along the way
and what impact that might have had on their promotion is hard to say. At
any rate, women are not yet equally employed in the more visible posts, for
example, as diocesan assistants (stiftsadjunkt), a demanding and influential
position.

Number of Colleagues

Eleven percent of the women work alone, running their own parishes or
doing their own thing in whatever specialized ministry they have chosen,
without clergy colleagues. Seventy percent of the men—and this is a significant difference—do not have a woman colleague in their parishes. Thus, while
women learn to work with men (72% of the women have one and up to eight
male colleagues) as well as with women (39% have one and up to four female
colleagues), most men priests have not yet had the experience of working
together with a woman priest.

Place of Study

On the average women were older when they finally decided to become
priests. Many of them attended Stockholm's Theological Institute rather than
going to the universities of Uppsala and Lund where the majority of men
studied.[2] Hence men and women hardly have the opportunity to become
friends and learn to cooperate during their time of study, an experience which
commonly provides a basis for future bonds.

View of Theological Studies

A learned ministry is a strong Protestant heritage. Both women and men consider academic theological studies as a necessary prerequisite for the priesthood. However, more women look upon their studies as an end in themselves rather than a means to become a priest. More women than men indicate that a theological book or a professor of theology has influenced their thinking. Both men and women priests feel a need for continuing education, and in several dioceses continuing education courses are compulsory. These courses provide opportunities for men and women to compare notes and hear each other out. This is one place where women could air their views, and the men would have to listen to "a different voice."[3] Women definitely think they have something to add to the interpretation of the Bible. Sixty-nine percent of the women answered yes to that question while only 24% of the men agreed.

When asked whether or not they had read any feminist theology, the majority of both women and men answered no, but 48% of the women and 37% of the men said yes. These studies, however, they have undertaken mostly on their own. The theological faculties have hardly had any women teachers. Uppsala has one tenured woman professor. Only during the very last years has Uppsala started a program in Women's Studies.[4] But women interested in feminist theology have begun to publish Swedish translations of foreign essays, as well as their own works.[5]

BACKGROUND AND PROFESSIONAL ASPIRATIONS

Second, it is important to find out whether men and women have the same background, whether they come from the same sector of society, or if the entrance of women has widened the field. Is new intelligence, new experience roped in? Do they come from traditional and bourgeois homes? Did they and their parents attend church? What or who made them think of becoming priests? Did they experience a personal call? What was their main motivation in choosing the profession? Did they aim for a specialized ministry?

Parents

In terms of parent's education and occupation there is not significant difference between the men and the women. They came to the priesthood from all walks of life and from all levels of education with only one significant difference: 17% of the men have fathers in the priesthood and 65% of the men, during the time they grew up, had mothers who were full time homemakers. Eight percent of the women had minister fathers and 54% had mothers who were full time homemakers.[6]

Religious Heritage

The parents of the men were church-goers to a greater extent: 37% attended church regularly while only 22% of the parents of the women went regularly to church. It can be assumed that the men come from more traditional and religious homes. When we consider that only 7% of the whole Swedish population are regular church-goers (*Aktiva i Svenska kyrkan*) it cannot be concluded that the majority of the clergy is recruited from this minority. Thirty-two percent of the women come from homes where religion did not play a natural part of their upbringing. Thus, it is intriguing to notice that the women as children, in a manner of speaking, were more devout than the men: 71% of the women said nightly prayers, compared to 63% of the men.

The overwhelming majority of both men and women were confirmed as teenagers. Confirmation was, until recently, an unbroken cultural rite of passage. In Stockholm only approximately 60% of the children between the ages of 13–16 are now being confirmed. Although the country has undergone a steady process of secularization, confirmation is, however, still "the thing to do" for youngsters. This is the age when they become acquainted with the church and with a priest and take a course in Christian dogma and morality. The confirmation ceremony and first communion are celebrated family occasions. The teaching of confirmands is one of the major tasks of the priests. The confirmation teacher is reported as a major influence in the choice of the priesthood.[7]

Although there are many churches in Sweden other than the Church of Sweden, hardly one-third of the priests has attended services in any of these churches, Baptist, Methodist, Pentecostal, Mission Covenant, Salvation Army, Roman Catholic, Greek Orthodox and Russian Orthodox churches, to mention some and not to forget that within the Church of Sweden there is also an evangelical branch that broke away in the late nineteenth century, called the National Evangelical Foundation (*Evangeliska Fosterlandsstif-telsen*).[8] Those of the priests who had prolonged experience from any of these churches, however, were very positive in their appreciation of their religious heritage. The low degree of interest in ecumenism that this investigation exhibits might have its explanation in this narrow experience of other traditions, of other ways of worship. The priests in the Church of Sweden seem rather isolated without special incentive to experiment with exchanges and dialogues. The Church of Sweden might, therefore, easily be perceived of by its priests as the "right" church for Sweden.

The Call

The call is a central concept in the Lutheran tradition. In his interview Bishop Giertz spoke of the inner and the outer call. The inner call is not to be understood as a voice or sudden revelation but as a personal decision.[9] Eighty percent of the men and 74% of the women declare that their call was a slowly maturing decision. But when the question was rephrased: Did you have a distinct experience as a basis for your decision to become a priest? Fifty-four percent of the women to 36% of the men answered yes. This is a significant difference. Could this be so because women, to a greater extent, have a tendency to think with memories and explain with images than men who might suppress personal memories for the sake of a clean reasoning process?

At any rate, there was a willingness both among men and women to refer to specific experiences as the incentive to become a priest when it was not labeled a call. Besides the conventional impulses coming through parents, confirmation teachers, church groups, counselors, the Student Christian Movement, and so forth, they volunteered specifics. A wide variety, indeed.

There were those who had a special experience in church or free-church settings: "At first communion when I did not take part"; "At a church drama performance"; "I was confirmed as adult"; "I came to (the ecumenical meeting) Uppsala '68"; "At a sickbed communion on the missionfield"; "I had a conversion in the charismatic movement"; "I had a strong religious experience, I was speaking in tongues"; "I was a (free-church) pastor"; "I was saved"; "I encountered the Jesus-movement."

Some related to a dream or vision: "I heard a voice calling my name three times"; "I saw the kerchief of St. Veronica in a dream, and the face of Christ"; "I was called on a certain date"; "Experienced absolute clarity during prayer"; "Jesus said to me personally that I should become a priest." Some related the influence of other people and places: "Martin Luther King"; "Margaret Murray"; "Martin Buber"; "Hugo Odeberg"; "Gunnar Rosendal"; "Gustaf Wingren"; "Frank Mangs"; "Sven Lidman"; "Stig Hellsten"; "Ingmar Ström"; "A Roman Catholic priest"; "A Finnish woman and priest"; "A hospital priest who became my role-model"; "A long stay in Israel where I met real piety"; "A stay at Taizé."

Some referred to the suffering in the world: "I saw people's fright and insecurity, their search for meaning in life"; "The troubles of my friends"; "Disappointment with the social work I did for the state and with its 'system'"; "Starving people."

For some, theological studies or other work led to a decision: "I was in a bible-study group"; "I read Giertz's *The Church of Christ*"; "I was a deaconess"; "I was a Roman Catholic priest and wanted to become a missionary."

Some told about experiences in connection with a change or move: "At my divorce"; "When my husband was very ill"; "At a deathbed in India"; "It happened in my car (while traveling) I was most surprised." Some had come to clarity over a period of time: "During psychoanalysis"; "Work among the sick while I was parish-assistant"; "All threads came together"; "I experienced a series of calls. This was the will of God"; "Many impulses coalesced."

Some mentioned that the shortage of priests had been a factor: "It was easier to be accepted at the Theological Faculty than at any other professional school. Then (when I had finished my studies) there was no other job available for a person with a theological degree"; "A job I thought I could manage while I also was bringing up my children"; "Lack of alternatives for my bent"; "I did not get another job for which I had applied."

There were some who had entered the priesthood for inverted reasons: "I had to speak up"; "Absurd to be silent about my experience therefore I changed to become a priest"; "The inability of the clergy to take laity seriously made me change to become a priest. I felt strongly about the sloth and lack of courage in the church"; "Against the milieu in which I had grown up."

Motivation

When Bishop Ström was interviewed, he mentioned that he used to ask the priests-to-be why they wanted to become priests and that they then answered that they did not want to shoulder an authority role but wished to do specialized ministry.[10] When the questionnaire was designed, this remark was kept in mind. The categories of alternative choice were deliberately kept traditional: Help the sick; work for the poor; preaching; liturgy; youth work; ecumenical work and better relations between peoples. These categories were used three times with slight variation.

The first time they show up in the question: What was your main motive to become a priest? Sixty-five percent of the men and 55% of the women answer: to lead people to faith in Jesus Christ through *preaching*. Surprisingly the old authority role comes to the fore. However, the high percentage in this category probably has its explanation in the fact that *Jesus Christ* was placed in the question. Since it is only through their preaching that many priests are given a natural platform to speak about Jesus, the center of their faith, it cannot be presumed that a great many of those who checked this category evangelize and do special outreach programs.

To help the poor and the sick attracted some but not many—4% of women, 2% of men—although it is a natural and traditional Christian task to exercise charity. An explanation close at hand here is that the welfare state has taken over the social work, and the rationalized care for the sick and needy is so efficient that it has made personal initiatives and efforts seem futile and inefficient, and, at times even counterproductive. Counseling, a person to person relationship, as Alva Myrdal remarked, is seen as the task proper for the priests to take on. Ecumenism and better international relations do not fire the imagination but the category "other" was indicated by 21% of the men and 27% of the women. This would point toward interest in specialized ministry.

However, when the comments by those who checked the category of "other" are scrutinized they seem to confirm another remark by Bishop Ström, namely, that people answer the question, Why do you want to become a priest? as if you had asked, Why did you become a Christian? Here are some examples of these answers: "I wanted to realize a Christian lifestyle"; "I wanted to be a Christian full time"; "To be of use for God as a tool for his love"; "To develop my personal resources"; "To share my faith"; "To inspire outsiders who have lost their trust in the church."

Some are conscious of the importance of role-modeling: "To do something meaningful and become a role-model"; "To be a kind of Don Camillo"; "To be a sojourner to everyone"; "To be a mirror for all people"; "Afraid that I would not be able to witness to God otherwise."

Some are realistic about the conditions of the time: "The only job available and a job that fits me"; "There is a shortage of priests and the Lord needs workers in his vineyard."

Specialized Ministry

When asked directly if they had hoped to do specialized ministry the majority answered no, but 36 percent said yes, and among these women and men split in their preferences. The women preferred hospital work, counseling, and "other," while the men wanted to do evangelization, youthwork, liturgical life, counseling, and "other." When asked to specify "other" the list included family counseling, work with immigrants, "My Latvian compatriots needed a priest," inner-city work, industrial and worker priests, the seamen mission work. One answered that he wanted to become a monk and live in a monastery. Some of these priests emphasized that they "wanted to walk among people" and "to cater to people's needs" rather than to have them come to church to sit and listen.

The next question followed: Do you work within this specialty? Sixty-eight percent do and 32% do not. Apparently it is possible within the structure to do specialized ministry. The question is, does it take an extraordinarily strong personality to land such a position?

Nevertheless, both men and women seem to think that they pretty much fulfill the role expected of them, as is seen from responses to the following question: To what extent have your expectations of the priesthood been fulfilled? The majority think that the priesthood has lived up to their expectations. Seventy-four percent of the women, 72% of the men, check that the priesthood has lived up to their expectations 80–100%. It is the younger clergy—35 years old and under—who are less satisfied. Twenty-six percent of the women, 28% of the men, register that the priesthood has not lived up to more than 50% of their expectations. The priests evidently experience many causes for satisfaction, wonder, and challenge in their everyday life, in those events that fall in and between the traditional categories. The work they do is with people and is therefore so varied that categories seldom fit.

WORK AND LIFE STYLE

Third, it is important to know how many of the priests are single or married. Does the household take much of their time and energy? What do priests consider to be their most important task, and what task in their work takes most of their time? What do they do in their leisure time, and where do they get their best support for their work? Have they reflected on the question whether perhaps it would be better for a priest in our time to remain unmarried?

Marital Status

The table on marital status exposes significant differences. While only 9% of the men are single, 39% of the women are single.[11] Keeping in mind that the women are younger, we find that the differences are, nevertheless, significant. The men also have more children, on the average between two and three, while the women have between one and two. The pattern seems to be that married couples have children. Couples without children are rare.

The vast majority of the priests work full time. Only 3% of the men and 14% of the women work part-time and half-time. Institutions are generally against half-time work, and particularly with the irregular working hours of the clergy there must occur difficulties in arranging half-time positions. Looking at the employment of the spouses, however, the conditions differ dramatically. While 88% of the women's spouses are employed full time, only half that number, 44% of the men's spouses, have full time employment. Eighteen percent of the men are married to full time homemakers, 23% to nurses, and 31% to teachers and childcare workers. These numbers suggest that many men priests are well cared for at home, in old style families.

The women have found their spouses wherever a good man was to be found—for instance, in church, 27% of the women are married to clergy or people employed by the church. Homogamy seems to be as common among women clergy as within other professions, but their spouses are also to be found in business, civil service, among engineers, farmers, professors, students, skilled and unskilled laborers, artists, and musicians.

Living Space and Household Management

Since the men in the sample, on the average, are older and have advanced further in the career, they also occupy larger and more prestigious housing. Although large families no longer are the rule, they still exist. There are households with up to thirteen members. The rule is, however, the small father-mother-and-two-children-size family. Who is in charge of the household chores? The answers prove that the women still carry the heavier load but that changes have taken place. Sixty-five percent of the men check that they do 20% of the household work while 33% of the women check that they do 80% of the work. Interestingly, 58% of the women report that they share 50/50 with their spouses while 30% of the men have that kind of sharing relationship with their spouses. One man answered: "We do 20/20, the rest remains undone," a familiar scene in a modern two-career household.[12] The question is difficult to answer in today's society where "invisible work" has increased for both men and women. Who keeps track of household expenses, does the car pooling for children, scans the consumer report, repairs the basement door, and on and on.[13]

Most Important Task

What do you consider to be the most important task in your work? The list of traditional tasks recurred in this question, and 56% of the men to 38% of the women checked preaching and teaching. Counseling is considered among the women to be their most important task, while the Sunday service is seen by the men as the most important task. However, it was difficult for the participants to stick to the instructions of this question and only check one alternative. The drop off became rather big due to this factor. And many checked "other" and specified: Work with children and youth; with church-drama; with language; with art; with small groups; with other people than church-goers; to build parish life; to make the church a "living-room"; to do outreach and evangelize; to do long-range planning; to organize fellowships; to work with handicapped; with immigrants; to do peace work; to research. The list reveals how varied and pliable the workload can be.

Many commented that most tasks are about equal in importance. One woman says: "(these tasks) are like pieces in a mosaic. Together they make a pattern."

The next question read: What task takes most of your time? Now the amazing reversal takes place. Administration, which had received no attention in the most-important-task table, is marked here by 31% of the men as their most time-consuming task. Only 14% of the women checked that administration takes most of their time. It suggests that the more responsibility, the higher status, the more time has to be spent in the office doing "the chores" of administration—chores, not challenges, since only one (a woman vicar) has singled out administration as her most important task. Both men and women divide their time between teaching, sermon preparation, services, and counseling. But while men spend more time in the office, women spend more time on performing baptisms, funerals, and weddings. Both men and women answered about equally on the amount of time spent on homecalls.

Leisure Time

What do the priests do in their leisure time? Are they sociable, belonging to clubs and associations? Do they work for peace, and are they members of political parties and trade unions? Do they get together with other priests, or are they spending their time with their families, or in solitude, meditating or reading?

It seems that priests have precious little time to spare.[14] Many of their evenings are taken up by working with church groups. When asked if they belonged to any women's groups, surprisingly twelve of the older men answered yes, they belonged to sewing circles. Traditionally, it belongs to the duty of a priest to attend the meetings of the parish sewing circle, to read aloud while the ladies busy themselves. Neither men nor women are much involved actively in politics. The majority answered no. But the women are somewhat more involved with associations: in women's associations, in peacework and environmental groups, and also in small professional groups where they discuss and study theological issues. Men are involved with sodalities, religious societies, Masons, Rotary Clubs and sport associations.

Support

Where do you get the best support for your work? was another question meant to gauge a priest's involvement with other people and measure their importance for the work. Sixty-eight percent of the men answered that they received the best support from their wives. Forty percent of women priests answered that they find the best support from their husbands. This is a strong witness to family unity, perhaps unique for a professional group in a modern society. Can we detect something of the Lutheran ideal of the family as "the little church," a model for society? Or has Swedish social policy with its family oriented legislation, its day-care centers, sick leaves and long vacations made professional life easier to combine with family life, so that husband and wife become each other's best friends and advisors concerning each other's problems and surprises in the office?

Other alternatives to the question of best support were "old friends." Women answered 19% yes; and for colleagues 17% yes. Men answered 2% yes; and for colleagues 11%. Women, as well as men, marked the category "other" and specified for instance: My confessor; an older priest. Several men mentioned the support of the deaconesses in the parish. They also pointed to the support of "the team we have"; the Church Council; the deacons; the parish assistant; parishioners; my free-church connections; and many named individuals. However, also among these "others" the category "family" comes in. Parents and siblings, children and relatives, "my home" and "my family" are written in.

Therefore it is not surprising that to the question: Do you think that a priest today perhaps should remain unmarried? Seventy-four percent of the men answer no and 64% of the women. What is more surprising is that 12% of the women answer yes (8% of the men) and 24% answer don't know (18% of the men). Modern women have to grapple with this dilemma of combining marriage and professional life to a greater extent, and for them it is far more an existential problem. Thirty-nine percent of the women priests are single. It can be presumed that they watch their colleagues. What these 39% have learned could be instructive for society. Priests should not be shy about what they learn. It is their duty to tell.

TRADITION AND SHAPE OF MINISTRY

Fourth, the questionnaire asked the priests questions that directly concerned their coexistence and cooperation with each other in order to find out what perception men have of women and what women think of themselves in the priesthood. Do they prefer to work with colleagues of the same sex? Does it bother them to work with colleagues of the opposite sex? Do they ever think about the fact that the priesthood historically has been shaped by men? Do they discuss the question and its implications? Do they think that women have any special gifts to bring to the priesthood? Is it their opinion that the press has overemphasized the particular issue of women priests? Do people in general think it to be an important issue?

Cooperation

To the question, Do you prefer to work with colleagues of the same sex? Twenty-nine percent of the men answer yes. Of course, a great many men priests, almost two-thirds of them, have never cooperated with women as priests. Another factor is also that the women priests they have seen, and perhaps met, have in many cases been younger than themselves. They know how to deal with younger men, but how do they deal with a younger woman colleague? Can she be ordered about in the same way? The whole question of a hierarchical order is coming under scrutiny. Women as wives, as deaconesses, as parish assistants, as secretaries, are apparently fine to cooperate with, but these women priests do equal work. They step inside the altar rail. They challenge the order of creation, St. Paul, and a tradition so long unchallenged that it has become a state of mind for some men priests and is labeled "Bible and Confession." That 67% of other male priests say that male or female makes no difference does not impress the 29% and that 89% of the women, who without exception at one time or other have worked with colleagues of the opposite sex, say that to them it makes no difference only aggravates the 29%.

The question that followed tried to pry a little further by asking on a scale of 1 to 5, Does it bother you to work with the opposite sex? Again the 29% show up among the men. Ten percent of them are "very bothered." Seventy-one percent of the men answered "no bother" as did 93% of the women. Thus we are dealing with a significant difference in attitude toward cooperation.[15]

How aware are the priests of built-in hierarchical and authoritative patterns in the priesthood? The question was asked, Do you sometimes think about the fact that the priesthood historically was shaped by men? Alternative answers were: Often, Seldom, Never. Twenty-one percent of the men and 39% of the women think often of that fact; 47% of the men think of it now and then, and so do 38% of the women. Add these together and 77% of the women and 68% of the men have reflected on this historical fact, but when the next question is asked, Do you discuss this fact with your colleagues? only 9% of the men and 13% of the women have repeatedly brought up the issue for discussion among colleagues. This, the most sensitive and vital subject that has threatened to rend the church asunder, has been avoided among colleagues. The press has brought it out in many and peculiar ways, but the priests—51% of the men and 36% of the women—have never talked to their parishioners about it. Only 5% of the men and 11% of the women have repeatedly discussed it with their parishioners. How can this be explained? Could it be that men did not know what to think about the *Amt* after the women had entered? The traditional image was shattered, and no new books were written. The women did not speak up either, partly because of insecurity but probably because they did not want to rock the boat again. In almost total silence the women have formed an idea of what they are doing and who they are as priests. Likewise, the men have formed ideas from their perceptions, but no common language has developed and no dialogue taken place. This is evident from the answers to the next set of questions.

Tasks and Special Gifts

41% women, 12% men think women have special gifts as preachers.

16% women, 3% men think women have special gifts as liturgists.

68% women, 32% men think women have special gifts as counselors.

25% women, 13% men think women have special gifts as teachers.

60% women, 10% men think women have special gifts for performing weddings, baptisms, funerals.

16% women, 11% men think women have special gifts for arranging meetings.

A look at the division between men's and women's opinions in this table reveals the tragedy that there has been no dialogue between them. Women who spend more of their time in performing weddings, funerals, and baptisms have come to hold the opinion that they have special gifts for these tasks.

Since they also spend more time in preparing their sermons, they have come to appreciate their own way of handling texts. Men do not generally think that women have any special gifts. What new element that women are contributing to the priesthood is not seen or heard as a contribution by their male colleagues except for what they do in counseling, as a private guidance and comforting service. In the open-ended "other" category the most frequent comment was: "There are no special feminine gifts, only individual gifts as it is expressed in the Epistle to the Corinthians. Gifts are not gender-related."

The comments from men span a wide spectrum of opinions. From the categorical: "Women should care first for home and family"; "Women priests do not belong in the Church. They do not have the right call"; to "The priesthood is becoming richer"; "Women's emotional life is more developed." They are "more human"; "closer to people"; "It is easier for them to establish contact"; "The expectations to fill a role are not so heavy on women."

The women write: "We are not tied to the old role but can be ourselves"; "Women respond to women"; "Since the majority of the church-goers are women they are less frightened by a woman priest"; "We have not yet begun to discover our feminine gifts." The women believe they have special skills: in counseling "owing to better relationship with our mothers." "Better work with families and children"; also "greater ability to reach agreement with the Church Council." As hospital priests "especially in maternity wards"; "as theologians"; and "as researchers."

Some women have listened to other women priests preach and discovered something special that they have not seen or heard before. But only a small minority of men have seen and understood the same things.

Influence of the Press

The process of the integration of women into the priesthood has been followed closely by the press, and at times with a certain glee the papers have reported on cases of discrimination: This persecution of women priests is a scandal! Is this behavior to be expected among priests!

When the question was asked in our questionnaire, Do you think that the press has focused too one-sidedly on the question of women priests? there came a ringing yes from 86% of the men. Of the women 66% agreed, but 21% of the women said no and 13% don't know. Many of the women are aware how the press has both helped and aggravated their cause. This became abundantly clear when the open question followed, What aspects would you rather see the press discuss?

The many comments to this question reflect the frustration of the priests with the newspaper material they have seen. First, there is the simple reaction that any professional group feels when the headlines attack their guild: Scientist cheats, Dentist drugs patient, Baker bites waitress. Too many times they have read: Man priest persecutes woman priest. Almost all ask for "objectivity, please," and one adds "no anonymous letters to the editor!"

Some of the comments reflect the pain they feel: "Forget it!"; "It's ridiculous!"; "The papers don't understand"; "It's too dominant"; "It hurts"; "It is nonconstructive"; "The volume should be turned down"; "No sensations, please"; "The Gospel is a scandal but it should be the right scandal."

Since this question came toward the end of the questionnaire, people were into the subject and were ready to contribute their reactions. Two views of the Bible were expressed, "(In this debate) the view of the Bible is *the* question. There must be faithfulness to Bible and Confession"; "Revelation came to men"; "People don't care what the Word of God says"; "There are no words in the Bible about women priests"; "The Bible does not permit a woman to become a priest."

On the other side "(The journalists) never bring out the Bible in support of the ordination of women. People get the impression that the opposition has the Bible on its side"; "Ordained women are just as biblically motivated"; "Report on our way of interpreting the Bible. Tell about Jesus' way of speaking with women."

On Cooperation

"The papers should report on the positive and good cooperation that exists in a normal parish. The complementary work that is done. The harmony and one-ness felt in spite of disagreement in this question"; "The papers should write about the parishioners' need of women priests"; "About the work in the parishes. That the church functions"; "Ask the parishioners!"; "The papers should help to spread the knowledge about new work-methods, give good hints and tell about real experiences among the Swedish people"; "Report on the actual role of the Church of Sweden"; "(They should write about) how to evangelize rather than women priests"; "How to turn the process of secularization around"; "Emphasize what is important for the nourishment of faith."

On the Call

"The papers should investigate what types of ministers are drawn to the different camps and why the opposition is greatest among the ministers themselves"; "The important thing is *who is suitable* to take the job"; "Why are so few priests recruited by the women-friendly priests?"; "The call is the most important thing for a priest. Who can judge whom the Lord will call?" "The press should show respect for other people's conscience. There is no longer freedom of speech in the country or in the church. People with inner certainty cannot proclaim it."

On Ethics

"Write about justice"; "About peace"; "About unemployment"; "About equal rights and theology"; "About human rights"; "The question (of the ordination of women) is ridiculous compared with the seriousness of the next twenty years in the future of the church. What is it good for? What do people expect from it? War, violence, unemployment, lack of faith in the future. How is the church engaged?"

On Theology

"The papers should explain how theology has changed during the course of history. How the views of the Bible and the Tradition are in interplay"; "What change has meant for the status of women"; "About Christianity as liberation."

On Parish Affairs

"The papers should focus more on the Church Councils. Their power and sometimes misuse of power"; "That the workload be restructured in order to give every priest greater possibility to choose the work that fits him or her."

Several priests suggested that the journalist should go to church once in a while "to understand what is going on." One woman had a short and penetrating comment: "It is important that bad things are reported."

What Do People in General Think?

On the final question, How do you think people in general evaluate the question of women priests? the priests were asked to mark the importance on a scale of one to five. The intention was to find out how the priests have accepted the fact that this question is of little importance to people in general and how they live with a problem which lay people see as an internal struggle within the clergy. Twenty-nine percent of the men and 21% of the women answer that they think the question has little importance to ordinary people. But 71% of the men and 79% of the women think it is important for people in general. They have hesitated before the choice. The drop off is large. Some marked two alternatives. The reasoning behind their hesitation is that they know that people in general do not think the question is important. If they only knew more, if they really understood the implications, then they would agree that it is an important question. But the priests have not solved the problem of how to communicate the importance. The isolation of the church from society is once more documented. Although the majority of the priests have had some other kind of employment before they entered the priesthood, their socialization into "the system" has occupied their time and minds.[16]

As is customary, there was room for comments at the end of the questionnaire. The priests were invited to write down what they thought of the questions and to express their criticisms of the procedure. They were right, of course, in commenting on how incomplete an investigation of this kind seems to be. How can an attitude towards a call by God be measured? Some were critical of the superficiality of the exercise and the artificial choice that the alternatives forced them to make: "Nobody gets a chance to formulate the spirituality that is essential. I distrust all questionnaires. They are intended to achieve statistically manipulated people who do not exist in reality. I detest questions that are nothing but guesswork. The danger is that the questioner overestimates his own intelligence and his own view of reality while underestimating the answerer."

Many comments were thoughtful and illuminated hindsight: "That the Swedish debate has become so devastating and has made many people so unreasonable may depend upon the fact that people never made the division of functions the way you do. According to one prominent view only a limited number of functions need ordination: Absolution, the Words of Institution and Baptism. To preach is reasonably the main function but who does it is unimportant. If we could agree on that point then the people of the High Church Movement and moderate women priests probably would have been able to unite. Had the problem been worked out theoretically before it was set in praxis in 1958 then there would have been less animosity in the pursuing debate and in the parishes. If that had been the case it would have put an end to the view that the priest, especially the rector or vicar, should do and know and decide everything in a parish. That is now what destroys both priests and laymen."

Many were those who by their comments testified to the fact that they thought the project was worthwhile at this point in time: "Thank you for doing it"; "Excellent that it is an international project"; "Fun questionnaire. Each question whetted my appetite for the next after I had got started. Had been nice to be able to tell more about how my view of women priests has changed and become a conviction which in turn has led to further change etc., but there were no squares to cross to declare such change. Thanks, however, that I got an opportunity to take part."

Some intimated that they thought there were other questions more important than ordination of women: "Personally I am for women priests. I have had no difficulties in cooperating with those I have met. But for the church there are more important things, like peace questions, destruction of the environment, unemployment, etc. However, it is also generally known that we have women priests who do not function well. Some of the reasons I believe are the following: These women have let themselves be ordained for some kind of feminist conviction: 'I shall teach them that women are just as good as men,' and perhaps less for reasons of faith. Others have great difficulties in keeping their private life apart from their work. It is not possible to be both an 'obedient housewife' at almost full time and at the same time be a priest. Then I have noticed a detail: The preaching by women priests lacks almost completely a social dimension while it often is psychologizing, displaying quasi-psychology"; "Do something more important. Treat suicide problems, our drug situations, our relations with immigrants. Shake up the bishops so they do something"; "Secularization is a more hard-core reason for the conflict in the church than the ordination of women"; "The ignorance of theological students of today is the reason for the demise of the church"; "There is a dwindling belief in the creed also among the priests themselves."

Some of the women expressed their dilemma in the church: "How can we get the church to function? How to teach, counsel and express a contemplative view in a world of action?" "I want to get together with other women to interpret the gospel"; "Women do *re*productive work (in the terminology of Rita Liljeström) and thereby they have less time for productive work, for advancement. I miss this aspect in the questionnaire"; "To be a priest means to move away from home and family for many women. Men usually get their families to move with them."

Concerning ecumenism these two comments are most revealing. One writes: "The question of the ordination of women is for me a question of 'home-ecumenism.' I look upon women priests as colleagues in the work of the church. They are like the deaconesses, the parish-secretaries, etc. They themselves have experienced that they have received a call and that they are ordained. The difference in perception feels very difficult for me. My view becomes insulting to them. But I myself must experience the same, namely that my ordination is not valid, when I am together with a Catholic priest. Similarly I have also difficulties to accept someone 'ordained' in one of the free-churches. Yet, I can see that this is not a basic question. The basic thing is our common belief in Christ. All Christians whether High or Low Church have gifts to administer and the right to do so in accord with our conscience. We need each other's support until we become one Shepherd and one flock"; The other writes: "I have no difficulties whatsoever in cooperating with a woman Baptist pastor who worked in the parish where I just served precisely because she belonged to another church and its inner policies were none of my headaches. Without hesitation I opened my church for her funerals and was even present at one. Within the Church of Sweden it is a completely different matter. At retreats or at continuing education courses etc., I behave with normal politeness. We exchange shop-talk but I have the feeling of being a Peter denying in the courtyard of the high priest."

Some commented on the Lutheran dogma of the priesthood of all believers. One person writes: "If we were real Lutherans we would have no difficulty with this question." And another: "The focus is too strong on *Amt*. Every Christian belongs to God's household—but there must be a small number who carry on full-time as priests. If *Amt* is stressed too much as to call and suitability then the opposition is strengthened to an equal extent. Every human occupation is a call before God. Both men and women are needed today for the care of Swedish society. This is especially true about the priesthood."

Concerning equal rights the comments often reflected a fear of mixing this aspect with the "serious" question of the ordination of women. "It is a matter of faith, not of equal rights." A woman writes: "I did not become a priest in order to score for equal rights"; "The papers have unfortunately made the opposition to the ordination of women to a question of equal rights thereby exploiting the sexual bias people have to incite them against those who oppose women priests. This has forced me to take a stand. For this reason and for ecumenical reasons do I belong to the minority. Inter-church matters should be handled and decided by the church and not by secularized opinion-makers and their manipulated majorities"; "Too many militant women have unfortunately become priests. They drive the question of equal rights and come with arguments that are horrible and unreasonable. Then on the other hand there are men priests who have locked themselves into a pattern of thoughts in such a manner that they are unable to reason and to discuss. The woman priest in our parish is good. She has respect for the conviction of others."

In question after question the answers show little variance between men and women. Twenty-four years have been enough time to bring women into the mainstream of the Church of Sweden and domesticate them in the old clergy role. Although their number is still small, there are now women in all the dioceses, in all the theological schools, and in all kinds of parish work. And women have begun to be promoted to more senior positions.

There are differences: Women more than the men come from the mainstream of Swedish society; their mothers worked outside the home to a greater extent; their spouses have full-time employment; their childhood environment was not so religiously active, and they themselves had to initiate their socialization into the church; they were older when they decided to become priests; their theological studies were often a goal in themselves not a means to reach the priesthood; they have experience in working together with men, while the majority of men have not worked together with women in the priesthood, and 29% of the men are bothered by the thought of having to do so; women think more about the fact that the priesthood has been formed by men; they think they have special gifts for tasks in the priesthood and that they can contribute new insights into biblical interpretation.

Hence, twenty-four years have not been enough to solve the underlying conflict. A full educational program lies ahead before men can hear and see what is on the agenda of the women and cooperation for the future of the church can become reality.

6

CONCLUSION: THE FORCE
OF TRADITION

In many and diverse ways we have encountered the force of tradition. The voices, the issues, the laws, the arguments, the proclamations that have emerged out of our study; all bespeak in one way or another the power and ambiguities of tradition. So much so that a more careful attention to the connotations, uses, and meanings of that very word may well serve toward a conclusion to our study. For the aim was not to dramatize an ecclesiastical conflict in a small country far away. I rather saw in that conflict attitudes of more general significance for women and men far beyond one church and one land, and I saw them writ large, and hence more capable of study.

Tradition is not a particularly theological or religious phenomenon, and its force makes itself felt in all areas of human endeavor—politics, culture, science, fashion—and to seek one's roots is "in" these days. But in religion and theology it tends to get higher density and the study and the consciousness of tradition is a central part of the enterprise.[1]

Thus it stands to reason that when radical change occurs, much of the world will muddle through, but for many religious people the force of tradition will assert itself as a counterforce. When the change pertains to millennia of patriarchalism, it is not surprising that the church becomes a crucible for tensions less visible but far from absent in society at large.

All those on the scene in this case study deal with tradition and witness to its force, whether in various configurations they fight it, defend it, depend on it, define it, debunk it, deride it, affirm it, foster it, see it as a vehicle for change or as a bulwark against change. Whether fought or embraced, whether a force for change or for stability, there it is, as indispensable and inconspicuous as the air we breathe.

TRADITION AS FACT IN
SWEDISH LIFE

At this point we need to spend few words on the fact that the tradition of Swedish church and society was patriarchal in structure. In that respect it

119

hardly differs from the vast majority of cultures. If there is any special aspect of the Swedish edition of patriarchalism, it could be that the century-old monopolistic compound between church, state, and culture added force to the tradition.

One can see this tradition both expressed and reinforced by the language. While the Swedish language is happily free from the plague of generic "man/men"[2] for human beings and humanity, many titles are of the type "congressman,"[3] and the titles for the major professions had a derivative female form used when addressing the wife of such office holders, for example, *general/generalska; professor/professorska; doktor/doktorinna; biskop/biskopinna; prost* (dean)/*prostinna*.[4]

The way Swedes at large dealt with tradition is perhaps illustrated by the fact that the "-man" titles like *riksdagsman* came to be used also for the quite large number of women members of Parliament, and there seemed to be no need to make the language inclusive. The maleness of those words were relegated to the etymological notations.

As to the titles for consorts which clearly defined the woman by the position of her husband, by now they have disappeared in most circles, as have the use of titles in general. If and where they linger, they may be used in a half serious, endearing manner, or in jest. There are, however, pockets of society, in the military and in the church, where they still function.

Perhaps especially in the case of the clergy spouses (*prästfru/prostinna/biskopinna*) these words had once been functional and not only honorific in a derivative manner. As we saw in chap. 2, above, the wife of the priest really had a profession with extensive expectations and duties beyond her own family. The *prostinna* was certainly experienced as a person in her own right and as the center of the "culture of the manse" which served as the prototype for proper family life in the parishes across the land. It still functioned in my youth in the 1940s. But by now the socioeconomic basis for the semiprofession of the *prästfru* and the life of the traditional manse is nonexistent. Even if our survey showed relatively high figures for full-time homemakers among clergy wives, the two-career family dominates the scene.[5]

In matters of religion Swedes are traditionalists in many ways. Much has been written and said about Sweden as a secular and nonreligious country. Yet it is a fact that approximately 93% are members of the Church of Sweden. It is easy to show that few of them go to church or claim much interest in the church. It is harder to gauge their degree of attachment to the Christian tradition. When asked about reasons for church membership, one of the highest scores is on the answer: "It is natural for me as a Swede."[6] Perhaps one should also note that in a country with high taxes, it must mean something that only a very small number of people have availed themselves of the opportunity to avoid paying the taxes that the state levies for membership in the Church of Sweden.

As we think about the force of tradition, we must note that by that very force the Swedes consider themselves in the Christian tradition—often unwilling to assess the specifics of their allegiance. In a vague but deep manner they are often convinced that what seems right and just and moral is in continuity with the Christian tradition and should be the concern of the church. They think of the church as the national guardian of the values of society. As people of tradition they are not expecting an adversary relation between church and society.

TRADITION AS A FORCE TO
COUNTER CHANGE

In such a traditional setting it came as a shock to many when the opponents to the ordination of women affirmed the patriarchal tradition for the priesthood as being a constitutive part of the church's essence and function. Tradition now came to serve as a bulwark against change. The affirmation that the male structure of the priesthood was an abiding and binding part of tradition—while one could admit that other elements of tradition were open to change—was intensified in the Swedish conflict by the joining of forces between High Church groups and Evangelical Biblicists. Hence the more catholic idea of tradition as development was made inoperative by the Evangelicals' insistence on literal interpretation of the Bible.

Thus it happened that Swedes were treated to a conflict where theologians in the name of tradition hailed patriarchalism as divine will and took pains to point out how ideas like "rights" and "equality" were alien to the Christian tradition since they were fruits on the tree of godless Enlightenment. And even many who defended the ordination of women were anxious to stress and prove that "of course" the issue was not one of "emancipation" of a secular kind. Such hermeneutical, or rather nonhermeneutical, use of the history of ideas was much in vogue in the Swedish theology emanating from Anders Nygren and Anton Fridrichsen.[7]

TRADITION AS A FORCE FOR CHANGE

But also those who were in favor of the ordination of women could claim tradition with equal right. For the classical Christian tradition has often served as a mighty force for freedom and liberation and for unmasking the ways those in power repress and oppress. The vision of how in Christ the distinction between men and women is broken down constitutes the third panel where the first is the abolition of slavery. And as the nineteenth century proved a milestone in the latter case, the twentieth no doubt has done the same in the former.

The force of this classical Christian tradition of liberalism and development

is one of the major forces in Western history, engendering even new perceptions like "rights" and "equality." It is a tradition with deep roots in the faith
and piety of millions. It is the classical manifestation of seeking the spirit
rather than the letter. It is a tradition of piety in which one is guided by the
simple question: What would Jesus have done? Therein lies the force of this
tradition and its openness to new situations. Or as James Russell Lowell
expressed it: "Time makes ancient good uncouth."[8]

TRADITIONAL PRIEST ROLES AND WOMEN CLERGY

In many ways women have adjusted well to the expected roles and duties of
clergy. And due to the system of promotion within a state church and its
relatively few positions of specialization, women are advancing to more
senior positions. They have not been shunted off into special chaplaincies and
educational assignments as has been the case in other churches ordaining
women.[9] And they have adjusted well into a role shaped by men for millennia
and by Swedish culture for centuries. One of the striking results from our
survey was how little difference there was between women's and men's
attitude toward their call, their duties, and their expectations.

It is only more recently that the women priests have begun to draw closer to
one another in caucuses and support groups. During these first twenty-five
years it seems that women saw as their first priority to show that they could do
what men had been doing—and do it well. And not to gather in cliques but
relate—often as a token woman—to the team where they were placed.

It is also in the area of priestly duties that one of the greatest differences
occurs between the perceptions of men and women clergy. Men think of
themselves as more suited for the more official duties (preaching, sacramental
acts, liturgy) and think of women more suited for counseling.

The women saw themselves quite differently. They felt that they had much
to give exactly in these more official duties, and the interviews indicated that
the sacramental acts were experienced as most central in their ministry.

The perceptions of the women in those matters have very special significance in a church with what we earlier called traditional Christianity. For it is
in the sacramental acts in the sanctuary and in the crematorium chapel that
people meet the church. The vast majority of the eight million members of the
Church of Sweden see the church primarily as a dispenser of those services
along the stages of life. Secular "christenings," confirmations or funerals have
not taken hold, and there is no landslide of secular weddings.

Thus the traditional nature of majority Christianity reinforces and makes
natural the more priestly perception of ministry in the Church of Sweden. I
would even argue that a major factor in the trend toward High Church

thinking and liturgical style in Sweden during the twentieth century is the response of clergy to a role expected by the people. In order to make it bearable to serve as a kind of master of ceremonies (as perceived by the people) those ceremonies have to be understood as far more than "ceremonies," and the role of the celebrant needs transcendent dignity sufficient for the wear and tear of a ministry in which these traditional and even conventional ceremonial acts constitute such a large part. Thus we find that just as the so-called folk-church actually led to a priest-church, so now the service-church feeds into a church where the clergy become mesmerized by the *Amt*. A complex of traditions are interwoven in this state of affairs.

WHAT NEXT?

Our survey, interviews, and observations have also detected another dimension than the priestly one in the ministry of the Church of Sweden. Both in the call that drew them to the priesthood and in the vision of their calling we often found the role of the missionary, the builder of Christian community, the enabler in people's lives, both as individuals, families, and groups. All these roles require closeness to people, sustained times of cooperation, ability to guide without directing.

These dimensions of ministry are not much part of or in contemporary expectations of the majority of members in "the service church." But they are a strong undercurrent in the souls of the clergy, both women and men.[10] Actually the very future of the Church of Sweden may partly depend on the wise resolution of the tension between the force of the traditional service church and power of the vision of the church as a community of faith and as a movement for the kingdom of God. The latter has weak roots in Swedish history with its once monolithic union between church and society. But speaking of the force of tradition, that is the orginal force of Christendom and has its own tradition in many lands. As the theological isolation of the Church of Sweden is broken by serious ecumenism, both to the right and the left,[11] the force of the tradition will no doubt assert itself increasingly.

We have not taken our study much beyond the Church Assembly of 1982, the last one within the old structure of relationships between church and state. The present structure is radically different, especially in having abandoned a quota for clergy delegates to the Church Assembly. A lay leadership of the church seems guaranteed.[12]

It now remains to be seen whether this lay leadership will opt for an even more pronounced "service church," or whether the force of the other, more ecumenical, classical and biblical tradition will be able to assert itself. It is too early to say. In either case the women priests will increasingly give special gifts and accents to all their duties. I say "increasingly" since it is clear that the support groups that are now emerging will raise their consciousness about women's studies. The hermeneutics of suspicion will be applied to much that was inherited as shaped by males.[13]

But if the force of the ecumenical, classical, and biblical tradition will shape the future of the Church of Sweden, then it is reasonable to expect many among the women to teach all how ministry can be done naturally by the role of enabling and community building. For the force of tradition has made women the great artisans in those tasks. And once fully equal, they will enjoy bringing those gifts to the community.

RESPONSES TO CLERGY
INTERVIEW/QUESTIONNAIRE

	Women	Men	
1. Number in total sample	313	308	621

2. Age   (percentage)

	Women	Men	
35 and younger	51	29	
36–49	30	37	
50 and older	19	36	
	100	100	SD

3. Position   (numbers)

	Women	Men
Bishop	—	—
Dean of the cathedral (domprost)	—	—
Vicar or Rector (kyrkoherde)	26	129
Associate Rector (komminister)	125	102
Church Associate (kyrkoadjunkt)	83	32
Pastorate Assistant (pastoratsadjunkt)	52	16
Diocesan Assistant (stiftsadjunkt)	5	10
Regional Assistant (kontraktsadjunkt)	2	2
Other	18	16
	311	307

Diocese   (numbers)

	Women	Men
Uppsala	28	24
Linköping	20	23
Skara	12	24
Strängnäs	16	16

Västeras	13	24
Växjö	12	26
Lund	65	43
Göteborg	2	33
Karlstad	23	18
Härnösand	20	17
Lulea	19	19
Visby	1	4
Stockholm	82	31
Other (missionaries, seamen churches, study leave, etc.)	0	6
	313	308

4. How many years have you been a priest? (numbers)

Less than 10 years	251	120
Between 10 and 30 years	59	148
Over 30 years	0	35
	310	303

5. Have you worked mainly in (percentage)

City	56	40
Densely settled	22	25
Country	21	33
All	1	2
	100	100

How many men priests in your present parish? (numbers and percentage)

none	32	11%	—
one	50	17%	94
two	62	21%	62
three	57	20%	62
four	47	16%	34
five to nine	43	15%	36
		100%	SD

How many women priests in your parish?

none	—		187	70%
one	182		51	19%
two	58		24	9%

three	38	4	2%
four	18	1	—
five	3	2	—
			100%

How many parishioners in your
parish?

More than 50,000	2	0
40,000–50,000	5	3
30,000–40,000	12	2
20,000–30,000	21	14
10,000–20,000	21	17
1000–10,000	33	56
Less than 1000	6	8
	100	100

6. Was religion a natural part of
   your upbringing?

Yes	68	76
No	32	23
	100	100

How often did your parents
attend church?

Regularly	22	37	
1–2 per month	31	31	
Once a year	35	23	
Never	12	9	SD
	100	100	

How often did you yourself
attend church?

Regularly	30	31
1–2 per month	48	46
Once a year	16	15
Never	6	8
	100	100

Did you say evening prayers?

Regularly	71	63
1–2 per month	7	12
Once a year	2	2
Never	20	23
	100	100

Were you confirmed as a
teenager?

Yes	94	97
No	6	3
	100	100

Did your family attend any
other churches than the Church
of Sweden?

Yes	32	31
No	68	69
	100	100

If yes, which church?

Mission Covenant	37	42
Pentecostal	12	7
Baptist	10	9
Methodist	1	3
Evangelical (Fosterlandsstiftelsen)	16	22
Others	24	17
	100	100

7. What were your feelings about
your religious heritage?

Very positive	32	36
Positive	27	26
Neutral	31	31
Negative	7	4
Very negative	3	3
	100	100

8. How old were you when you
first thought of becoming a
priest?

Before 15 years of age	16	25
15–21	48	59
22–31	18	11
32–52	18	5
	100	100

How old were you when you
finally decided to become a
priest?

Before 20 years of age	18	31
20–24	31	39

25–30	21	15	
31–56	30	15	
	100	100	SD

9. From where did you get the main impulse to become a priest?

SCM (at the university)	3	4
SCM (in high school)	6	13
Voluntary Corps	0.36	1
Church group	12	13
Book	6	4
Political organization	1	0
Father	4	9
Mother	4	3
Relative	3	4
Confirmation teacher	11	13
Counselor	1	1
Movie	0.36	0
Other	49	35
	100	100

10. Did you receive a call at a certain point in time?

Yes	26	20
No	74	80
	100	100

Was the call rather a slowly maturing decision?

Yes	86	89
No	14	11
	100	100

Did you have a distinct experience on which you based your decision?

Yes	54	36	
No	46	64	
	100	100	SD

11. Was the priesthood your first choice?

Yes	44	46
No	56	54
	100	100

12. What was your main motivation in becoming a priest?

Help the sick and dying	4	2
Justice for the poor and helpless	3	2
Preaching the gospel of Jesus Christ	55	65
Prayer and liturgy	5	6
Work with youth	4	3
Better relations between people and religions	2	1
Other	27	21
	100	100

13. Where did you study theology?

Lund	37	36	
Stockholm	24	7	
Uppsala	32	51	
Other	7	6	
	100	100	SD

14. Do you consider theological studies a necessary prerequisite for the priesthood?

Yes	88	91
No	6	6
Don't know	6	3
	100	100

Were your studies a means of attaining the priesthood or were they an end in themselves?

Means	57	74	
End	37	21	
Both	6	5	
	100	100	SD

Do you feel a need for continuing education?

Very strong	43	33	
Strong	27	39	
Weak	23	21	
Very weak	5	5	
None	2	2	
	100	100	SD

15. What kind of education did your father have?

Elementary school	58	60
High school	14	9
Baccalaureate	9	8
University	19	23
	100	100

What kind of education did your mother have?

Elementary school	63	69
High school	25	20
Baccalaureate	5	4
University	7	7

What was your father's occupation during the time you grew up?

Business and management	13	20
Art and design	3	2
Teaching	8	4
Clergy	8	17
Farming	13	16
Science and engineering	7	4
Health and social work	1	1
Military, law, and law enforcement	7	4
Clerical work, skilled and unskilled labor	27	32

What was your mother's occupation at the time you grew up?

Business and management	2	2
Arts and design	2	1
Teaching	6	9
Homemaking	54	65
Science and engineering	1	0.3
Farming	5	5
Health and social work	2	5
Clerical work, skilled and unskilled labor	16	10

SD

16. What is your marital status?

Unmarried	25	5	
Married	60	92	
Divorced	10	3	
Widowed	4	1	
Cohabiting	1	0	SD
	100	100	

How many children do you have?

None	28	8
One	19	11
Two	28	32
Three	15	28
Four	7	12
Five	2	6
Six or more	1	3
	100	100

17. Do you work?

Full-time	86	97
Half-time	9	1
Part-time	5	2
	100	100

Does your spouse work?

Full-time	88	44	
Half-time	4	29	
Part-time	8	27	
	100	100	SD

What is your spouse's occupation?

Business and management	10	2
Arts and design	9	4
Teaching	13	31
Clergy	27	7
Homemaking	1	18
Farming	1	0
Science and engineering	12	0.3
Health and social work	9	23
Clerical work, skilled and unskilled labor	6	9
Military, law, and law enforcement	2	—

Politician	5	1
Student	4	1
Deceased	4	0.4

18. How big is your share of the household chores?

100%	3	0
80%	33	1
50%	58	30
20%	4	65
0%	2	4
	100	100	SD

19. How many rooms in your home?

Less than 4	30	10
4–6	42	38
7 or more	18	51
	100	100

How many members of your household?

One	32	5
Two	25	25
Three	17	17
Four	15	25
Five	7	18
Six	3	7
Seven or more	1	3
	100	100

20. Do you think that perhaps it would be preferable today if a priest remained unmarried?

Yes	12	8
No	64	74
Don't know	24	18
	100	100

21. When you began as a priest had you hoped to enter some specialized ministry?

Yes	40	33
No	60	67
	100	100

If yes, which special field?

Hospital and social work	31	10
Mission and ecumenical work	5	14
Counseling	28	27
Student and youth work	9	14
Liturgical life	10	22
Artistic work	3	1
Other	14	12
	100	100
	(N) (105)	(N) (81)

What other special field?

Family and school, children	27	17
City or factory priest	13	8
With the handicapped	6	0
With immigrants	27	17
Seamen churches	7	8
Evangelism	7	42
Research journalism, movies, drama, etc.	13	8
	100	100
	(N) (15)	(12)

Do you work within this special field?

Yes	66	70
No	34	30
	100	100
	(N) (119)	(N) (108)

22. To what extent have your expectations of the priesthood been realized?

0%	1	1
20%	4	3
50%	21	24
80%	51	54
100%	23*	18*
	100	100

*Percentage in age groups:

35 and younger	12	13
36–49	30	23
50 and over	36	18

23. What do you consider the most important task in your work?

Home calls	6	5
Sermon preparation	9	13
Services themselves	23	31
Counseling	27	23
Baptisms, weddings, and funerals	8	2
Teaching	6	12
Administration	0.45	0
International and ecumenical work	2	1
Other	19	13
	100	100

What task is most time-consuming?

Home calls	9	9
Sermon preparation	18	11
Services	4	11
Counseling	15	10
Baptisms, weddings, and funerals	24	10
Teaching	12	13
Administration	14	31
Ecumenical work	0.40	0.38
Other	4	5
	100	100

24. Where do you get the best support for your work?

Spouse	40	68
Colleagues	17	11
Old friends	19	2
Parish group	8	9
Prayer group	4	2
Other	12	8
	100	100

25. Do you generally prefer to work with colleagues of your own sex?

Yes	3	29
No	8	4
No difference	89	67
	100	100	SD

26. Are you bothered by working together with colleagues of the other sex?

No bother	93	71
A little bothered	3	5
Bothersome	4	9
Quite bothersome	0.65	5
Unpleasant	0.32	10
	100	100 SD

27. Do you somctimes reflect on the fact that the priesthood has been historically formed by men?

Often	39	21
Seldom	38	47
Never	23	32
	100	100 SD

Do you discuss this fact with your colleagues?

Often	13	9
Seldom	51	53
Never	36	38
	100	100

Do you discuss it with your parishioners?

Often	11	5
Seldom	53	44
Never	36	51
	100	100

28. Do you think that women priests have special gifts as preachers?

Yes	41	12
No	44	67
Don't know	15	21
	100	100 SD

Do you think women priests have special gifts for liturgy?

Yes	16	3
No	62	75
Don't know	22	22
	100	100

Do you think women priests
have special gifts as counselors?

Yes	68	32
No	23	46
Don't know	9	22
	100	100	SD

Do you think women priests
have special gifts as teachers?

Yes	25	13
No	56	61
Don't know	19	26
	100	100

Do you think women priests
have special gifts conducting
weddings, baptisms, and
funerals?

Yes	60	10
No	28	67
Don't know	12	23	SD
	100	100

Do you think women priests
have special gifts for arranging
parish affairs, meetings, etc.?

Yes	16	11
No	62	62
Don't know	22	27
	100	100

29. Is it your experience that women
priests can add something new
to biblical interpretation?

Yes	69	24
No	13	52
Don't know	18	24
	100	100	SD

30. Have you read any feminist
theology?

Yes	48	37
No	52	63
	100	100

Do you belong to any women's
associations? (Numbers)

Yes	70	13
No	173	283

Do you belong to any men's
association? (Numbers)

Yes	13	63
No	287	183
Political clubs or unions	70	54

31. Is it your experience that the
media focus too much on
women priests?

Yes	66	86
No	21	8
Don't know	13	6
	100	100

32. How do you think that people in
general judge the importance of
the question of women as
priests?

As very important	20	12
Moderately important	30	26
Important	29	33
Of little importance	16	24
Absolutely unimportant	5	5
	100	100

The data processed material is available at the Henry A. Murray Research Center: A
Center for the Study of Lives, Radcliffe College, 10 Garden St., Cambridge, Massachusetts, and at the Institute for the Study of Sociology of Religion in Stockholm,
Sweden, Religionssociologiska Institutet, Klara Västra Kyrkogata 18A, 11121, Stockholm.

STIR IN THE
ECUMENICAL MOVEMENT:
THE ORDINATION OF WOMEN

INTRODUCTION

This is the story of the discussion, debate, and conflict over the ordination of women in the ecumenical movement. It includes the World Council of Churches, founded in 1948, and those churches outside of the Council's membership with whom it cooperates. Controversy in a single church and its resolution are mirrored on another level in a global, ecumenical, and crosscultural setting. Though the Church of Sweden is not the focus of this chapter, together with the preceding chapters, its struggle and unique role will become apparent.

At an international level many factors, tensions, and forces influence the treatment of this topic. From the beginning two key forces have been 1) women's participation in the ecumenical movement and 2) negotiations for church union. Later, the influence of the Orthodox churches becomes more prominent, both in terms of their conversations with Anglicans and Roman Catholics and in terms of questions of women's full participation within the Council itself. The impact of Vatican II on this question is also substantial, not only on the WCC and its Faith and Order Commission but also on the scholarly community and on Roman Catholic women. Of long-term importance is the burst of theological work on this topic from the 1960s to the present. This historical backdrop exists in tandem with some extraordinary actions such as the 1974 decision of three Episcopal bishops in the United States to ordain eleven women and the 1977 Papal Declaration against ordaining women. Within the WCC itself the 1981 Sheffield international consultation on "The Community of Women and Men in the Church" reverberated the impact of these forces, and, in turn, they resounded in the 1981 WCC Dresden Central Committee and in the 1982 Lima meeting of the Faith and Order Commission with the report of the Sheffield findings. Taken together, all of these events weave an elaborate background for approaching the current ecumenical discussion on the ordination of women focused around the converging ecumenical texts on *Baptism, Eucharist and Ministry,* which is now before the churches.

This appendix on the ordination of women is organized historically. The first section, "The First Twenty Years," examines the development of this topic in the World Council of Churches, beginning with its First Assembly in Amsterdam in 1948. The second section, "Finding the Right Place," focuses on hopes and constraints of the 1960s, and section three, "The Turbulent Years," concentrates on events of the late 1970s. The fourth section, "Tradition and Equality in Confrontation," builds up to the WCC Dresden Central Committee of 1981, while the fifth section, "Looking Ahead," is directed beyond Lima and the WCC Sixth Assembly in Vancouver (1983) to essential points for further ecumenical work. At the end I assess the present status of the debate, looking toward the Fifth World Conference on Faith and Order scheduled for the end of this decade.

THE FIRST TWENTY YEARS

Concerns for the Church as a Whole

In the movement for Christian unity, the ordination of women is an unresolved issue. As early as 1916, in the midst of World War I, William Temple, later archbishop of Canterbury, an advocate for the rights of women and one of the chief architects of the World Council of Churches, stated that "he would like to see women ordained but would have no part in a big rush for it. Desirable as it would be in itself, the effect might be (probably would be) to put back the reunion of Christendom—and reunion is more important."[1] As early as the 1927 founding meeting of the Faith and Order movement in Lausanne, Switzerland, the women present drafted a memorial cautioning the churches that in pursuit of the goal of reunion the concerns of women in the church, their status and roles, must not be overlooked. An excerpt from their memorial reads:

In this great Conference assembled to try to discover the will of God for His Church, it has been laid upon the hearts of the women delegates to ask the Conference to realise the significance of the fact that out of nearly 400 delegates only seven are women. We do not wish to raise any discussion on the subject, but we believe that the right place of women in the church and in the councils of the Church is one of grave moment, and should be in the hearts and minds of all.[2]

Twenty-one years later, in 1948, Faith and Order became an integral part of the structure of the World Council of Churches at its founding assembly in Amsterdam. During the thirty-five years of WCC assemblies, the "right place of women" has been dealt with by two major units of the Council: that section where the voice and actions of women are reported presently, called the Sub-Unit on Church and Society, and the Faith and Order Commission.

The concerns expressed by women today still echo those made known at Lausanne in 1927, namely, that these are not women's issues alone but issues of "grave moment" for the church. From the beginning, the WCC program on women has played a major role in the support for and advocacy of women—making sure that this worldwide ecumenical body not overlook the majority of its people. The Faith and Order Commission, twenty years older than the Council itself, continues to echo the sentiments of Bishop Temple, as it gives its priority to overcoming barriers of dogma, ameliorating differences, and seeking common grounds for Christian unity.

The first WCC assembly in 1948 took place in war-ravaged Europe amidst urgent needs to rebuild destroyed and disordered churches and Christian communities and amidst the tensions yet to be overcome between Christians as a result of the East/West political divisions of World War II. Many of the women present at the first assembly had held responsible leadership positions themselves during the war; they arrived at the Amsterdam assembly viewing their task as one of complete integration, addressing and taking responsibility for the church, its mission and work, on equal levels with men. However, in the course of the assembly, comments made by Karl Barth brought the force of tradition regarding women's subordinate place to the fore. This resulted in the women calling a caucus to challenge the eminent Basel theologian. Barth maintained that the women's use of the Pauline phrase that in Christ there is "neither male nor female" (Gal. 3:27–28) failed to take into account other texts such as Genesis 2 and Ephesians 5 where, he said, though male and female are equally created in two kinds, they are nonetheless assigned different functions in the order of creation. These remarks prompted a heated exchange between Barth and the women participants.[3] David Gaines, in recounting events around the assembly, stated that Barth made a remark "concerning the place of women in the Church, which was understood as adverse to their (the women's) claim to the right of full participation. . . . At a press conference he (Barth) explained that he was not opposed to women having positions in the Church, as in society, but wished only to stress that there are differences of function between them and men. . . ."[4]

Henrietta Visser't Hooft, wife of Willem Visser't Hooft, the first WCC General Secretary, viewed this exchange quite differently. She had had a correspondence with Barth beginning in 1934 and continuing to 1948 on the issue of women's subordinate status. Barth's position on the issue was not new; that he would be so unyielding is what created the stir, reflected in a post-Amsterdam letter from Mrs. Visser't Hooft to him. She writes:

> Why did it have to be that in this underdeveloped area of women's work in the Church and for the Church that Professor Barth had to act so totally non-constructively, to the point of being almost destructive. . . . I am writing you in the hope that you will gain some insight into my position and, if possible, make some amends for the calamity you have caused.[5]

The Conference "The Life and Work of Women in the Church" that occasioned the controversy was chaired by Sarah Chakko of India. The minutes indicate some negative rumblings among the delegates about the independent thinking of the women participants. This prompted Sarah Chakko to explain in the preface of their report that not only women but also men were involved in its drafting. Furthermore, she reminded the assembly that the subjects being raised were "the concern of the Church as a whole and not the problem of women alone."[6] Echoing the women at Lausanne, women at Amsterdam were also certain that the status of women in the church must not be discussed apart from the status of men.

It was in this feisty atmosphere that the issue of the ordination of women was first raised as one dimension of concern for human wholeness within the church as the body of Christ. The particular text of the report concerning the ordination of women has the familiar ring of many reports that have been drafted since the 1948 assembly. It reads:

> The churches are not agreed on the important question of the admission of women to the full ministry. Some churches for theological reasons are not prepared to consider the question of such ordination: some find no objection in principle but see administrative or social difficulties; some permit partial but not full participation in the work of the ministry; in others, women are eligible for all offices in the Church. Even in the last group, social custom and public opinion still create obstacles. In some countries a shortage of clergy raises urgent practical and spiritual problems. Those who desire the admission of women to the full ministry believe that until this is achieved the Church will not come to full health and power. We are agreed that this whole subject requires further careful and objective study.[7]

The Amsterdam minutes indicate considerable discussion of the issue, with an intervention by Major Robinson of the Salvation Army asking "whether any good purpose was served by embarking upon the discussion of one particular aspect of this enquiry, namely, the full ordination of women, when it was fully known that there was no hope whatever of anything like agreement."[8]

Traditionally Incompatible Images

Not to be discouraged, the women at Amsterdam, and the men who joined them, would not allow the question of ordination of women to be overlooked; radical changes in the status of women in the twentieth century needed to be acknowledged. To recognize the full partnership of women and men must mean to increase the participation of women, to lift up before the world community of churches their leadership, and to point to the equal status already attained by women in some church and societal settings.

Yet, the real achievements of Amsterdam do not relate per se to advancing the discussion on the ordination of women, but to two recommendations that would prove to be influential for future work:

a) The establishment of a Commission on the Life and Work of Women in the Church in order to identify and follow more closely women's participation in the churches.

b) The preparation of a major report on the same subject. (This report would be written by Kathleen Bliss.)[9]

Both recommendations were accepted. A commission was then established, and Bliss began her research, the results of which were published in 1952 as The Service and Status of Women in the Churches.[10] The Bliss report was the first worldwide study of its kind: it interprets and evaluates information gathered from fifty-eight countries regarding the status and ministries of women in the churches. It documents the increasing number of churches that ordain women, and it points to the new positions of women in society, partly encouraged by the church's emphasis on women's public education.

In spite of this pioneering work, by the time of the Second Assembly in Evanston (1954), the topic of the ordination of women had disappeared from the WCC agenda, and, as is the fate of many studies, there was no direct follow-up of the Bliss findings.

For the future of women what was important at the Evanston assembly was the transition from a provisional commission that dealt with the special concerns raised by women to the founding of a permanent women's department within the WCC. Entitled "The Department on Cooperation of Men and Women in Church and Society," this new department had a fourfold mandate, one of which was to encourage the churches to accept the contributions of women "to a fuller extent and in more varied ways." [11] Further work on the ordination of women would become one of the implications of this phrase, though nothing explicit was said at the time. This structural change within the Council itself guaranteed that the concerns of women would not be channeled through a separate worldwide women's organization or auxiliary body, but they would become an integral part of the Council's central ecumenical vision, the Amsterdam commitment: "We intend to stay together."[12]

Similarly, the Faith and Order section at Evanston made no direct mention of women's ordination. Its attention in 1954 was focused on the results of the Faith and Order meeting in Lund (1952), where hope was quickened regarding steps to common understandings of baptism and common affirmation of a theology of the crucified and risen Christ. The Lund meeting signaled a turn in the ecumenical "growing together" with its cautious word that the churches should act as one in all matters, except where deep differences compel them to act separately.[13] Up to this point, the ordination of women had been more or less looked upon as an issue of individual church practice.

Many churches of the Reformed, Lutheran, and Free church traditions were already ordaining women, and Biship R. O. Hall of the Anglican diocese of Hong Kong had ordained the first Anglican woman to the priesthood in 1944.[14] International theological debate on the subject had not yet begun. Signs that women's ordination could become an ecumenical issue signifying deep differences were just beginning to emerge, particularly in church union negotiations. In Canada, for example, in 1956 the question of ordained women was made a subject of union negotiations between the United Church of Canada which had ordained women since 1936 and the Anglican Church of Canada which at that time did not ordain women.[15]

During the years between assemblies, several other churches opened the way—among them the Methodist Church in the U.S.A. granted "equal status to women" in 1956[16] and the Church of Sweden ordained its first women priests on Palm Sunday, 1960. Whereas previously those churches supporting ordination of women in the ecumenical movement were doing so largely on the basis of theological arguments for equality and needs for mission and service in the face of a diminishing number of men pastors, now, with the Swedish ordinations, additional questions began to emerge. These revolved around the representative and symbolic character of the ordained priest. The British patristic scholar G. W. H. Lampe signaled this shift in an article written for the *Manchester Guardian* describing his eyewitness account of the first women being ordained in the Church of Sweden. He uses the phrase "traditionally incompatible mental images."

> That a woman should occupy a pulpit may not seem to be altogether strange. But that she should stand before an altar is different—something which at first sight seems to involve a clash between traditionally incompatible mental images. It was the more striking to find the whole emphasis in this ordination being firmly laid upon the Catholic conception of priesthood and upon the priest as the celebrant of the Eucharist.[17]

The Swedish ordinations were the first indication of what would become a shift in the debate from equality to representative function. Women could preach, but could they represent the whole church? This was to be the new question.

The Charisma of Representing Christ Borne by a Man

More women within the ordained ministries of member churches prompted the topic to be raised again at the Third Assembly in New Delhi in 1961. One initiative came from the newly established Department of Cooperation of Men and Women which recommended that "churches which employ women and women professional workers, study the ways in which they are being used and consider how best they may be enabled to make a distinctive and significant contribution."[18] A second initiative came from the Faith and Order section, from those charged with establishing the guidelines for planning the Fourth World Conference on Faith and Order scheduled for 1963. The Working Committee recommended that a study be undertaken in Europe "of the theological, biblical and ecclesiological issues involved in the ordination of women."[19] However, objections were raised about limiting the study to Europe, and individuals pointed to experience with church union negotiations in Japan, Canada, and India where some churches, so engaged, ordained women and others did not.[20]

A hint of what was to come in the years ahead erupted during the discussion of the report from the Department on Cooperation of Men and Women. Commissioner Norman Marshall of the Salvation Army urged the New Delhi Assembly to "encourage a wider opportunity for the use of women as ordained ministers."[21] This was immediately opposed by Anglican and Orthodox voices. The archbishop of Melbourne, the Most Rev. Frank Woods, spoke against it on the grounds that "such encouragement lay outside the mandate of the WCC."[22] This was underlined by Archimandrite Pitrim from the Moscow patriarchate who argued that "ordination of women is a question of principle not to be debated in the Assembly." Pitrim maintained that "more careful consideration should be given to the theological factors involved."[23] Christian Howard of the Church of England intervened suggesting that inasmuch as there are "divergent views on the ordination of women the Department should continue to remain unaligned with a particular point of view."[24]

These stirrings at the New Delhi assembly led to a recommendation that a consultation be held to explore this subject in depth. This took place in May 1963, and from it a study booklet was prepared as background material for the Fourth World Conference on Faith and Order held later that year in Montreal. Published jointly in 1964 by Faith and Order and the Department on Cooperation of Men and Women under the title *Concerning the Ordination of Women*,[25] the report contains articles from Protestant, Orthodox, and Anglican theologians, including among them one woman, a New Testament scholar, Dr. Marga Bührig of Switzerland.[26] She demonstrated how specific Scripture passages are often used to argue either pro *or* con the ordination of women, leaving, she felt, the biblical evidence "inconclusive."[27]

Bührig argued that the issue is not one of biblical texts for or against, but one of ecclesiology. She states:

> The regulative criterion for all texts discussed here is the building up of the body of Christ. . . . The contemporary question about the ordination of women should help to shake up all orders of ministry which have become too solidified. For

example, it would be a pity if the admission of women to the traditional ministries, which bear the masculine imprint, were to hinder a new appraisal of the rightness of these ministries, by means both of the Scriptures and the contemporary situation. Or, to say the same thing in another way, the question of ordination of women is primarily a question of ecclesiology. . . ."[28]

The final report of the consultation stressed that new theological attention to this topic is occasioned not by "feminist demands or agitation by a few enthusiasts"; rather "it concerns the total understanding of the ministry of the church."[29] The final report affirmed the biblical concepts of wholeness and partnership as essential categories. It states:

> In our day there has been a rediscovery of two theological factors particularly relevant to our present study: a new insight into the nature of the wholeness of the body of Christ and a better understanding of the meaning of the partnership of men and women in God's design.
>
> a) It is a basic tenet of the New Testament that the whole body is called to witness to the name of Christ; all members—men and women—have therefore their appropriate ministry to which they are called by Him. This basic Christian truth was for many centuries overlaid. It has been rediscovered in our own day by all parts of Christendom.
>
> b) It is an essential element of the Christian message that men and women are created in the image of God and are therefore of equal dignity and worth before him. The developments of our time have shown us that this truth has not always been sufficiently understood and emphasized. All the churches are confronted with the necessity of finding a new expression for this basic truth.
>
> It is in this context that the question of the ordination of women is raised. Even the churches which oppose such ordination will realize that these new theological emphases have a relevance for them. The question involves many controversial points of exegesis, of dogmatic formulation and of ecclesiastical life.[30]

This 1963 consultation marks another turning point in the discussion about the ordination of women in the ecumenical movement because it makes clear that the topic, whether a particular church ordains women or not, demands a theological reconceptualization of issues of church and ministry. Consequently, it calls for a basic reassessment of traditional teachings regarding female/male relationships in light of the wholeness of the church's witness as the body of Christ and the full dignity of male and female persons who are created equally in the image of God.

Within the consultation, however, there were strong counterarguments. Theological opposition to the ordination of women to the priesthood came from both Orthodox and Anglican participants on the grounds of 1) representative function, 2) the tradition of male apostles, and 3) threats to intercommunion. Orthodox theologian Archimandrite George Khodre argued that the central issue for Orthodox churches revolved around the bishop's representative function. He stated:

[The bishop] carries the fullness of the priesthood and of his Church. The bishop is not the delegate of the congregation; he is the representative of Christ. He holds the power of Christ to preach, celebrate the Eucharist, prophesy and guide God's people. He is the living image of the Lord, His sacrament, the Head which renews the members. The Church is the Bride of Christ. The bishop carries out the functions of the Bridegroom toward the Church. That is why in principle he holds office for life. It is therefore normal that the charisma of representing Christ in relation to the Church (the Bride) should be born by a man.[31]

For the Anglicans, the arguments in opposition revolved around points of apostolic ministry and intercommunion. The Rev. Henry R. T. Brandreth, O.G.S., representing this position, quoted the Anglican theologian E. L. Mascall who maintained that, though the primitive church gave witness to the absolute equality of women and men through their baptism as members of the body of Christ, it "restricted the Church's ministerial functions to men. And behind the action of the Church in this matter there lies the example of her Founder, who was full of sympathy for women but who nevertheless founded the Church's ministry by giving it a purely male Apostolate."[32]

Regarding intercommunion with other churches, Brandreth issued a warning aimed at relations between the Church of England and the Church of Sweden. He said:

Many Anglicans have shown themselves openly sympathetic with those elements in the Swedish Church which are opposed to the ordination of women, and such sympathy with a part of the Church of Sweden opposed to the official policy of its Church could, if it became widespread and vocal, introduce a considerable element of restraint in the relation of the two Churches.[33]

Already by 1963, it was clear that two very different visions of church unity and ministry were emerging: one with equality in Christ as a central model, the other with male hierarchy as the ecclesiological given.

A Measure of Recognition as Their Due

Exposing for the first time some of the complex ecumenical problematics of this issue these papers were entered into the Montreal Fourth World Conference on Faith and Order during the summer of 1963. Present at that meeting of over four hundred delegates was a significant new ecumenical partner: five Roman Catholic observers and many Roman Catholic guests. In the atmosphere of Vatican II and in a Roman Catholic city, they had a major impact on the deliberations. The papers concerning ordination of women were background documentation for the section "The Redemptive Work of Christ and the Unity of His Church," a section that dealt with issues of ministry. Ministry was a topic "which has not been prominent" in Faith and Order discussions for twenty-five years.[34]

An important breakthrough at the Montreal Conference was an agreed definition of the ministry as the royal priesthood of the whole people of God, rather than limiting the word "ministry" exclusively to the ordained clergy.[35] Consequently this took some of the heat out of the centuries-old controversies over order of ministry and apostolic succession. It allowed the churches' appointed theologians to step back and look again at ministry in a broader theological perspective. Together with this emphasis on the royal priesthood of the whole people of God, there was a parallel emphasis on the missionary thrust of the church in order that the "redemptive work might be proclaimed and attested to the ends of the earth."[36] Only after these two essential agreements were in place was the link established that could enable the Montreal meeting to tackle the sensitive issue of the apostolic ministry. It was agreed that the apostolic ministry could be defined more inclusively and vocationally, its members being defined as those who are chosen by Christ and committed to the reconciliation and salvation of all peoples.[37] In principle, this agreement appeared to be closer to the equality and partnership model.

However, this broad definition was immediately qualified by defining two categories of ministry. In addition to the ministry of the whole people of God, those gathered at Montreal developed the designation "special ministry."[38] This was used to take the place of words such as "ordained ministry" or "priesthood." A second new category of ministry was also developed, referred to as "more flexible forms of ministry."[39] This was to designate the ministry of the whole people of God who live and work in the world (laity) and there find their testimony and service. Further, these ministries are to equip members with a variety of gifts for service to one another and for mission. It was not under the category of "special ministry" that the ordination of women study was proposed to continue but under the category of "other ministries." The Faith and Order Commission, building on the Montreal report, made three recommendations regarding study on the ordination of women: 1) that it continue to be viewed theologically relative to studies in Christology and the ministry as a whole; 2) that it be considered under the rubric of "other ministries" rather than "special ministry"; 3) that women be included in the study, along with specialists in fields of sociology and psychology. Added to these recommendations was a significant, small paragraph, stating that contact be maintained both with the Department on Cooperation of Men and Women and with member churches whose theological convictions must be respected.[40] This meant that whatever study might follow it must be situated between those most committed to understanding the church in terms of equality and wholeness and those most committed to explorations of unity in terms of a hierarchy of male authority.

In writing about the post-Montreal debate on ordained ministry, Stephen Neill in *The Church and Christian Union* summed up the flavor of the times and the sentiments of many. He argued for the full but not necessarily equal status of women in ministry in the following way:

> In the nineteenth century the Church was faced with a new problem which no one could have foreseen. Missionary work had been man's work; now, overwhelmingly, it became women's work. Most Protestant missionaries had been married. The extent to which the wives took part in their husbands' work naturally varied very much according to capacity and predilection. But in no case did the women have any official status in the work, any more than the wife of an English country clergyman. The unmarried woman missionary was unknown in the Protestant world until the middle of the nineteenth century. The penetration of the Roman Catholic Orders for women began about the same time. But, once in the field, the unmarried woman far more than justified her existence; she showed herself indispensable at every point.
>
> Inevitably the question came to be raised whether women, who were in fact carrying out all the functions of the ministry, could any longer be excluded from official recognition as ordained ministers of the Church.
>
> It is clear that a vast amount of ministry is taking place outside the traditional ministry of bishops, priests and deacons, though at times overlapping it, and that these less regular types of ministry are now recognized as being indispensable to the church. This being so the question must be raised whether we do not need a total reconsideration of the question of the ministry, extending its scope far beyond the limits of the traditional order, and providing for official recognition of those types of ministry which actually exist in the Churches, but which have so far only had a marginal existence without that measure of recognition which is their due.[41]

This meant that by the mid 1960s the time had come for the churches in the ecumenical movement to recognize the ministry of the whole people of God and the work of "women's ministries" as a category, but there was still considerable reluctance to recognize women's ordination within "the traditional order." Though steps toward mutual recognition of ministries were viewed by some church leaders as a major breakthrough, by others the mutual recognition of ministries was seen as a step backward for women. One dream of Lausanne (1927) was coming closer to realization: the demand for a "ministry acknowledged by every part of the Church of Christ as possessing not only the inward call of the Spirit, but also the commission of Christ and the authority of the whole Body."[42] But, the other Lausanne dream signified by the six women signatories of the 1927 memorial still remained: could the designation "other ministries" be acknowledged by them and those to follow as "the right place of women in the Church"?

Major hurdles were passed during these first twenty years. First, the issue of ordained women came to be viewed no longer as one that should not be raised even if there could be "no hope whatever of any kind of agreement." Second, it was acknowledged that the ministries carried out by women must be recognized as part of the general category titled "ministry," if not yet of the "special ministry," which means the ordained. Third, during this time, the initiative for raising both the practical and theological issues of women's ordination came most often from women. While women from the beginning saw this as a question of the theology of the church as a whole, men raised the topic of the ordination of women primarily where negotiations for church union were at stake.

FINDING THE "RIGHT PLACE"
Women in the Church's Apostolate

By the time of the Bristol meeting of Faith and Order in 1967, the topic of the ordination of women was still not positioned within the discussion on ministry, which was by now a major Faith and Order endeavor; rather, it appeared together with baptism and confirmation as "other ministries." Yet, in the Bristol minutes there is an instruction to the Faith and Order Secretariat that it approach world confessional bodies to see whether, in view of the questions arising in church union negotiations,[43] any of them would sponsor ecumenical study groups on this topic. At that time church union processes were underway in several churches of the Southern Hemisphere: Nigeria, Ghana, Ceylon, and New Zealand. Simultaneously, Faith and Order was making an effort to widen its community of work to include not only the "younger churches" but also greater participation of the Orthodox and joint work with the Roman Catholics who since the end of the Vatican Council in 1965 had begun to widen their ecumenical circle, including membership in Faith and Order. In addition, some conservative evangelical churches that had been part of the International Missionary Council before it merged with the WCC in 1961 took similar steps.

During the same period Rome was beginning to experience some changes as well. In 1963, Pope Paul invited thirteen laymen as auditors to the Vatican Council. It was only after considerable pressure from Roman Catholic women's organizations, plus a public plea from Cardinal Suenens of Belgium, that seventeen women were finally invited as auditrices in 1964, at the third session of the Council.[44] The women were both lay and religious, some representing international women's organizations such as the World Union of Catholic Women with thirty-six million members. At one point in the deliberations it was proposed that the head of this organization (the largest lay organization in the Roman Catholic Church) should speak in the basilica in the debate over the "Pastoral Constitution on the Church in the Modern World" (*Gaudium et Spes*). This was rejected by the Secretary General of the Council.[45] Similarly, in the Vatican documents the contributions of women are hardly mentioned; women's participation was thought to be covered under "laity," not ministry, and it was only during the final draft of "The

Decree on Apostolate of the Faith" that the following sentence acknowledging the need for reexamining the role of women was inserted:

> Since in our times women have an even more active share in the whole life of society, it is very important that they participate more widely also in the various fields of the Church's apostolate.[46]

The official invisibility of women at Vatican II has had an impact not only on Roman Catholic women but also on the ecumenical movement and on the movement for recognition of the ministries of women in other churches. Networks of women leaders in Roman Catholic women's organizations, increasingly aware of their marginalized status in the church's power structures, have responded by reaching beyond their own ecclesiastical framework to women in the larger ecumenical community and in society. This began in 1965 when women from the WCC and the auditrices at Vatican II held a joint consultation.[47] On the initiative of Roman Catholic women a second meeting took place in 1966. They identified as a common task the necessity to "bring the ecumenical idea into the various local situations."[48] Women leaders began to see that if the church was going to change it would have to be from the bottom up, for it was at local levels, where women are a majority, that their leverage could increase on issues of ministry and status. Furthermore, Roman Catholic women theologians and writers since that time have helped to sensitize women in all churches to the functioning of highly hierarchical and patriarchal church structures, their limited flexibility, slowness to accept change, and their male symbolic—as well as decision-making—power over the attitudes about, the placement of, and choices open to women.

The Vatican Council made a striking impact on the Fourth Assembly of the WCC in Uppsala (1968). The memory was still fresh of the meeting between Pope Paul of the Roman Catholic Church and His All Holiness Athenagoras, Ecumenical Patriarch of Constantinople. On 5 January 1964 the embracing of these two men marked a turning point away from nine centuries of hostility and division between the churches they represented. Members of the Vatican Secretariat were present at Uppsala as official observers, and, as mentioned earlier, Roman Catholic participants were now fully engaged in Faith and Order work as Commission members, though the Roman Catholic Church itself was not a member of the Council. At the same time, representatives from other non-WCC member churches were added to the Commission, such as representatives from the Seventh-Day Adventists and the Southern Baptists. It was in this changing context that the concerns of Faith and Order at the Fourth Assembly were developed under the theme "The Nature of the Church's Unity." The three major agenda items were: 1) hopes for intercommunion between the churches, 2) relationships with world confessional families, and 3) church union negotiations.[49] In this setting the topic of

ordination as such became firmly situated in the paragraphs on intercommunion related to "an inquiry into the meaning of commitment to Christ in his
Church,"[50] but as yet there was no mention of the ordination of women
though the Church of Sweden (which ordained women) and the Church of
England (which did not) were still in intercommunion.

Two points made at Uppsala could be useful in the future relative to
women's ordination, though they were not made with this purpose in mind.
The first was that "terminological distinctions need to be more carefully
made between those instances where substantial differences of doctrine are
concerned and those referring to the discipline of the churches."[51] Though
future debate on women's ordination would be mainly theological, a possible
new direction for discussion could be that of church discipline and specifically
how much variety and autonomy of practice in discipline is possible within
local and national contexts of mutual recognition. The second point was that
further work on ministry would be influenced by the enlargement of the area
in which the unity of the church must be pursued: the recognition that it must
be integral with the steps toward the unity of the whole human community
and of the creation. This point brought justice and equality as theological
issues within the parameters of discussion about the very nature of the church
itself and its ministry.

Meanwhile through another channel of the assembly, the Department on
Cooperation of Men and Women generated a request related to women's
ordination. It recommended a survey of those churches that already ordain
women (such as the Church of Sweden in whose context the assembly was
taking place). The recommendation read:

> [We] realize that the question of the admission of women to holy orders has been
> the subject of several studies. We urge that these be continued, especially taking
> into account the experience of the increasing number of churches which now
> ordain women, so that in the light of this experience there may be further
> theological reflection on the ecumenical implications of this development.[52]

During the same year (1968), the Lambeth Conference of the Anglican
Communion met, gathering representatives from Anglican churches worldwide. In a report regarding theological research on the ordination of women,
it made a major breakthrough, establishing that: "We find no conclusive
theological reasons for withholding ordination to the priesthood for women
as such."[53]

Admitting Women to the Priesthood

Within the hopeful and moderately encouraging ecumenical atmosphere of
the late 1960s, a second consultation on the ordination of women was
organized in 1970 by the WCC Department of Cooperation of Men and

Women with twenty-five participants from six continents. A follow-up of the Uppsala recommendation on the experience of the churches with ordained women, it also included Roman Catholic and Orthodox participants. Faith and Order staff were involved in the leadership of the meeting, but the Commission itself was not a cosponsor. The final report, entitled *What is Ordination Coming To?*[54] was edited by Brigalia Bam and published by the Department on Cooperation of Men and Women. Starting from the perspective of practice, the consultation explored psychological and sociological factors of women's ordination, cultural perspectives on the issues from Africa, Asia, and Latin America, and a case study of attempts made from within the Roman Catholic Church of the Netherlands to request the ministerial priesthood of women. In terms of church union negotiations, the consultation reported:

> The ordination of women has been mentioned as one of the obstacles to negotiations for church union. 55% of the women who replied agreed that this was true in their situations, but still it was not considered to be the major issue. When the Lutherans in Sweden decided to permit the ordination of women, they were afraid that their relationship with the Church of England would be strained, but there has been no significant crisis in nine years.[55]

From the perspective of this consultation organized by the women's sub-unit, findings regarding obstacles for ordained women turned out to be not so much theological in nature as psychological, having more to do with attitudes that have been codified through the force of tradition. The report stated:

> Women who are ordained suffer from the fact that they live in a church and society which for hundreds of years has been patriarchal. In that pattern they feel they have only a limited place and fixed role, and to find a new identity they must push against high walls. Very often they sense attitudes of unconscious superiority among men, especially when, as by ordination, they have entered fields traditionally thought of as male. They are confronted with conservative ideals of women and the family, both in male colleagues and in parishioners male and female, and with old stereotypes such as physical and mental feebleness, unpredictability, lack of nervous stamina and the like.
> They also have to face in church and tradition the myth of the unholiness or uncleanness of the female. Such myths have no place in the modern world.[56]

The consultation's approach to the issue of ordination of women was seen not merely from the perspective of past patriarchal tradition but also with a view toward the present experience of women and the church's future. The link was made regarding the necessity to see the unity of the church in the context of the church's mandate for mission and renewal.[57] The report of Group I stated:

> Creative thinking about ordination has been encouraged by what has been called by some, the eschatological aspect of the church, and by others the need to think

with the future always in mind, with the mark of hope always predominant. Our conviction is that the church of our grand-children is as important as the church of our grand-fathers.[58]

One sign of combining tradition and present experiences, reported as the "high point" of the meeting, was the closing mass celebrated according to the rite of the Church of Sweden and presided over by a Swedish woman priest, The Rev. Caroline Krook of Lund.[59]

Professor Catherine Halkes, Roman Catholic theologian in the Netherlands, provided insights and background information on efforts toward the ordination of women in the Roman Catholic Church. Her appraisal of Vatican II regarding Rome's view of women's ordination was as follows:

The time of the Council was not a very favourable time to speak about the ordination of women, because there was that difficult question regarding celibacy, and most of the time was spent in very hot discussion on celibacy and all the implications in connection with Rome and the Dutch Bishops.[60]

However, she continued, a request was made later to the Roman Catholic Church in the Netherlands for the ministerial priesthood of women. This, she argued, "was an historical date, for it was the first time in a Roman Catholic Church that it was considered that this question required to be discussed officially."[61] An initiative similar to that in the Netherlands was reported from Canada where in 1971, sixty-five Canadian bishops and sixty women participated in a dialogue on the status of women, arriving at a set of recommendations, one of which was to accept in principle to "ordain qualified women for the ministry."[62] The basis for these efforts came as a result of the paragraph in the Vatican document "The Pastoral Constitution on the Church in the Modern World," which stated that all types of discrimination should be eradicated:

True, all men are not alike from the point of view of varying physical power and the diversity of intellectual and moral resources. Nevertheless, with respect to the fundamental rights of the person, every type of discrimination, whether social or cultural, whether based on sex, race, colour, social condition, language, or religion, is to be overcome and eradicated as contrary to God's intent. For in truth it must still be regretted that fundamental personal rights are not yet being universally honoured.[63]

Since Vatican II within renewal movements of the Roman Catholic Church, there have been two major directions with respect to the ordination of women. One movement has been aimed at women's ordination, a first step being to open up the ordained diaconate to women. The other movement focuses on working for continual renewal of the church, searching for more equal expressions of priesthood and ministry, updating theological and liturgical interpretations of the role of the president of the Eucharist and new forms of collaboration in pastoral teams— lay and ordained, women and men. Both movements advocate a church structure that is less hierarchical and patriarchal.[64] Those representing the first direction take the position that the present rules governing the ordination of men to the priesthood ought to be opened to women as well. Those representing the second maintain that the very concept of priesthood must be renewed, restructured, and re-imaged in ways appropriate to modern Christian ethics, to life styles of equal partnership and justice.

For the Anglicans, a significant shift occurred at the Anglican Consultative Council in Limura, Kenya, in 1971, largely in response to women's ordination in the Anglican church in Hong Kong. In reply to a request of the Council of the Church of Southeast Asia, the Council 1) gave their acceptance to the bishop of Hong Kong to ordain women if it were done in good order (that is with the approval of the Synod and of other bishops of the Anglican Communion within the province), 2) asked that in the future heads of the churches consult with other churches on this matter, and 3) requested that member churches continue in communion with one another.[65] The importance of the Orthodox church as an "other church" was made apparent in a 1973 response from the Orthodox members of the Joint Orthodox-Anglican Consultation. They warned that "admitting women to the priesthood and episcopate . . . will obviously have a decisively negative effect on the future of the Anglican-Orthodox dialogue."[66]

These various initiatives had a cumulative effect. By 1974 the topic of ordination of women was creating a lively stir. In addition to movements within the Roman Catholic Church in Europe and the United States and bilateral conversations such as the one cited between Orthodox and Anglican theologians, the Episcopal Church in the U.S.A. was challenged from within by eleven women and three bishops who announced that they would ordain women. In an open letter they stated:

On Monday, July 29, 1974, the Feasts of Sts. Mary and Martha, God willing, we intend to ordain to the sacred priesthood some several women deacons. We want to make known as clearly and as widely as we can the reflections on Christian obedience which has led us to this action. . . .

This action is therefore intended as an act of obedience to the Spirit. By the same token, it is intended as an act of solidarity with those in whatever institution, in whatever part of the world, of whatever stratum of society, who in their search for freedom, for liberation, for dignity, are moved by that same Spirit to struggle against sin, to proclaim that victory, to attempt to walk in newness of life.[67]

Though Faith and Order had not yet settled on the place for the discussion of the ordination of women, actions from within member churches brought it sharply into the ecumenical forum.

Recognizing Small Advances

All of these forces converging within a short span of time prompted the Faith and Order Commission, meeting in Accra, Ghana, in 1974, to take up the topic of ordination of women, not in one but in two different projects of the Commission's work: a) in the newly proposed study on the "Community of Men and Women in the Church," and b) after ten years of discussion, finally, in the work on "The Ministry" under "Ordination" in the draft formulation of the agreed statements on "One Baptism, One Eucharist and a Mutually Recognized Ministry."[68]

At this point in the history of Faith and Order, though there were objections to including ordination of women as a topic of the ordained ministry, it was acknowledged by all members that this subject was a potential source of conflict and of increased division. It therefore called forth from the Commission the need for a deeper and expanded dialogue between the churches in the search for unity. At Accra, the time had arrived, not to argue pro or con ordination of women, or to consider it as "other ministry," but rather to find suitable contexts with enough leeway so that the churches could come together for honest dialogue.

The three texts of mutual agreement on "Baptism, Eucharist and Ministry" were published in 1975, in time for the Fifth Assembly of the WCC in Nairobi. Within point III of the Ministry section under "Ordination" are six paragraphs with the heading "The Ordination of Women."[69] A major turning point since Montreal 1963, the issues dealt with include theology, tradition, Scripture, and church practice. The final paragraph addresses the fact that churches are on different time trajectories regarding this topic. It states that because there is as yet no common instrument for conciliar action, churches must act in this matter in obedience to their own convictions. The paragraph reads:

> For some churches these problems are not yet alive. While recording a position, they have not yet determined whether the decisive factors are doctrinal or simply related to a longstanding traditional discipline. Nor are individuals within the different confessions in agreement about the doctrinal and disciplinary factors or about their relation. Differences on this issue could raise possible obstacles to the mutual recognition of ministries. But these obstacles should not be regarded as insuperable. Openness to each other holds out the possibility that the Spirit may well speak to one Church through the insights of another. Ecumenical awareness and responsibility also demand that once a Church has decided what is timely and right, it should act in obedience to its own convictions. Since the opinion appears to be growing that doctrinal considerations either favour the ordination of women or are neutral, the possibility is open that a future ecumenical council might deal with the question. Ecumenical considerations, therefore, should encourage, not restrain, the full, frank facing of this question.[70]

Appropriately at the WCC Fifth Assembly in Nairobi (1975), the topic of the ordination of women arose in two of the six sections. Faith and Order concerns were expressed through section II, "What Unity Requires," and the concerns of the Sub-Unit on Women in Church and Society through section V on "Structures of Injustice and Struggles for Liberation." Concerns for unity and justice were positioned on two separate tracks, yet the assembly was meeting on a continent where the separation of these concerns was viewed by many as a major roadblock to furthering the gospel.

A statement regarding ordination of women came to the assembly floor from section V and had to be redrafted. A finally agreed-upon resolution called for ecumenical relations to be continued between churches that do and do not ordain women. But it maintained that where ordination of women has been agreed upon in principle, churches should "take immediate action to admit women to all their ordained ministries," and where ordination was not possible, this position not be overlooked but given "serious consideration."[71]

Two recommendations from section V were as follows:

Those member churches which do ordain women and those which do not continue dialogue with each other and with non-member churches about the full participation of women in the full life of the Church including ordained ministries, according to the measure of their gifts;[72]

Those churches that ordain women to give them the same opportunities and pay as men, according to the measure of their gifts (I Cor. 12).[73]

In the section of the resolution dealing with Faith and Order concerns, the churches were asked to "study the three agreed statements approved at Accra, and return their responses to the Faith and Order Secretariat by December 1976 to facilitate further work."[74] In addition, it recommended to the churches that they participate fully in a new study called "The Community of Women and Men in the Church," which would consider issues of theology, Scripture, tradition, and ministry with special attention to "the significance of the Virgin Mary in the Church and the question of ordination of women."[75] They also recommended that concern for unity be pursued in relation to contemporary social conflicts and divisions giving "a new urgency to the work for unity by setting it in wider context of concern for the whole of humanity."[76] At this point a new conceptual framework, begun at Louvain in 1971, was starting to develop in Faith and Order, which attempted to integrate issues of unity and justice as part of the movement toward one common goal.[77]

The approach to ordination of women in the unity section at Nairobi dealt with how and in what future context the discussion should be pursued, while the discussion in section V on "struggles for liberation" was more concerned with the reality of ordained women's lives in the churches and the precarious discriminatory situations of many. The section V report takes an advocacy

158

APPENDIX 2

position on behalf of women in the church. This is summarized under the heading "Sexism":

> Recognizing that small advances in the position of women in the church and society have been made, we are nevertheless convinced that it is vital for the WCC and the member churches to open all service opportunities to women and to encourage the study, by both men and women, of a deeper and more thorough participation of women in church life with special attention to the question of ordination and the employment of women in the Church.[78]

The Nairobi assembly actions that dealt with the ordination of women prompted several critical questions. Is it possible to locate precisely where the issues around the ordination of women fit? Is there only one "right place" in which it ought to be discussed? Does it come under the rubric of "struggles for liberation, a justice issue"? Or does it fit more appropriately under the "Unity We Seek," relating to convergencies on church understandings of ministry and ordination or to as yet a far-off goal of "conciliar fellowship"? Should it be placed under the study of the unity of the church and the renewal of the human community, a broader focus that recognizes that the very issues which divide in societal life—race, sex, and class (issues of conflict and power)—are also obstacles to the unity of the church? Under what category, for example, should questions of Christian teaching regarding anthropology be placed? What lies behind biblical and theological misinterpretations of the nature of women and of female/male relationships where women are cast as the "weaker," or subordinate, sex? Is this a question of equality and human rights, or is it one that lies at the heart of theology, requiring a fundamental revision of our understanding of the nature of the church itself?

It would become the task of the Community of Women and Men in the Church study, recommended by both sections II and V of the Nairobi assembly, to open up several aspects of these questions. At the Nairobi assembly recognition was given to the fact that the identity and status of women in the church is changing, that relationships between women and men are in a process of transformation. In the call for mutual recognition of ministries there was some realization that there can be no "right place" for either women or men, ordained or lay, unless expression of the church's vocation is set within the wider context of the unity and renewal of humankind.

THE TURBULENT YEARS

Post-Nairobi writing on this subject was catalyzed and accelerated by certain events:

1. The ordination of women in churches of the Anglican Communion—in Hong Kong, Canada, the United States, and New Zealand—brought the churches in the Lambeth Conference who ordain women to an even greater

number. Further, eight other member churches, including the Church of England and the Anglican Church in Australia, had announced that there were no theological obstacles to the ordination of women.

2. Theologians from Orthodox churches responded sharply to these ordinations in the Anglican Communion.

3. In the Roman Catholic Church, 27 January 1977, a public declaration against the ordination of women was released by the Sacred Congregation for the Doctrine of the Faith.

4. Some "fundamentalist" traditions began to ordain women.

Holding Diversity Together

With the situation in the Anglican Communion in flux, the archbishop of Canterbury, in a letter dated 9 July 1975, consulted with Pope Paul VI about the growing consensus in the Anglican Communion "that there are no fundamental objections in principle to the ordination of women to the priesthood."[79] A reply came back from Paul VI on 30 November 1975 saying that the Catholic Church "holds that it is not admissible to ordain women to the priesthood for very fundamental reasons."[80] The reasons he listed were: 1) Christ choosing only male apostles, 2) the constant practice of the church, and 3) the teaching of the magisterium which has consistently held that women are excluded from the priesthood "in accordance with God's plan for His Church."[81]

Parallel with this, opposition became more vocal both inside and outside the Anglican church. Internal voices of dissent most often used ecumenical arguments, that is, the relationship with Roman Catholic, Orthodox, and Old Catholic churches, as the basis for their opposition. External voices in opposition came forcefully from theologians in the Orthodox churches. Not only were many articles generated arguing why women should not be ordained but Orthodox members of the Joint Orthodox-Anglican Consultation issued another statement in 1976, saying that women's ordination was counter to the "order of creation." It read:

> The biblical, conciliar, patristic and canonical evidence affirms that only men, and only some men, are eligible for the offices of priest and bishop. This scriptural and traditional evidence—reflecting and protecting the order of creation— cannot be challenged or relativized by references to historic or social changes, unless one rejects the very idea of God's revelation in Christ once and for all, transmitted to us by His Apostles and by the Church.[82]

At the Lambeth Conference of 1978, an entire day of debate was given to this subject. It resulted in an eight-point resolution on "Women in the Priesthood." The resolution accepted those member churches that both do and do not ordain women, recognized that those dioceses which have ordained women have received them into the historic priesthood, and encouraged continuing dialogue with other churches on theological issues of ministry and priesthood. For those members who oppose women's ordination it put restrictions on the exercise of the priesthood of ordained women in provinces where women were not ordained. In inviting dialogue with "other churches" that oppose women's ordination, it made clear that this is part of its movement toward a fuller catholicity and a deeper fellowship in the Holy Spirit. In other words, Lambeth was able to find a way through a heated conflict between "equality" and conventional church order by embracing both sides and affirming this range of practice as part of the centuries of Anglican heritage, namely, the ability to "hold together diversity within a unity of faith and worship."[83] These resolutions were then communicated to Orthodox, Roman Catholic, and Old Catholic churches in such a way that the doors of dialogue, carefully cultivated over many years, could remain open.

A Wedge Between the Sexes

A different situation emerged within the Roman Catholic Church. The 1976 Declaration on the Question of the Admission of Women to the Ministerial Priesthood prompted a shocked reaction in some theological faculties and pontifical commissions, as well as among a growing number of trained women theologians, some of whom were specialists in Scripture, theology, and canon law.[84]

During and after Vatican II considerable research and writing had been devoted to this topic. As early as 1960, Jean Daniélou of France addressed the subject favorably, as did Jean-Marie Aubert and Yves Congar somewhat later.[85] Some voices were more cautious than others, favoring the admission of women into the order of the ordained diaconate but not yet ready to consider women in the priesthood. German theologians, such as Karl Rahner and Bernard Häring, and the Swiss theologian Han Küng were among those who stated that there were no theological obstacles in the way of women's ordination. Karl Rahner in a letter to a Lutheran pastor in Bavaria stated that:

> The practice which the Catholic Church has of not ordaining women to the priesthood has no binding theological character. . . . The actual practice is not a dogma; it is purely and simply based on a human and historic reflection which was valid in the past in cultural and social conditions which are presently changing rapidly.[86]

Parallel with the theological writings, local movements developed working for the ordination of women in France, Switzerland, West Germany, Belgium, England, and the United States.[87] In November 1975, at the same time as the WCC Nairobi assembly, more than a thousand women and men gathered in Detroit, Michigan, for the first of what would become several conferences on this and related topics.[88]

During the same period, there were formal initiatives in many areas to restore the diaconate for women, an office which women held in the early church at least to the twelfth century.[89] The Catholic Theological Society of America in 1971 maintained that "the early church followed the example of St. Paul in availing itself of the service of women, most notably in the diaconate where women played a full part in the preparation of women and children candidates for baptism, assisting the bishop in the administration of sacraments, taking the eucharist to the sick, and performing certain other functions in the eucharistic assembly. She is seen as the counterpart of the male deacon."[90] Arguments for restoring the diaconate for women include 1) that it is ancient tradition, maintained in the East much longer than in the West; 2) that it is a sacramental order, where the functions of male and female deacons are similar, including parallel rites of ordination—the laying on of hands by the bishop and the invocation of the Holy Spirit; and 3) that it could meet pastoral and evangelistic needs, if restored in a creative way.[91]

After an extensive survey of the state of the question of ordination of women in the Roman Catholic Church, the French theologian Herve-Marie Legrand summarized the sentiment as follows:

> In the year 1975—in the Catholic Church of the West at least—the idea of women being ordained to the priesthood is a possibility to be considered by official groups of Christians, by sisters, by theologians of repute, and by bishops who, in the eyes of all, are conscious of their pastoral responsibilities. In the Catholic Church today, then, the idea of ordaining women is no longer a novel one emanating from marginal groups.[92]

It was a little more than a year later that the Vatican issued a declaration against the ordination of women, *Inter Insigniores*. In the history of the Roman Catholic magisterium, it is the most decisive statement against the ordination of women, creating a stir in the Roman Catholic Church which is equal in recent times only to the 1968 statement on birth control, *Humanae Vitae*. The declaration was criticized extensively for overlooking the scholarly work that had been done on the subject of ordination over the last twenty years within Roman Catholic faculties, as well as the work of two special pontifical commissions mandated in 1975 to study the role of women in the ministry, including the question of priesthood. The final report of the Pontifical Biblical Commission published its findings with the conclusion that: "Scriptural grounds alone are not enough to exclude the possibility of ordaining women."[93]

Criticism of the declaration's decision-making process was matched by criticism of its arguments, in particular the following paragraphs which refer to a concept of "natural resemblance":

> The Christian priesthood is therefore of a sacramental nature: the priest is a sign, the supernatural effectiveness of which comes from the ordination received, but a

sign that must be perceptible and which the faithful must be able to recognize with ease. The whole sacramental economy is in fact based upon natural signs, on symbols imprinted upon the human psychology: "Sacramental signs," says St. Thomas, "represent what they signify by natural resemblance." The same natural resemblance is required for persons as for things: when Christ's role in the eucharist is to be expressed sacramentally, there would not be this "natural resemblance" which must exist between Christ and His minister if the role of Christ were not taken by a man. In such a case it would be difficult to see in the minister the image of Christ. For Christ Himself was and remains a man.[94]

This argument has been opposed publicly by many Roman Catholic scholars on the grounds of both dogma and justice. In terms of dogma, critics argued that in Roman Catholic theology the priest does not directly represent Christ. Rather, the priest represents Christ only through first representing the church, for the priest is called by the church in ordination. In the words of St. Thomas Aquinas, "in prayers of the Mass, the priest speaks in 'persona Ecclesiae,' occupying the place of the Church."[95] In addition, others from the perspective of Trinitarian theology saw the argument of "natural resemblance" as neglecting the integrity of the Trinity by inappropriately assigning sexual categories to one of the three persons. These critics held that the Christ who is part of the mystery of the Trinity, is not sex-linked, for the persons of the Trinity are not distinguished from one another by biological categories.

The declaration argues for an order of priority moving from Christ who is the head of the church to the priest as male who then represents Christ. In opposition, prominent Roman Catholic theologians reasoned that the priest represents first the church by virtue of the ordination bestowed, and through this and because of it the priest at the Eucharist represents Christ. While the argument used in the declaration puts heavy theological weight on the maleness of the historical Jesus and on male hierarchical authority, the argument of critics puts more emphasis on the church of the risen Christ of the Eucharist and the authority of the church as the inclusive people of God guided in salvation by the intervention of the Holy Spirit. The latter position, looking at the entire christological event and its implication for the future as well as the past, is more open to both women and men serving in the ordained diaconate and priesthood. It can be argued further that because the church consists of women and men, both are therefore needed at worship to image the wholeness of the church of the risen Christ.

In March 1977, a formal letter of protest was sent to the pope by members of the Jesuit School of Theology at Berkeley, California. Among other theological considerations, it addressed those of justice pointing out the necessity to argue more cogently and biblically if one is to argue for a status of equality and exclusion at the same time. It reads:

The Declaration correctly maintains that no single person can lay claim to ordination as a personal right. The profound issue of justice does not arise because one woman has been denied presbyteral orders. The issue of justice is engaged when an entire class of Catholics is antecedently excluded on principle even from the possibility that Christ might call them to this ministry, so that simply because they are women it is impossible to admit them to this service of *word* and sacrament.

The exclusion of any group of Christians from a life or from a function to which they feel a call is so serious an action by the Church that it should be supported as an obvious demand of the Gospel. Any evidence should be overwhelming which makes discrimination an imperative. This Declaration does not contain such evidence.[96]

Sister Elizabeth Carroll, staff member of the Center of Concern in Washington, D.C., reflected in a Center memo, on how the papal declaration would be received by women.

Far from being life-giving and creative of love and unity, the document drives a divisive wedge between the sexes. It sacralizes roles at a time when these are widely perceived as arbitrary limitations placed upon women by a male society. For a believing woman it saps the spiritual motivation of her life.

Women will respond to this document in myriad ways. Some will take no notice of it. Some will abandon the church and its ministry. Some will continue in the church but with a weakened self-concept, wounded in their deepest spiritual motivation as "co-workers of God," with loss of enthusiasm and commitment to ministry. Hopefully many will have their consciousness raised 1) as to their own truth, 2) as to reform of unjust structures and sexist language in the church, and 3) as to the needs of people for good pastoral ministry and wise use of authority by both women and men.[97]

As is the case today that many Roman Catholic couples do not follow the pastoral advice in *Humanae Vitae* regarding birth control, so one wonders how much the declaration against the ordination of women might undermine the spiritual fabric of the church's strongest support system—its varieties of ministries served by committed women, lay and in religious orders. For the first time in its history, the highest authority in the Roman Catholic Church declared that it would be difficult to see in the priest the image of Christ if that priest were a woman.

Biblical Authority and "Re-creation of a New Race"

An added dimension of the ecumenical movement of the 1970s with yet another set of issues was that of "fundamentalist" churches who were beginning to ordain women. Though many of these churches do not belong to the World Council, some of their members belong to the Faith and Order Commission. One of the largest of these church bodies is the Southern Baptist

Convention where a woman was first ordained in 1964. Since that time over one hundred women have been ordained, and about sixteen hundred women in 1982 were attending seminaries of the Southern Baptist Convention, with half of them looking forward to ordination. In the words of Leon McBeth of that convention: "Ordination does not remove subordination."[98] Because of the fact that those favoring ordination have looked freshly at Scripture, arguing essentially for the equality of women and men in Christ, subordination has appeared not on the level of theological arguments but on the level of practice. Women desiring to serve as ordained ministers find that it is easier to get ordained than it is to find suitable placement. Most ordained women serve in "non-preaching roles, such as chaplains in hospitals and correctional institutions, teachers, counsellors, and in non-pastoral church staff positions." Yet, McBeth observes, the trend in the convention toward ordination of women has moved rapidly and he identifies several reasons why:

1. Women in the church are now better educated and better trained; this means that the pool of leadership is larger;
2. Southern Baptist women are also influenced by the general movement for women's emancipation;
3. The ordination of women in other churches, on an equal basis, has influenced the attitudes and changed the minds of Southern Baptist women (and men);
4. Perhaps most important, a "growing number of Southern Baptists do not find in the Bible final barriers to a more active church role for women."[99]

Although the issue of ordination of women continues to be a point of controversy, McBeth maintains that:

> Baptists have always been, and are now, firmly committed to the authority of the Bible. Although that deep commitment to biblical authority abides unchanging, Baptist *interpretation* of the Bible can vary and has varied at different times and places in our history. In the past more Southern Baptists interpreted the Bible in such a way as to keep women in silence and subjection, making much of the so-called "Pauline restrictions" upon the religious roles of women. In recent years, however, a growing number of Southern Baptist scholars, pastors, and lay persons are reading those same passages in a different light. They profess to find in both testaments an emphasis upon human dignity and equality and find new dimensions of biblical truth when passages are interpreted in context and in light of the teachings and practices of Jesus.[100]

What appears to be turning around the thinking in these churches more than anything else is the emergence of women in new positions of leadership. This change within the life of the community itself has enabled Scripture to be interpreted in a new light without undermining its authority.

In the late 1970s the issue of the ordination of women was indeed turbulent across the ecumenical spectrum; no church escaped some level of conflict and self-examination. This, in turn, has had its repercussions on the discussions within Faith and Order, the Sub-Unit on Women, the WCC as a whole, groups for and against ordination in the Roman Catholic Church, and relationships between the churches.

TRADITION AND EQUALITY
IN CONFRONTATION

Given this ferment, the question of the final placement of the discussion on the ordination of women in the mutually agreed statement on the ministry was up in the air again at the time of the 1978 Bangalore meeting of the Faith and Order Commission. In spite of new research and more Lutheran, Reformed, Anglican, and Free churches ordaining women, no decision about placement was reached. The mood was one of caution and restraint.

The Unique and Eternal Priesthood of
the Great High Priest

A follow-up consultation by the Community of Women and Men in the Church study on the subject of "Women in Ministry" was recommended at Bangalore with particular attention to how the question of ordination of women should be included in the revised statements. Topics to be considered were 1) the churches' experiences of women in ministry, 2) ecumenical relationships, and 3) mutual recognition of ministries. Among the theological points to be covered were those of theology of the Eucharist (the nature and function of the role of presiding priest) and authority of the Bible and its interpretation. Practical studies were also requested to elicit further documentation on questions of whether women and men priests exercise their ordained ministries differently and how various concepts of the priestly role affect women, including as well what impact women might have on the shape and function of the office. Also recommended for study was the influence of bilateral and multilateral discussions between churches on policies regarding ordination of women, and finally how women's ordination affects processes underway toward mutual recognition of ministries in local situations.[101] On this latter point, the Churches' Council for Covenanting in England was an important case study underway at the time.[102]

This recommendation formed the basis for a 1979 consultation of the Community of Women and Men in the Church study on "Ordination of Women in Ecumenical Perspective." It was the third major meeting on this subject in the history of the World Council of Churches, with eighteen women and twelve men participating from a range of churches—Protestant, Orthodox, Anglican, Old Catholic, and Roman Catholic—and from fourteen countries. Held at Klingenthal in France, the conference published a report which was designed for long-term practical use by persons and groups within and between churches and which recognized that much more ecumenical consciousness and sharing must be developed on local levels. If mutual recognition of ministries is to be fostered, it is important for ordained women and men, in local councils, ministerial associations, and seminaries to find occasions for study and practical exchange that can build more understanding and mutual respect for each other's ministerial office.[103]

The orientation of the Klingenthal meeting was not primarily about what different churches believe about ordination or about women but about what can be said together and what must be said separately. Included in the book are stories of women's experiences in ministry linked to the questions previously posed and reflections about gender-linked symbols for God. Alternatives for male androcentric theological images are also explored. One important question dealt with was the issue raised by *Inter Insigniores*, the relationship between God's incarnation and the concept of priesthood: "Is the maleness of the historical Jesus essential to the meaning of incarnation? Does Christ have to be represented by a male priest?" The paragraph responding to these questions affirmed that the basis for all priesthood—regardless of sex, class, or status—was the priesthood of Christ:

> The universal priesthood of all believers and the sacramental priesthood both derive from the unique priest (of Christ). The bishop and the priest only actualize, by the grace of the Holy Spirit in time and space, the unique and eternal priesthood of the High Priest.[104]

This is expanded by a paragraph aimed at opening a way, theologically, for further ecumenical research around the ordained diaconate for women and the priesthood. Decisions for and against an ordained role for women were placed within the context of a principle of unity/diversity within the unique, redemptive priesthood of Christ in the church of the new creation. The reasoning was as follows:

> On the basis of biblical anthropology, men and women are different and at the same time one, both in accordance with the order of creation and the order of redemption. This unity/diversity can be signified in the reconciled new creation which is beginning in the Church here and now, through the presence at the altar of a man and a woman, both ordained to the ministries of equal dignity, though of different symbolic significance. Others would ask yet further, is not this truth of creation and redemption best exemplified when both women and men stand at the altar as priests?[105]

Although this argument seemed too cautious for some, for others it offered a theological way to mutual understandings of ministries while still maintaining respect for different traditions and for variance in forms of church order.

The next development of this paragraph took place in July 1981 at the Sheffield international consultation on the WCC Community of Women and Men in the Church study. Among its recommendations to the Faith and Order Commission, it asked that 1) more theological work be done on the significance of the representation of Christ in the ordained ministry, with particular reference to the ordination of women; 2) more encouragement be given for the development of the ordained diaconate for women and men; 3) further explorations be undertaken regarding "the possibilities of different churches being in Communion with each other when they have different policies with regard to the ordination of women"; and finally 4) that work be undertaken on the question of fundamental human rights as they relate to the calling of women and men to the ordained ministry.[106] Participants at Sheffield were made keenly aware of the pain that this issue causes to those women who look toward ordination, yet who are members of churches that do not ordain them. This refers mainly to women in Roman Catholic and some Anglican churches. But there were others, mainly women and men from Orthodox churches, who made the counterargument that there was not enough sensitivity expressed toward those churches who feel they cannot, for theological reasons, adopt the practice of ordination of women.[107] Though these churches would affirm women's equality, they also contended that equality has no bearing on the issue of priesthood which is based on tradition.

Equality and Loyalty to Tradition

These Sheffield recommendations were submitted to the WCC Central Committee meeting in Dresden, the German Democratic Republic, in August 1981. At Sheffield the recommendations regarding ministry had been carefully worked through by a group of Lutheran, Reformed, Anglican, Roman Catholic, and Orthodox participants. The recommendation that could move the discussion further was point 3;[108] however, the recommendation that drew the most attention was point 4, which had to do with fundamental human rights. Its intention was to study those situations, such as the Church of Sweden, where equal rights legislation in the government had been an important factor in the church debate. Because few countries have such legislation, yet questions of equality and justice are continually being posed, it was hoped that such an ecumenical study could benefit all the churches faced today with women and men wanting to serve in a diversity of ministries, yet holding equality in church and society as a norm.

Discussion and debate on the topics of ordination of women and women and men as equal partners in decision making proved troublesome for the Dresden Central Committee. Sensitivity to the word "equality" led to long and heated debate. It occurred over a resolution from the Sheffield consultation that at the 1983 WCC Sixth Assembly "50% of all membership elected to sub-units and committees of the WCC be women."[109] After an arduous exchange, the Central Committee was able to agree. However, the Orthodox members did not participate in the vote; they considered that the question involved theological and dogmatic issues that should not be legislated. The Dresden recommendation reads:

> The (Central) Committee appreciates:
> 1) that women make up over half the constituents of the member churches and half of the human family;
> 2) that the principle of men and women in partnership means equal participation.
>   Therefore, it affirms that this principle of equal participation between men and women be a goal towards which we move, starting with the composition of the WCC decision-making and consultative bodies during and after the Sixth Assembly.[110]

Paul Crow, a member of the Faith and Order Commission and representative of the Church of the Disciples of Christ in America, made an intervention in the debate about the relationship between tradition and equality. His comments, as recorded in the minutes, are:

> The Central Committee had begun a deep theological debate. It was important to realize that all churches in the WCC claimed the Tradition. In his own church it was a dynamic Tradition and faithfulness to it led to the dogmatic affirmation of equal participation of women and men in the life of the Church. But it must be recognized that the churches, while standing under the same Tradition, have different interpretations of it and therefore there are theological differences between them. But that was why the WCC existed and it was here that they brought their differences, but in loyalty to that one Tradition.[111]

From the Dresden Central Committee, the Sub-Unit of Women received recommendations to continue providing support and advocacy for women in the ministry. Following its predecessors since the First Assembly in Amsterdam, it was asked to 1) "collect case studies of the experiences of lay women and men as they relate to ordination and hierarchical church structures and that this collection be a basis for further discussions" and 2) work to build a network of women in ministry, both ordained and non-ordained ministries, so that women in all parts of the world can share their experiences and "take seriously the burden women carry in the discussion which needs to be shared equally by men and women."[112]

Though ordination of women was not a highly focused topic over the four years of the community study, some of the underlying issues began to surface that are still to be faced by the Faith and Order Commission and the WCC as a whole. At no prior time in the history of the WCC had so much formal attention been catalyzed in a confrontation between those committed to "equality" and those committed to "tradition." Emerging out of the larger study on the Community of Women and Men in the Church, the specific point of conflict was not ordination of women, but women's equal participation in the ministries of decision making within the Council's structures. It was another echo of Lausanne 1927: the question of the right place of women in the "councils of the church." This controversy made clear the need for a long-term ecumenical examination of the role of equality within the "one tradition."

LOOKING AHEAD

Unity That Is Less Than Honest Will Not Work

Looking to the future, it is not clear what will come from the studies done and what follow-up there will be of recommendations made. During the Lima meeting of the Faith and Order Commission in January 1982, reflections on the findings of the Community of Women and Men in the Church study prompted an excited, suggestive, and much-needed dialogue among Orthodox participants, followed later by a Protestant response. Reported in the minutes and quoted below, the exchange points to the necessity for new dimensions of ecumenical research and sharing on issues of equality and tradition, particularly in the areas of Christology and the theological anthropology as they relate to the nature of the Trinity, the church, the human person, and the practice of the eucharistic life. The minutes read:

> Several Orthodox members of the Commission explained their difficulty with the ordination of women in a variety of ways. It was said that since Jesus Christ was incarnate as a male, it is necessary that the priest at the eucharist, who is a typology or icon of Christ in that role, must necessarily be male as well. However, it was also observed that the Christ of whom the priest is a type is the eschatological Christ, and it remains unclear whether the eschatological Christ is to be described a male, or male/female, or entirely transcendent of sexual categories. It was suggested that a helpful perspective is to look at the incarnation as God entering into the process of history. Then the question is not whether one historical moment is determinative but how are we to understand God's activity in historical change. It was also argued that the understanding of God as Trinity reveals that there are both masculine and feminine qualities in the Godhead, and hence there is no theological reason not to ordain women. In contrast, it was contended that God entirely transcends sexual categories, which are therefore inappropriate in discussion of the Trinity. Serious theological reflection is still needed on this issue.
>
> In responding from the Protestant perspective, some commissioners found it difficult to understand the logic of concluding that the maleness of Christ required the maleness of the ordained person, any more than the fact that Jesus was a Jew would require ordained persons to be Jews. The central importance of this issue was strongly held. It cannot be avoided on the false premise that to raise it would threaten the emerging consensus. Unity that is less than honest will not work.

Advocates of the ordination of women were cautioned not to speak of ministry as the "right." Ministry is not a right but a gift of God to the Church. Arguments should be based on theology rather than democratic concepts.[113]

It is evident from this exchange how much there is yet to sort out and how far there is to go. Yet this exchange does represent another turning point because the ordination of women is acknowledged not as a seperate theological issue but as an unfolding of new dimensions of theology for fundamental examination within an ecumenical framework.

Speaking to One Church Through the Insights of Another

In the period following the 1983 WCC Sixth Assembly at Vancouver one point of focus is the paragraphs on "The Ministry of Men and Women in the Church" which finally found a place under "The Church and the Ordained Ministry" in the three converging statements *Baptism, Eucharist and Ministry*.[114] These statements, now before the churches, are an important test in bringing divided Christians into closer relationship. They "represent the converging lines of the faith of the separated church communions."[115] The churches are being asked to study these texts and respond to them by the end of 1985. These responses are to form an essential part of the preparations for a Fifth World Conference on Faith and Order, projected for the end of this decade.

Paragraph 18 of *BEM* on the ordination of women represents the present unresolved status of this question in the ecumenical movement. With growing numbers of women studying theology in a variety of church and crosscultural contexts, with a deepening sense among both laity and clergy of their need for each other as equals in the royal priesthood of all believers, with many people wanting to serve the church in ministries that give witness to the wholeness of relationships between women and men, considerable attention will be given to this paragraph in the converging statements. It now reads:

Where Christ is present, human barriers are being broken. The Church is called to convey to the world the image of a new humanity. There is in Christ no male or female (Gal. 3:28). Both women and men must discover together their contributions to this service of Christ in the Church. The Church must discover the ministry which can be provided by women as well as that which can be provided by men. A deeper understanding of the comprehensiveness of ministry which reflects the interdependence of men and women needs to be more widely manifested in the life of the Church. Though they agree on this need, the churches draw different conclusions as to the admission of women to the ordained ministry.

An increasing number of churches have decided that there is no biblical or theological reason against ordaining women, and many of them have subsequently proceeded to do so. Yet many churches hold that the tradition of the Church in this regard must not be changed.[116]

Commenting on the Ministry text, Father Emmanuel Lanne, a Belgian Benedictine monk who has been close to this twenty-year process of dialogue, writes:

> The exegetical, doctrinal and pastoral questions arising from the admission or non-admission of women to ordination were not tackled by this document. This is undoubtedly a real limitation in this new text, which is specifically intended to make it possible for churches to reach a truly common concept of ministry.[117]

Though the substantive issues were dealt with in the special consultations of 1963, 1970, and 1979, the Faith and Order Commission as a whole has not yet worked through this question. Lanne points to paragraph 54, mostly developed in 1974 at Accra, as a possible way forward. It reads:

> Some churches ordain both men and women, others ordain only men. Differences on this issue raise obstacles to the mutual recognition of ministries. . . . Openness to each other holds the possibility that the Spirit may well speak to one church through the insights of another. Ecumenical considerations, therefore, should encourage, not restrain, the facing of this question.[118]

Openness to Each Other

In the final analysis, what impact has the debate on ordination of women had on Christian unity? Does the 1916 opinion of Bishop Temple still prevail: first church unity then women's ordination? What can be said about these years of constraint in facing the issue? Depending on one's point of view, advances have been made since early in this century: 1) more women are included in the concern; 2) all churches are involved in the topic and/or the dialogue; 3) many more churches ordain women without "threats" to unity; 4) the topic has become more public; and 5) there is more participation in the shaping of decisions in many churches—among lay and ordained leaders. Yet, this historical study reveals that while there is more agreement so also are differences more clear and sharp. True, the ordination of women is no longer an isolated concern. It has found "a place" in the discussions, but the development of that "place" is still open to debate.

References to "further study" may seem like one more excuse to avoid or soft-pedal a highly controversial topic. Yet the ecumenical movement, slow and frustrating as it is, must be tested by open, honest, and hard dialogue, expanding the base of shared understanding if not agreement. As a guide for evaluating the past and moving toward the future, the following areas are singled out:

1. *Intercommunion.* A place where intercommunion was first threatened because of ordination of women was in relationships between the Church of

Sweden and the Church of England, yet they continue to remain in communion with one another. Similarly dioceses of the Anglican Communion that do and do not ordain women also remain in communion, "holding together unity and diversity" (Lambeth, 1978).

2. *Church Union Negotiations.* The formation of the Church of South India in 1947 meant that the Methodists had to relinquish their practice of ordaining women in order to conform to the Anglican practice of the time. Today, the Church of South India ordains women as does the Church of North India, in a similar union. In Canada, both the Anglican church and the United Church now ordain women, but union negotiations between them are at a standstill for other reasons.

At the 1981 Faith and Order consultation on "United and Uniting Churches," the question of women's ordination was lifted up as a priority, a significant change from the 1968 position described by Stephen Neill. The report stated:

> There is an urgent need to continue the search for a consensus on the ordination of women to the ministry of the Church, and to seek new ways in which women and men can become partners in common decision-making, in mission and service, in spirituality.[119]

3. *The Force of Tradition.* It remains to be seen what the impact of the "force of tradition"[120] will be and how it will be interpreted. It has been the case in the past that, when some areas of tradition have been subjected to serious historical, theological, and liturgical inquiry, positions thought too deeply imbedded and immovable are uncovered in a fresh light. Apostolic succession and baptism are two such examples; the current Faith and Order study on the apostolic faith may be another.

Contemporary studies of the early church and its development have revealed, at local levels, a diversity of theological testimonies and structures of the church and of its ministries not unlike movements in the churches today, notably in the Southern Hemisphere. A deeper probing of the nature of the apostolic witness has uncovered not only links with the past but also continuity with renewed forms of ministries presently practiced in mission, service, evangelization, and eucharistic celebration.

Further, studies of the early diaconate have pointed to the integral liturgical and teaching roles that women carried on with men from apostolic times into the twelfth century. Communities of consecrated nuns in Orthodox, Roman Catholic, and some Protestant churches continue to attest to the fact that some form of diaconate for women still exists, surviving centuries of cultural transition and transformation in the churches.

4. *Tradition and Context.* More attention must be given to the experience of the churches and their starting points. This was precisely the plea made at the 1971 Louvain Faith and Order meeting and it was the theological method adopted by the community study from 1978 through 1982. Thomas Hopko's essay in *Women and the Priesthood* underlines how much the context of the partners in the debate influences the shape of the theology itself. He states:

> What we (Orthodox) want to affirm now is our conviction that no one really thinks, decides and acts on the issue of women and the priesthood (or, for that matter, on any other issue) in a vacuum. Everyone does so from within a living tradition, in a lived situation and vital context. No one comes to the "data" of the debate in a thoroughly detached and disinterested manner. Data by itself, as Fr. (Georges) Florovsky has said, is "mute." It responds to questioning and cross-examining. And the questioning and examining are always in a situation, from a perspective and towards a point. It cannot be otherwise. This is the only human way.[121]

5. *Irreconcilable Differences.* It is significant that to date no church that has ordained women has done so because of pressure from another church. The steps that have led to the ordination of women have begun from within particular church bodies themselves. It is highly unlikely that this will change, even with more ecumenical networks among women. The history of the discussion and the various steps in the process indicate that if churches are to truly respect one another, they must begin with the acknowledgment that differences may be irreconcilable but not necessarily divisive. This was the point of the 1975 Nairobi resolution regarding continuing the dialogue among member churches that do and do not ordain women, as well as with nonmember churches on both sides of this question.

6. *Anthropology.* In terms of a theological understanding of the human person, does Karl Barth's ordering of men/women relationships in creation and vocation still carry the "force of tradition"? The statement within the Ministry text of the *Baptism, Eucharist and Ministry* document that refers to "the ministry which can be provided by women as well as that which can be provided by men" appears to be a reminder of Barth's argument. Yet there is a renewed understanding of tradition emerging, acknowledged and affirmed at Vatican II: that all human beings (*homines*), "have the same nature and origin," "enjoy the same divine calling and destiny," the "basic equality of all." This kind of statement, similar to that expressed in the 1948 "Life and Work of Women in the Church" report, raises more than the question of women's ordination; it has theological implications regarding the very nature of being human, male and female, ordained or lay.

7. *Practice.* Since the Bliss report of 1952, many individual churches have

undertaken studies that have yet to be gathered, compiled, and evaluated ecumenically as part of the experience of women in the churches' ministries and as part of the church's experience with ordained women. Thus far, most material published is from Western churches, similar studies will have to be undertaken in other parts of the world. What is still at stake in Barth's 1948 argument about women's roles is not only theology but theology applied to half of the *homines* in its practical treatment of women in the church, a first and continuing concern of the WCC Sub-Unit on Women in Church and Society.

8. *Equality and Tradition.* The Church of Sweden was the first of the churches within the apostolic tradition to ordain women. As a result of its action, it has heard threats of breaking communion, but this has not happened. It has faced the real danger of division within itself but has kept its unity with diversity. It continues its life in the historic apostolic succession, yet it lives in a society where equality is an established norm, the will of the people since early in this century. Brita Stendahl's research on the Church of Sweden shows how that church has struggled with whether or not it could be true to tradition—biblically, theologically, and liturgically—and yet ordain women. Because of its decision and unique situation, it will continue to be an important ecumenical case study.

9. *Authority.* Finally, how much is the issue of equal partnership versus male hierarchy an indication of widely differing visions regarding the nature of the church itself, its exercise of authority and ministry,[122] and its relationships with the culture in which it lives? Specifically, what is the relationship between hierarchy in church and society as social reality and theological concepts of hierarchy in creation and human relationships? Similarly, how do concepts of equality in society influence and shape theological understandings of creation, Christology, and the church? These questions, touched on at Lima, may well be the hardest of all in that they raise the topic of the nature of the church and its institutional structure, a subject not given attention in Faith and Order since the report on "Institutionalism" in Montreal 1963.[123]

Finally, having looked both backward and forward at advances made and at what is yet to be undertaken, the question still stands: how will faithfulness in the body of Christ and openness to each other be translated into concrete actions so that the separated churches can find their way through what appear to be "substantive hindrances"?

From the perspective of this study, it is evident that some issues stir in the ecumenical movement for a long time and that those around the ordination of women are destined to be among them—issues of the nature of the church itself.

NOTES

INTRODUCTION

1. More than a third of the member churches of the World Council of Churches ordain women. The majority of these are in the tradition of the Reformation. They are primarily situated in the western cultures of East and West Europe and North America. Some churches in Asia, the Pacific, the Caribbean, Latin America, and Africa do ordain women, but opportunities for theological education and acceptance in the ordained ministry are less frequent. Within the Orthodox churches the issue is largely unraised. Some Anglican churches have approved women's ordination in principle, but few have implemented it. Others have decided against ordaining women, and still others have not as yet discussed the issue. The Roman Catholic and Old Catholic churches do not ordain women to the priesthood. Official statements are firm on that position. See Constance F. Parvey, ed., *Ordination of Women in Ecumenical Perspective* (Geneva: World Council of Churches, 1980), pp. 9–10.

2. Although I do not primarily approach the subordination of women from a psychological angle, even so, a book that has influenced my thinking to a great extent is Jean Baker Miller, *Toward a New Psychology of Women* (Boston: Beacon Press, 1976). Etching the contours of conflict embedded in the domination-subordination model, Miller points out that the methods of conduct in conflict do not have to be those we have always known. She admonishes people to ask not how *can* but how *should* institutions be reorganized in order to include women, and how the quality and the priorities of those institutions then might change.

3. As early as 1890 women scholars in Sweden tried to initiate special historical research focused on women, but the efforts faded away. The new orientation did not break through until the 1970s. Then the pioneer of women's history was a man, Professor Gunnar Qvist. See Birgitta Odén, "Forskande kvinnor inom svensk historievetenskap," *Historisk Tidskrift* 3 (1980): 244–65.

4. Although sex roles and social structure are often dealt with in historical and sociological material, the role of the clergy is not pointed out as central in the change of attitudes. Cf. Edmund Dahlström et al., *The Changing Roles of Women and Men* (Boston: Beacon Press, 1971) and Annika Baude, "Public Policy and Changing Family Patterns in Sweden, 1930–1977," in *Sex Roles and Social Policy: A Complex Social Science Equation*, ed. Jean Lipma-Blumen and Jessie Bernard (London and Beverly Hills, Calif.: Sage, 1979), pp. 145–75.

5. One visitor was Bertil Gärtner who taught at Princeton Theological Seminary between 1965 and 1969. Gärtner's home diocese was Göteborg where due to the strong Orthodox tradition the clergy had enjoyed extraordinary authority. He came to Uppsala to study theology and was ordained for the diocese of Göteborg but continued his studies in New Testament exegesis at Uppsala where he obtained his

doctorate and stayed as docent. His position concerning the ordination of women was argued in *Kvinnan och Ämbetet enligt Skriften och Bekännelsen*, pp. 83–113. He became a central figure in the resistance. In the United States he met pluralism and seemed to enjoy the many ways of living with the word of God that the country exhibits, but when he returned to Sweden, and especially when he became bishop of Göteborg, he resumed leadership of the opposition to women priests.

6. Fredrika Bremer, *Life in the North*, trans. Mary Howitt (New York: Harper & Brothers, 1849), is a slim volume intended to introduce Bremer's Swedish readers to the cultural life of Denmark where she visited in 1848. Among the many things she undertook during her stay in Copenhagen was to read galleys for the systematic theologian Hans Lassen Martensen, one of Kierkegaard's enemies. This did not help to endear Bremer in Kierkegaard's eyes. The manuscript was Martensen's *Dogmatik*, which for decades to come was to mold the minds of Danish theologians. The index of Kierkegaard's *Journals and Papers* lists five entries under Fredrika Bremer. All of them express his irritation with "this woman." Søren Kierkegaard, *Journals and Papers*, ed. and trans. Howard V. Hong and Edna H. Hong (Bloomington, Ind., and London: Indiana University Press, 1978).

7. At one occasion Böklin wrote: "If you have no inclination for family care, well! then develop your wonderful talents in art and language...." Another example from their correspondence shows how Böklin, in one small sentence, solved one of her crucial theological problems, namely, why God is always referred to in the masculine gender: "That the persons in the God-head are referred to in *masculinum* is merely an insignificant coincidence." Eva-Gun Junker, *Per Johan Böklin to Fredrika Bremer, Fredrika Bremer to Per Johan Böklin: A Selection of Letters* (Malmö: Allhem Förlag, 1965).

8. The feminist literature in theology is growing by the year. I have come to depend on the bibliographies prepared by Harvard Divinity School. To obtain an up-to-date bibliography write the Program of Women's Studies, Harvard Divinity School, 45 Francis Avenue, Cambridge, Massachusetts 02138. Three examples from the study of Old and New Testament and of the church fathers: Phyllis Trible, *God and the Rhetoric of Sexuality* (Philadelphia: Fortress Press, 1978); Elisabeth Schüssler Fiorenza, *In Memory of Her* (New York: Crossroad, 1983); Kari E. Børresen, *Subordination and Equivalence: The Nature and Role of Women in Augustine and Thomas Aquinas* (Washington, D.C.: University Press of America, 1981).

9. The subordination of women has been a popular theme for sermons over the ages. When the young Fredrika Bremer heard a sermon preached by the poet and later archbishop Johan Olof Wallin, in which he admonished women to be humble and obey their husbands, she went home and wrote him a letter asking for fair treatment. Cf. also a forthcoming book by Ian Siggins, *The Preaching of a Disciple* (Durham, N.C.: Duke University Press, 1984/85), where the author highlights the sermons by Johann Herolt (1390?–1468) as a telling source for how religion and morality were preached to the burghers of the empire on the eve of the Reformation. "Herolt faithfully repeats all the blindest male prejudices about women. It would be foolish to underestimate the cultural role of the priests and preachers who have transmitted men's prejudice and women's self-hatred, sanctioned men's power and women's subjection, from generation to generation" (quoted from section on "Woman").

10. In 1853, Antoinette Brown was the first ordained woman minister in the Methodist Church in the United States. The preacher of the sermon at the occasion

declared this break with the tradition justified because the Spirit of the gospel had led them: "Every Gospel minister is a prophet, and every prophet under the new dispensation is a Gospel minister." See *Women of Spirit: Female Leadership in the Jewish and Christian Traditions*, ed. Rosemary Radford Ruether and Elinor McLaughlin (New York: Simon & Schuster, 1979), p. 21. Women in the past have achieved recognition in the church by exhibiting extraordinary submission to the tradition, but very little material has survived to give us a clue to the ideas of the early mothers of the church. The essays in *Women of Spirit* give examples of spirited women who have attempted to create their own alternatives and made a difference as leaders, martyrs, and reformers.

11. For a full treatment of emerging models see chap. 4 on "Anthropology: Humanity as Male and Female" in Rosemary Radford Ruether, *Sexism and Godtalk: Toward a Feminist Theology* (Boston: Beacon Press, 1983), pp. 93–115.

CHAPTER 1

Bo Giertz

1. The titles given are my rendering of the Swedish *Stengrunden (The Rocky Ground)*. It was translated into English under the title *The Hammer of God* (Minneapolis: Augustana Book Concern, 1960). See also *With My Own Eyes* (London: Allen & Unwin, 1960).

2. For the text of *The 17 Points* (1960), see pp. 88–92.

3. According to results of one poll among the clergy where 92% participated, 43% were against and 37% were for ordination of women; 16% abstained and 4% sent in blank forms. There were perhaps other polls. In any case there were more priests clearly against ordination than clearly for it in the early 1950s.

4. Ernst Staxäng (d. 1967), a small farmer, a member of Parliament and of the diocesan council of Göteborg. Gustaf Adolf Danell, dean emeritus of the cathedral of Växjö.

5. "Special Commission" appointed by the government to prepare a question to be debated by the legislative body, the *Riksdag*. "Special Committee" appointed by the Church Assembly to prepare a special item of business.

6. The Church Assembly Meeting of 1958 was an extra session called expressly to solve the question of the ordination of women that otherwise would have had to wait until 1962, the statutory year for the next Assembly. Contrary to common practice to wait five years the government called a Church Assembly meeting the following year.

7. My translation of *The 17 Points*, pp. 88–92, includes the introduction.

8. The situation in Norway is both similar and different from that in Sweden. The Church of Norway ordains women. It too has gone through a bitter conflict and has listened to the same arguments for and against the ordination of women. There the women have had to put up a stronger fight for admission to theological studies, especially at Menighetsfakultetet which dominates the practical course required for ordination.

Ole Christian Hallesby grew up in a pious farming community. He studied theology in Oslo and then in Erlangen, Germany, where he received his doctorate in 1909. The same year he became professor at the orthodox Menighetfakultetet in Oslo that he, together with some others, founded because they considered the theological faculty at the University of Oslo too liberal. For information about the women priests in Norway see Kristin Molland Norderval, *Mot Strømmen; Kvinnelige teologer i Norge før og nå* (Oslo: Land og Kirke/Gyldendal Norsk Forlag, 1982).

9. Bishop Giertz, who asked to read the written text of the interview, found some parts of it to be either too general or too specific and wanted them changed or excluded. However, I find this kind of informal talk and argumentation important because each side of a conflict develops its own kind of shorthand. I have included the changes he made but kept in parentheses some material he found irrelevant when he read the text. At that time the Conscience Clause had been abolished. Cf. chap. 3, the section on Informal Arguments, pp. 68–69.

Ingmar Ström

1. Magda Wollter, *Annorlunda: Några tankar om kvinnligt prästämbete och andra kvinnofrågor inom kyrkan* (Stockholm, 1957).

2. Ingmar Ström is referring to SOU 1950: 48, a document produced by a commission appointed by the government to investigate the possibility of the ordination of women in the Church of Sweden. It was entitled *Kvinnas Behörighet till Kyrkliga ämbeten och tjänster* [*Woman's Right to the Ministries of the Church*] (Stockholm: Victor Pettersons Bokindustriaktiebolag, 1950). A significant part of this report is the exegetical statement in favor of ordination for women. This statement was written by Erik Sjöberg, a docent in New Testament exegesis (see pp. 30–47). Sjöberg argues that although the Bible is steeped in a patriarchal culture and has many sayings that speak for a view of women as inferior, there is no absolute connection between such dicta and the central gospel. To interpret them in "a mechanical biblicistic manner would be untenable and inconsistent with an evangelical-lutheran view of the Bible" (p. 42).

3. Called the "Green Book" because its cover was green and because it gave the green light to women. Ingmar Ström wrote the title essay in which he summarizes the essence of the contributions by the other authors. As he states: "It is of course the evolution of society that has brought about the question of women priests. The changes in society press clamoring questions on the church, questions that can neither be avoided nor circumvented," *Kvinnan-Samhället-Kyrkan* [*Women-Society-Church*] (Stockholm: Svenska Kyrkans Diakonistyrelses Bokförlag, 1958), p. 197. Krister Stendahl's essay was later translated into English and published as *The Bible and the Role of Women*, trans. Emilie T. Sanders (Philadelphia: Fortress Press, 1963).

4. *Women-Society-Church* was written as a study document for such study circles. In the first essay "Women in the Work Force," Karl-Manfred Olsson sorts out what principles are constitutive for the social ethics of the church, pp. 28–102.

5. Prior to this disagreement Giertz and Ström cooperated well. Giertz chaired the social ethics program. After the crisis of women's ordination social programs became suspect and were shied away from by the opposition which wanted to stick closely to Bible and confession.

6. The Folk-Church, a peculiar Scandinavian theological idea, sprung from the fact that the territorial parish and the Christian congregation once upon a time were one and the same. See pp. 53–54.

7. See the interview with Margit Sahlin, p. 30.

8. The proportion between men and women who study at the Stockholm Theological Institute is about 50/50, while in Uppsala and Lund men are in the majority. The practical course that is obligatory is, however, only given in Uppsala and Lund.

9. See pp. 86–88.

10. Holsten Fagerberg, *De homosexuella och kyrkan,* published by the Bishops' Council (Stockholm, 1974). It should be noted that the council has never taken an official stand as to the content of the book.

11. Stora Sköndal has now also an academic line open to women students for the study of social work.

12. A three-year course at Kyrkans Kursgård under the directorship of the Central Council.

13. See pp. 93–95.

Olov Hartman

1. Hartman's novel *Holy Masquerade* was translated and published by Wm. B. Eerdmans in 1952. His *Three Church Dramas,* translated by Brita Stendahl, was published by Fortress Press in 1962, as was his *On That Day,* a church drama written for the 1968 General Assembly of the World Council of Churches. One of his memoir books, *Fågelsträck* (Stockholm: Rabén & Sjögren, 1982), touches on the ordination conflict.

2. The SOU 1950: 48, see above, note 2 (Ström), also contained a report by those of the Commission who disagreed with the majority. Hartman's statement (pp. 109–19) stresses "the mystery in the male-female relation in the creation" and proposes to let "the ministry keep its masculine character" and "leave it to the women who are called to serve in a special capacity . . . not copied on the priesthood but free from its heavy masculine character . . ." (p. 119).

3. During the 1940s the Church of England instigated a new line for deaconesses. Women who had worked as "lay workers" for some years could apply to the Council for the Order of Deaconesses and be accepted at Gilmore House in London. The prospective deaconess could then study theology and take time for meditation and prayer, preparing herself for the consecration. After a time she would be ordained by laying on of hands by the bishop. As a sign of her consecration she is given a cross that she wears for the rest of her life as is customary also for the Swedish deaconesses. However, her duties are not much different from those of a lay worker. *The Order of Deaconesses* (London: published for the Council for the Order of Deaconesses, 1948).

4. Olof Linton, *Das Problem der Urkirche* [*The Early Church as a Problem*] (Diss., Uppsala, 1932), changed the theological climate in Sweden during the 1930s.

5. Kerstin Anér, a politician and an author with a lot of influence due to her double role, is a member of Parliament and was undersecretary in the department of education from 1976 to 1980. Like Olov Hartman, she is orthodox conservative and progressive in a unique mixture. Her Christian thinking is fresh and clearly stated in her many books; *God's Word and the Daily News* (1968); *Must We Stop the World* (1973); *Computer Power* (1975); *God Now* (1974); *God Is Here* (1978); *Women and the Bible* (1981).

6. Cf. *The Basic Writings of C. G. Jung,* ed. Violet Staub de Lazlo (New York: Modern Library, 1959), the essay "Psychological Aspects of the Mother Archetype," pp. 334–35. Erich Neumann, *The Great Mother: An Analysis of the Archetype,* trans. Ralph Manheim, Bollingen Series XLVII (Princeton, N.J.: Princeton University Press, 1963).

G. K. Chesterton's brilliant style, his suspicion of everything "modern," his devotion to paradox, and his sturdy personal piety as expressed in, for instance, *Or-*

thodoxy (1908), are traits that Hartman admires. These three authors were not mentioned randomly. Hartman's "mariological filter" had its lenses sharpened on these whetstones.

Margit Sahlin

1. *Vår Lösen,* an ecumenical, cultural monthly magazine of high quality containing commentary, essays, poems, and book reviews, was founded in 1909. It has outgrown the militaristic connotations of its title, "Our watchword and our password." The Young Church Movement that started it loved military metaphors. The present editor-in-chief, Anne-Marie Thunberg, is a woman with extraordinary wide reading and talent for putting the vital issues in perspective.

2. The Stockholm City Mission (*Stadsmissionen*) was founded in 1853 in order to help people who became homeless and helpless in the city. It built children's homes, vacation homes for tired mothers, study homes for students, homes for retired people, for the blind, for alcoholics, and for those just released from prison. The Rev. J. W. Johnsson became the director in 1923. During his forty years at the helm the work greatly expanded. Many thousands of people each year visited the different counseling bureaus the City Mission established. Being also an M.P., J. W. Johnsson was the priest whose motion in 1946 led to the appointment of the Royal Commission which recommended that there be no obstacle to the ordination of women.

3. This is the third time that the name Anton Fridrichsen occurs. Both Bo Giertz and Olov Hartman refer to him as their mentor, and now Margit Sahlin tells of his encouragement to her. Fridrichsen was born in Norway where he became a minister in 1911. He studied in Germany and became a docent in Strasbourg with the dissertation "Le Problème du miracle dans le christianisme primitif," Eng. trans. John Hanson, *The Problem of Miracle in Primitive Christianity* (Minneapolis: Augsburg Publishing House, 1972). Fridrichsen was one of those teachers who gathered and inspired students of quite diverse theological and intellectual styles. In his later years, however, he turned increasingly conservative and in 1951 he took the initiative together with Prof. Hugo Odeberg in Lund to prepare a declaration by academic teachers of New Testament stating that the ordination of women was contrary to the New Testament. See pp. 69–70.

4. Margit Sahlin, *Man och Kvinna in Kristi Kyrka* (Stockholm: Svenska Diakonis-tyrelses Bokförlag, 1950). Both Hartman and Sahlin said the idea died but Ström claims it still exists in the form of *församlingssekreterare* (see Ström, note 12).

5. It is common practice in Sweden that the priests wear a chasuble when at the altar. In the pulpit they wear an alb and stole. They have to remove the chasuble in the sacristy before they enter the pulpit and again put it on after they have preached the sermon. One of the formal duties of the sexton has been to assist with the change, but in Margit Sahlin's case he apparently thought it immodest to help a woman dress and undress in the sacristy. A striking example of how the sublime issues of theology are transformed into the petty and ridiculous.

6. Margit Sahlin, *Dags för Omprövning? Om bibel, kyrka och kvinnliga präster* (Stockholm: Proprius, 1980).

7. The program at Katarina in the spring of 1982 included the following titles for dialogue: "Violence and peace in the heritage of the religions of the Book (the Bible and the Q'ran)"; "Sweden—a society unkind to children"; "East meets West—Ways to

NOTES

renewal"; "Modern-physics-classical mysticism—Towards a new cosmology"; "In the public interest—The responsibility of the press."

Elisabeth Olander

1. In 1983 Elisabeth Olander became Sweden's first women *kontraktsprost* (dean). Each diocese is divided into several *kontrakt* (districts). The *kontraktsprost* is the deputy of the bishop within that kontrakt. He, and now she, has the right to give leaves of absence, and to call the priests together for discussions of theological and pastoral subjects. To become a *kontraktsprost* is considered a trust and an honor.

2. Hugo Odeberg was professor of New Testament exegetics in Lund. Extremely learned, he was a specialist on gnosticism and apocalyptic material. Together with Fridrichsen he issued a declaration against women's ordination. See pp. 69–70.

3. *Venia concionandi*, i.e., a special permission to preach given to those who study for the priesthood. Cf. Hans Cnattingius, *Diakonat och Venia Concionandi i Sverige intill 1800-talets mitt* (Stockholm: Svenska Kyrkans Diakonistyrelses Bokförlag, 1952). I have, however, never heard about the distinction imposed by Bishop Bolander between pulpit and altar when *venia* was given to theological students.

4. Ludvig Jönsson, now the dean of the cathedral of Stockholm and a chaplain to the court, has been assistant director of the Stockholm City Mission, and between 1962 and 1980 executive director in the Foundation for Ethics in the Marketplace, an enterprise that he founded.

5. The 1982 Church Assembly was no doubt one of the most important in recent Swedish history. A totally new structure for the national church was accepted with both more autonomy on internal matters and less power in matters of legislation. Legislation proper now resides entirely with Parliament.

6. Martin Lönnebo, bishop of Linköping since 1980, is one of the more visible leaders in the Church of Sweden. His peculiar blend of spirituality, unconventionality, and initiations cannot easily be pegged. Having done his doctoral work on Albert Schweitzer he has since written extensively in hermeneutics, homiletics, and spirituality.

7. Cf. the interview with Lillemor Hogendal, pp. 58–60. The two women agree that these two foundations at the universities of Lund and Uppsala do not inspire the students of theology to branch out. The students become politicized, and when they leave they get involved in "the network."

Else Orstadius

1. Each of the four institutions for deaconesses constitutes a "mother-house." When the deaconesses worked outside the institution their salary was paid to the mother-house, which in turn gave them an allowance. The money was used for the institution and toward a pension fund for the old age of the deaconesses. Thus they were tied to the institution with both spiritual and secular ties. The mother-house was like an extended family of sisters and mothers. When a sister grew old or developed some physical or psychological problems she could always return to the mother-house where her sisters cared for her well-being. The sisterhood was a very important ingredient in this community. Before social security plans in Sweden, it also gave extraordinary security.

2. An old custom of purification as women were readmitted to the church services

after having given birth. The custom more or less died out during the early part of this century but is still preserved in the Swedish Hymnal of 1937.

3. Although the universities of Sweden are supported by the state and charge no tuition, the student has to pay "room and board." Today there is state support for students in the form of low-interest student loans or even student "salaries." In the 1940s and 1950s, however, a family with many children had to carry a financial burden if all of them wished to attend the university. It could well happen that the boys took priority if there had to be a choice.

4. Saint-Etienne, known for its coal mining and gun industry, was the very town where Simone Weil taught school and demonstrated for workers' rights in 1934–35.

5. The Church of Sweden has strong ties with Tanzania. See Bengt Sundkler, once Swedish bishop of Bukoba, *Bara Bukoba: Church and Community in Tanzania* (London: C. Hurst & Co., 1980).

6. A foundation for the research and practice of pastoral psychology and counseling. A pioneering center in this field, founded in the 1940s and located in Stockholm.

7. An ecumenical community led by monks who live in Taizé, not far from the old Cluny monastery. Their services are open to whoever wants to come. At Christmas, Easter, and Pentecost, people come in the tens of thousands, especially young people, often unchurched, to learn and to participate in liturgy and meditation.

8. The study existed then only in mimeographed form. It was later published as *The Community of Women and Men in the Church: The Sheffield Report,* ed. Constance F. Parvey (Philadelphia: Fortress Press, 1983).

9. Martin Lönnebo, see Olander, note 6. Gustaf Wingren (born 1910), professor emeritus in Lund. Wingren is a systematic theologian who consistently has been thinking out of the Swedish situation. He has had considerable influence both within and outside of the country. The titles of his books show his progressively intensified concern for the theological issues and the religious climate of the country: *Luther's Teaching About the Call* (1942); *The Human Being and the Incarnation* (1947); *Preaching* (1949); *The Question of Method in Doing Theology* (1954); *Swedish Theology after 1900* (1958); *The Amt of the Church* (1958); *The Ecumenical Responsibility of the Church of Sweden* (1959); *The Gospel and the Church* (1960); *Democracy in the Folk Church* (1963); *The Folk Church Ideology* (1964); *Einar Billing* (1968); *Luther Liberated* (1970); *The Flight from Creation* (in English) (1971); *Change and Continuity* (1972); *Credo* (1974); *Two Testaments and Three Articles* (1976); *Openness and Particularity* (1979); *The Interpreter Keeps Silent* (1981); *A Human Being and a Christian: A Book About Irenaeus* (1984). Of these, *Credo: The Christian View of Faith and Life* is translated by Edgar M. Carlson (Minneapolis: Augsburg Publishing House, 1977). Hans Küng, a German Roman Catholic theologian, has written about how Christian faith can meet the challenges of today's world, *On Being a Christian,* trans. Edward Quinn (Garden City, N.Y.: Doubleday & Co., 1976).

CHAPTER 2

1. Hans L. Zetterberg, *Aktiva i Svenska Kyrkan—en livsstilsstudie* (Stockholm: Verbum, 1983), p. 10.

2. Ibid., p. 13.

3. Cf. Bengt Åberg/Thorleif Pettersson, *Identitet och roll* (Stockholm: SKEAB/ Verbum, 1981).

4. See Hilding Pleijel, *Hustavlans värld. Kyrkligt folkliv i äldre tiders Sverige* (Stockholm, 1970). This book on church folklore in olden times is extremely valuable to make us understand how familiar the Swedes were with biblical ethics and metaphors.

5. The story of Hjortberg is told by Sten Lindroth, *Epoker och människor* (Stockholm: Wahlström & Wistrand, 1972), pp. 147–78.

6. Anna Maria Lenngren (1755–1817), the daughter of a professor who found joy in giving her a classical education. Her marriage was childless. A much-appreciated writer of humorous realistic poems, she had ambivalent views of the emancipation of women. See Ruth Nilsson, *Kvinnosyn i Sverige: Från drottning Kristina till Anna Maria Lenngren* (Lund: Gleerup, 1973), pp. 328–64.

7. "Faith and knowledge are siblings" was one of Fredrika Bremer's favorite expressions. See Introduction, pp. 4–5. She saw science as propelled by faith and faith again as nourished by science, a view she had adopted from reading Hegel.

8. On the recruitment of the Swedish clergy. See Anders Bäckström, "Religion som yrke: En studie av de svenska prästkandidaternas bakgrund och rolluppfattning vid 1970-talets slut" ("Religion as Occupation. A Study of the Background and Role Conception of Swedish Ordinands at the End of the 1970s") (Diss., Uppsala, 1983). Bäckström includes a history of recruitment to the Church of Sweden and carries an exhaustive list of all the earlier literature.

9. Pietism, the movement begun in late seventeenth-century Germany with Spener and Francke, spread to Sweden, not least with the returning soldiers of Charles XII's disheveled army, whose chaplains, while they were prisoners in Siberia were in touch with Francke by correspondence. In 1717 the movement got its own hymnbook, which became enormously popular, *Mose och Lamsens visor (The Songs of Roses and the Lamb)*. The church and the government instituted a law against Pietists meeting in the homes for prayer and Bible readings if an ordained minister were not present, the so-called *konventikelplakatet*.

10. The Swedish brand is *"brännvin,"* aquavit, a hard liquor distilled from grain or potatoes. As in England, so also in Sweden it was customary during the nineteenth century to pay farmworkers in kind, and aquavit was then a common payment.

11. Two life style studies, companion studies to the *Aktiva i Svenska Kyrkan,* have been conducted among the people who frequent the free-churches and also the people belonging to temperance lodges, *Frikyrko-Sverige* (Stockholm: Moderna Läsare, 1979) and *Nykterhets-Sverige* (Stockholm: Sober, 1979). A comparison between the three life style studies shows that the people active in the Church of Sweden have less in common with each other than do the free-church people, whose pietistic life style is much more pronounced, and whose puritan traits overlap with the cycle of the temperance movement.

12. As the movement began, the baptism of every child was taken for granted. The theological meaning of baptism became identified with the doctrine of God's pure grace, without any act of will or faith by the child.

The inner logic of Swedish Folk Church theology tends now toward an agreement where "birth in Sweden" rather than baptism constitutes church membership—a rather unique position in Christendom.

13. All four of these men eventually became bishops. The leader of the movement, J. A. Eklund, wrote in 1909 the hymn that is characteristic for its program: "Fädernas kyrka i Sveriges land," #169 in the Swedish hymnal. Nathan Söderblom became world-known when he gathered the ecumenical Life and Work to a meeting in Stockholm in 1925. Gustaf Aulén wrote what became the most read work of systematic theology in the whole of Scandinavia, *Den allmänneliga kristna tron* (Stockholm: SKDB, 1929). In the care of Aulén and Söderblom the chauvinism of the movement lessened by their ecumenical and international contacts.

14. Cf. interview with Ingmar Ström, pp. 18–19.

15. For the history of preaching, for famous preachers, and for the composition of sermons from a Swedish perspective, see Yngve Brilioth, *Predikans historia* (Lund: Gleerups, 1945) (*A Brief History of Preaching,* [Philadelphia: Fortress Press, 1965]).

16. The author Selma Lagerlöf received the Nobel Prize in literature (1909) chiefly due to her novel *Gösta Berlings Saga* (1892), the story of a runaway priest in rural Värmland just at the beginning of industrialization.

17. Quoted from a Swedish prayer regularly used after a sermon.

18. For a short history of the Swedish church see Robert Murray, ed., *The Church of Sweden,* published in English and sponsored by the Bishops' Council, Stockholm, 1960.

19. Olov Hartman (see above) even claims that the people actually remembered the tunes perserved from the time when the hours had been kept in the parish, p. 25.

20. For instance: Ragnar Askmark, *Ämbetet i den svenska kyrkan* (Lund: Gleerups, 1949); Hugo Blennow, ed., *Prästämbetet* (Kallinge: Eginostiftelsen, 1951); Hjalmar Lindroth, ed., *En bok om kyrkans ämbete* (Uppsala: Svenska Kyrkans Diakonistyrelses Bokförlag, 1951); Per Erik Persson, *Ämbete som Kristusrepresentation* (Lund: Gleerup, 1961), a strong critique of the idea of ministry as representation of Christ.

21. In his essay "Den apostoliska successionens form och innehåll," Gunnar Rosendal, a pioneer in the High Church movement, holds the view that the succession is a charisma that gives the ordinand the right to teach, to loose and to bind, and to handle the sacraments in such manner that they "become real and true sacraments." The succession is "a transmission of charisma synonymous to the transmission of the Spirit" (Blennow, ed., *Prästämbetet,* p. 91).

22. Bäckström, "Religion som yrke," investigates the attitudes of the candidates for ordination concerning the Amt and finds that probably the greatest tension develops between what he calls "the vertical," i.e., a view of the Amt as given by God, and "the horizontal" understanding of Amt as given by the congregation. When he tested the candidates on their attitudes toward the Bible, he found a clear connection between the view of the Bible and that of the Amt. Those with a vertical view considered the Bible normative in a higher degree than those with a horizontal view, pp. 152–54.

23. See pp. 125–38.

CHAPTER 3

1. The first missionary to Sweden, St. Ansgar, arrived in 830. See Rimbert, *Vita Ansgarii.* Rimbert became Ansgar's successor as bishop in Hamburg. Both were considered saints. Also Rimbert got his hagiography, *Vita Rimberti.*

2. *Denarius Petri*, a kind of tax money and a common custom all over Europe during the Middle Ages. Each household paid a "penny" to the pope to get St. Peter's protection. In Sweden the custom lasted until the Reformation. See Yngve Brilioth, *Den påfliga beskattningen av Sverige* (1915).

3. *Acta et processus canonizacionis beate Birgitte* (Stockholm: J. Collijn, 1924–1931).

4. *Societas Sanctae Birgittae*, a High Church Society, holds its annual convention in Vadstena around July 23, Birgitta's "heavenly birthday" as the day of her death is called. The society's members, mostly clergymen and their wives, and young theological students, come from all over the country. They celebrate mass, read the hours, meditate, walk in processions, sing, and chant. SSB has accomplished much for the revival of old church customs. A kind of "a third order," it requires that its members take vows.

5. *Västerås ordinantia*, the most important part of the decisions at that meeting by the four estates declares the king to be head of the church. It gives him the right to tax the church and to reorganize its structure.

6. From the Constitution (*Regeringsformen*) of 1809. Full freedom of religion became law in 1951.

7. A favored expression ever since *Uppsala möte* in 1593 when the clergy united around the Bible as norm for the faith and accepted the Augsburg Confession as the pure evangelical one.

8. An excellent historical review is to be found in SOU 1964: 16, written as an introduction to an investigation of the relationship between church and state by Per-Olov Ahrén, pp. VII–LIII. The exhaustive report itself is written by Arne Palmqvist, pp. 1–324.

9. According to the law (1982: 943) the bishops have the duty to attend the meetings but only have the right to vote if they are elected delegates.

10. According to the law (1982: 1052) a church council elects its own chair. The clergy are members of the church council.

11. *Aktiva i Svenska Kyrkan* reports that the majority even among the church attending-people, when asked about "how important do you think that religion will be in the future for the people in our country," answered "about the same as now," p. 143.

12. The Myrdal-Gustafson proposal that would have put the Church of Sweden on a more equitable footing with the free-churches was a generous deal that was rejected by the Church Assembly in 1979. The actual report was made by Myrdal during her time as minister of the church. Her successor in the bourgeois coalition government was Gustafson who put the proposal forward.

13. Jackson W. Carroll, Barbara Hargrove, Adair T. Lummis, *Women of the Cloth* (San Francisco: Harper & Row, 1983), p. 208.

14. For a detailed account of all moves and proposals see Sahlin, *Dags för omprövning*.

15. The motion was raised by a clergyman, the director of the Stockholm City Mission, J. W. Johnson.

16. See Erik Sjöberg, *Exegeterna om kvinnliga präster* (Stockholm: Svenska Kyrkans Diakonistyrelses Bokförlag, 1953), in which Sjöberg defends his stance and argues against his colleagues Fridrichsen, Odeberg, Riesenfeld, and Reicke, and against the systematic theologian Hjalmar Lindroth.

17. SOU 1950: 48, pp. 120–26.

18. *Pastoraltidskriften,* founded in 1958, is supported by the Church Consolidation *(Kyrklig Samling)* and the Community Working for Renewal of the Church *(Arbetsgemenskapen Kyrklig Förnyelse).*

19. In the months between the 1957 and 1958 Church Assemblies two collections of essays were published, one for and one against women's ordination. In the volume for ordination, *Woman-Society-Church* [*Kvinnan-Samhället-Kyrkan*] (Stockholm: SKDB, 1958), the contributors were chosen from different fields—historian K. G. Hildebrand wrote on "Some Aspects of the Historical Development of the Question of Women"; ethicist and sociologist of religion Karl-Manfred Olsson on "Women in the Jobmarket: Structural Background and Actual Engagement"; educator and politician Birgit Rodhe on "Women's Contributions within the Church of Sweden," dividing their contributions in two categories: a) as professionals and b) as volunteers; physician Greta Hedenström on "The Biological Causes of Female Behavior and the Social Repercussions" (sexuality, menstruation, pregnancy, and birth); exegete Krister Stendahl on "The Bible and the Role of Women"; theologian Ruben Josephson on "Ordination from the Evangelical Lutheran Point of View." The book has a wide outlook and an awareness that the status of women in the church is interdependent with her status in society.

The volume expressing opposition to the ordination of women equally gave a signal by its title: *Woman and Amt According to Scripture and Confession (Kvinnan och Åmbetet enligt Skriften och Bekännelsen).* Exegete Bo Reicke wrote on "Women and the Amt of the Church in the Light of the Bible"; exegete and historian of religion Ake V. Ström on "The Background to Jesus' Choice of the Apostles"; exegete Bertil Gärtner on "The Teaching of the New Testament Concerning Women and the Amt"; Bishop Bo Giertz on "Faithfulness to the Confession"; systematic theologian Hjalmar Lindroth on "Woman—Church—Amt." Three women added "Lay Views on the Ordination of Women," and finally a clergyperson, Eric Grönlund, entitled his piece "Women priests—No!"

In *Kvinnan och Ämbetet enligt Skriften och Bekännelsen* there is a claim by the women that every woman "instinctively feels that (subordination) is right," p. 207. Cf. Kari E. Børresen, *Subordination and Equivalence,* thoroughly documents how androcentric the teaching of the church fathers is, to the point that women themselves disclaim equivalence.

20. Rodhe in *Kvinnan-Samhället-Kyrkan,* p. 25.

21. Tord Simonsson, *Kyrkomötet argumenterar; Kritisk analys av argumenttyper i diskussionerna vid 1957 och 1958 års kykomöten om "kvinnas behörighet till prästerlig tjänst"* (Lund: CWK Gleerup, 1963).

22. Ibid., p. 5.

23. Ibid., pp. 17ff.

24. Ibid., pp. 66ff.

25. Minutes from the Church Assembly of 1957, p. 81 (in *Allmänna kyrkomötets protokoll*).

26. Simonsson, *Kyrkomötet argumenterar,* p. 163.

27. Ibid., p. 165.

28. Ibid., p. 167.

29. Cf. interviews with Giertz and Ström.

30. Quoted from SOU 1981: 20, pp. 26–27.

31. Minutes from the Church Assembly of 1982, p. 215.

32. Ibid., p. 216.
33. Ibid., p. 217.
34. Ibid., p. 230.
35. Ibid., p. 236.
36. Ibid., p. 240.
37. Ibid., p. 245.
38. Ibid., p. 247.
39. Ibid., p. 255.
40. Ibid., p. 272.
41. Ibid., p. 276.
42. Ibid., p. 285.

CHAPTER 4

1. *Towards Equality: The Alva Myrdal Report to the Swedish Social Democratic Party*, trans. Roger Lind (Stockholm: Prisma, 1971).
2. Ibid., pp. 22–23.
3. Ibid., p. 23.
4. Ibid., p. 14.
5. Ibid., p. 64.
6. One of the few Swedish loanwords in English is "ombudsman," an independent office to which the citizens can turn when they think they have been treated unfairly, somewhat in the style of the Roman Tribunes.

The ombudsman is appointed by the Parliament, not by the government. Two such offices have long been in operation, the JO *(justitieombudsman)* handling cases of law, and the MO *(militieombudsman)* handling military cases. The JÄMO *(jämlikhetsombudsman)* judges alleged cases of discrimination.

7. To counteract the alienation of immigrants, a law was passed in 1975 giving immigrants who had spent more than two years in the country the right to vote in local elections.

8. One agency active for the promotion of expanded equality for women is the Fredrika Bremer Society founded in 1884. There is also the Tercentenary Fund of the Bank of Sweden, which supports research projects that deal with issues of equality in fields where they hitherto have been hidden. The published material has contributed greatly in opening people's eyes to sex discrimination in many cases, not least in the ways traditional research itself has been carried out. A presentation in English of the work is given in *Women and Men in Swedish Society: Research Projects Supported by the Bank of Sweden Tercentenary Foundation* (RJ 1983: 1), ed. Ann-Sofie Kälvemark, trans. William P. Michael (Stockholm: Liberdistribution, 1983).

9. Ester Lutteman, a woman theologian, B.D. in 1924, member of YWCA, and early leader for women's ordination, wanted to become ordained. She left the Church of Sweden after the Church Assembly had voted no to ordination.

10. When a position is vacated, an election is held. The names of the three people who receive the highest number of votes are then presented to the government, which can choose anyone of the three for the appointment. The recommendation of the Minister of Church Affairs is usually heeded by the cabinet.

11. Not the women's ordination question but the question of state-church was the reason why Alva and Gunnar Myrdal terminated their membership in the Church of Sweden in 1982.

12. This aloof attitude is typical for Swedish office-holders *(ämbetsmän)*. In order to be objective such a person is not supposed to become personally involved.

13. A symptom of this malaise was the outcome of the election in 1976 when the Social Democratic Party was voted out and a bourgeois coalition took over. The people wanted a change, a cut in taxes and greater freedom to handle their own affairs. However, they did not want the social programs to be cut. Thus the change became minimal since the coalition could not agree on a policy. In 1982 the Social Democrats were again voted into office.

14. The Kinsey Report, published in the United States in 1948, was immediately translated into Swedish and published in 1949.

15. The letter was not published but only circulated in stenciled copies. The quotes are from a revised edition, stencil copy.

16. Ibid., p. 2.

17. Ibid.

18. Ibid., p. 3. Mark the repeated use of the word "mentality."

19. "Homologic insemination" means when the wife's husband is the donor.

20. Ibid., pp. 4–5.

21. SOU 1950: 48, p. 7

22. Cf. Eric Grönlund's essay in *Kvinnan och Ämbetet*. He remarks that when dressed in clergy attire he could not travel anywhere without being asked by strangers: "Are we going to get women priests?" p. 216.

23. *Riktlinjer utarbetade av Kyrklig Samling kring Bibeln och Bekännelsen,* (Stockholm: Offprint, Blomvists Boktryckeri, 1960). Reprinted in Margit Sahlin, *Dags för omprövning,* pp. 31ff., and in SOU 1981: 20.

24. In 1983 Bishop Gärtner refused to install Margeteta Berndtsson as vicar in Skaftö, a post to which she had been elected.

25. In Kävlinge parish, reports *Expressen* on 11 September 1983, all the people employed in the parish are women: the vicar, the assistant pastor, the secretary, the parish assistant, the organist, and the warden.

26. Such a synod was formed in 1983 with Bishop Gärtner as its head. It is a separate body within the Church of Sweden. It is yet too early to say how it will work out. The Church of Sweden has a precedent of a separate body within itself in *Evangeliska Fosterlandsstiftelsen,* founded in 1856.

27. SOU 1981: 20, p. 34.

28. Ibid., pp. 131–34.

29. Ibid., p. 63.

30. Ibid., pp. 65–66.

31. Ibid., pp. 11–12.

32. In 1983 Palm was appointed justice to one of the superior courts *(regeringsråd)*.

33. The interview was taped, but due to the noise from outside traffic, the tape is almost inaudible in parts.

CHAPTER 5

1. Cf. Ulla Carin Holm, *Hennes verk skall prisa henne; Studier av personlighet och attityder hos kvinnliga präster i Svenska Kyrkan* (Helsingborg: Plus Ultra, 1982). Holm's study of 138 women priests show that although the women hailed from all the

dioceses (11% of them from Göteborg), 30% were working in Stockholm and 26% in Lund (p. 134).

2. An investigation of all the candidates for the priesthood shows that the women candidates are older than the men and that they are overrepresented at the Stockholm Theological Institute while Lund has the lowest number of women theologians. Anders Bäckström, "Religion som yrke; En studie av de svenska prästkandidaternas bakgrund och rolluppfattning vid 1970-talets slut" (Diss., Uppsala, 1983), pp. 98–99.

3. Carol Gilligan, *A Different Voice: Psychological Theory and Women's Development* (Cambridge: Harvard University Press, 1982) reveals how male-directed psychology has misunderstood and ignored women, and she aims at correcting such misperceptions. The book has earned a great deal of recognition since its publication. Male development, according to Gilligan, has persistently been described as human development. She offers an alternative outlook on maturity. See chapter 6, "Visions of Maturity," pp. 151ff.

4. Under the leadership of Ragnar Holte and Kari Børresen, and subsidized by the Tercentenary Foundation of the Bank of Sweden.

5. Holm, *Hennes verk,* is one example. An ambitious attempt is a book put together for the core-program in religion at the Theological Institute in Uppsala by Carl-Henric Grenholm and Linda Fredriksson, *Religion, Könsdiskriminering och Kvinnokamp* (mimeographed edition, Uppsala, 1978). It features excerpts from a wide variety of literature illuminating the biases and offers an attempt to overcome them in the field of religion.

6. In his investigation Anders Bäckström, "Religion som yrke," found that among the candidates for the priesthood only 8% were children of clergy, which means that the percentage among the younger clergy is going down. Bäckström remarks that compared to other occupational groups, however, "children of clergy and academics are evidently overrepresented" (p. 200, cf. table of father's occupation, p. 104).

7. According to Bäckström, "Religion som yrke," 46% mention the priest in their home parish as the most influential individual for the choice of priesthood, p. 87, Fig. 3.

8. Holm, *Hennes verk,* reports that only 6% of the women priests have free-church background (p. 134). During the 1970s there was an increase of recruits from younger denominational churches (especially the Pentecostals)—Bäckström, "Religion som yrke," pp. 58–59. It seems that denominational lines are easier to cross over than to bridge the gap between those priests who held to the biblicistic tradition and the doctrine of *successio apostolica* and those who strive to incorporate doctrinal understanding with their everyday life in interaction with people.

9. Holm, *Hennes verk,* reports 40% of the women as saying yes to the question of call as a spiritual experience, 20% answered that it was a maturing decision, 14% that is was "a direction" *(ledning)* and 19% that the call was a force (to obedience) (p. 137).

10. In the beginning of this century there were almost no specialized posts in the priesthood. Still, in the country there is great uniformity. But during the last decades specialization has also spread in the priesthood as in all other professions. Priests are employed by the central agencies, the Swedish Mission Board, the Central Board, the Lutheran World Federation, the Diaconate Boards, etc. There are priests for hospitals, for immigrants, for students, for the deaf, for the mentally ill, for prisons, for industry, etc.

11. Ulla Carin Holm's sample (in *Hennes verk*) registers the proportion of single women even larger: 31% unmarried, 5% widowed, and 12% divorced (p. 142). Such a great percentage of divorced people in the priesthood ought not to be surprising since a personal crisis drives people to start questioning the meaning of life. The interesting thing to know would be whether they divorced after they became priests and in that case whether the burden of the dual career collapsed their family life.

12. This answer was given in the trial run of the questionnaire, sent out to twenty priests in the fall of 1981.

13. Holm, *Hennes verk,* reports that 80% of the women priests have experienced the conflict between the roles of priest and wife (p. 143).

14. Bäckström, "Religion som yrke," shows that the theological students are highly active in associations and union: 65% belong to a theological group, 53% to a cultural association or sports club, 52% to some kind of church group, 33% to a political party and 33% to a union (p. 95). He also points out that politically the priests had a definite bourgeois political leaning: 26% voted for the Center Party (the former Farmers' party), 7% for the Liberal (Folk-) Party, 30% for the Moderate (Höger-) Party, 11% for the Social Democrats, 2% for the Communists, and 15% for the Christian Democratic Party. Thus 78% are to the right while 13% to the left (p. 79). Two-thirds of the theological students come from homes where the parents vote for the bourgeois parties, yet the students themselves are not so united in the bourgeois fold as could be expected (pp. 82–83). Cf. also *Aktiva i Svenska Kyrkan* which shows that the majority of the laity votes for the bourgeois parties.

15. Holm, *Hennes verk,* reports that 76% of the women priests have experienced some kind of opposition or discrimination from theologians, priests, and laity; 40% did not take any action (pp. 144–45).

16. Holm, *Hennes verk,* p. 151, reports that 21% of the women had no other work experience before they entered the priesthood but 34% had for a longer period of time and 17% for a shorter period worked in some other capacity: 30% in teaching, 34% as clerks or secretaries, 35% in some kind of care, and 16% in religious work. Also Bäckström, "Religion som yrke," has a table showing that the majority of candidates are recruited from the teaching corps; another group of priests has formerly been employed by the church as parish assistants, deacons, youthleaders, and church wardens, or they have been free-church pastors (p. 101).

CONCLUSION

1. Cf. Francine Cardman, "Tradition, Hermeneutics, and Ordination," in *Sexism and Church Law,* ed. J. Coriden (Ramsey, N.J.: Paulist Press, 1977), pp. 58–80. In coming to grips with the term "tradition," Cardman uses as her point of departure two studies, one catholic and one ecumenical: Ives Congar, *Tradition and Traditions: An Historical Essay and a Theological Essay* (London: Burns & Oates, 1966), and the report on "Scripture, Tradition and Traditions," Section II of the Fourth World Conference on Faith and Order, Montreal, 1963. By combining the two and placing them in the context of contemporary discussions she arrives at a theological consensus. By distinguishing between the various senses of Tradition and tradition, Cardman resolves the earlier Protestant-Catholic polemic about the relationship between Scripture and tradition. The gap in the understanding of tradition "is due in part to the tendency . . . to equate Tradition with the Scriptural and written word" (p. 60).

Cardman uses the term "apostolic tradition" in contradistinction to Scripture which itself is a result of tradition. "The Scriptures are 'apostolic' only in the loose sense in which the early church felt them to possess that authority which the apostles represented in the church. . . . Just as specific books of the New Testament cannot be traced reliably to specific apostles . . . so too with other aspects of the church's tradition" (p. 77).

2. For which the word is *människa*, a feminine noun, *mänsklighet*.

3. For example *riksdagsman* (a member of Parliament), *lagman* (a judge), *ämbetsman* (an official), even *barnavårdsman* (social worker dealing with children), a profession predominantly staffed by women.

4. On the other hand, the still-lingering American convention of referring to the wife as Mrs. John Doe died out in Swedish society a few generations ago.

5. Since clergy are heavily located in rural areas where career opportunities for spouses may be limited, these figures may not express the desires or actual choices of either partner.

6. Cf. *Aktiva i Svenska Kyrkan*, table 31.

7. For Anton Fridrichsen, see above. Anders Nygren's research into Christian motifs led him to define what was un-Christian. Thus he declared Augustine un-Christian in his most famous book *Agape and Eros*, translated by A. G. Herbert and P. S. Watson, where Nygren defines what he sees as the Christian concept of love. In the Christian tradition love has been hailed over against justice, and love has been overemphasized to the disadvantage of equality.

8. A line from what perhaps became the poet James Russell Lowell's (1845) most-beloved hymn: "Once to every man and nation."

9. See Carroll/Hargrove/Lummis, *Women of the Cloth*, chapter 5, "Experiences of Women and Men Clergy in the Job Market."

10. Cf. Thorleif Pettersson, "Präster och lekmän om prästrollen," in B. Åberg/Th. Pettersson, *Identitet och roll* (Stockholm: Verbum, 1981). Pettersson investigates the discrepancy between what the priests themselves accept and adjust to as their role and what the laity expect from them in that capacity. He considers this discrepancy a challenge for the clergy to start a dialogue with the laity.

11. The Church of Sweden has tended more toward the right than the left. There seems to be more excitement about those churches that dress their clergy well, the Anglicans/Episcopalians, Eastern Orthodox, Roman Catholics, than with the Baptists and Pentecostals.

12. Concerning the new structure of the Church Assembly and the central organs of the church, see SOU 1981: 14, *Reformerat Kyrkomöte, kyrklig lagstiftning, mm: Betänkande av 1979 års kyrkomöteskommitte* (Stockholm: Gotab, 1981). Concerning the local government of the parishes, see SOU 1983: 55, *Församlingen i framtiden: Ett diskussionsbetänkande om svenska kyrkans lokala organisation från 1982 års kyrkokommitte* (Stockholm: Minab/Gotab, 1983). The debate concerning these proposals continues in *Kyrkans Tidning*.

A Free Synod of the Church of Sweden was founded in 1983. The synod is not a grassroot movement but is made up mostly by priests and theologians. According to the bylaws only one layperson from each *dekanat* (five such *dekanat* together make up the synod) is required to attend each Synod Assembly. The leader of the synod is Bishop Gärtner.

13. "Hermeneutics of suspicion," I am not sure who coined the expression but the

method is to be alert to the biases present in biblical writing and biblical scholarship. Women have to move from the mere reading of androcentric texts to the reconstruction of the history of women in early Christianity. This is the work that Elisabeth Schüssler Fiorenza has attempted in her splendid book *In Memory of Her: A Feminist Theological Reconstruction of Early Christian Beginnings* (New York: Crossroad, 1983).

APPENDIX 2

1. Joseph F. Fletcher, *William Temple* (New York: Seabury Press, 1963), p. 112. Fletcher states that Temple "constantly struggled against the subordinate and falsely humble place given to women in both Church and society." Frederick A. Iremonyer, *William Temple, Archbishop of Canterbury: His Life and Letters*. Iremonyer quotes Temple as saying: "Personally I want (as at present advised) to see women ordained to the priesthood. But still more do I want to see both real advance towards the re-union of Christendom, and the general emancipation of women. To win admission to the priesthood now would put back the former and to moot it would put back the latter," p. 452. (Also quoted in *Concerning Ordination of Women* [Geneva: WCC, 1964], p. 67, by Rev. Henry R. T. Brandreth, O. G. S.)

2. H. N. Bate, ed., *Faith and Order: Proceedings of the World Conference, Lausanne, 3–21 August 1927* (New York: Doubleday, Doran & Co., 1928), p. 373. Of the 104 members elected to the Continuation Committee appointed at Lausanne, three were women, two of whom were signatories of the Memorial from the Women Delegates. The women were: Dr. Elisa H. Kendrick, Miss Lucy Gardner, and Mrs. Kingman Mott Robins. From S. Wood, ed., *Lausanne, 1927* (New York: George Doran Co., 1927), pp. 189–92.

3. Karl Barth, *How I Changed My Mind* (Richmond: John Knox Press, 1966), p. 58.

4. David P. Gaines, *The World Council of Churches* (Peterborough, N.H.: Richard N. Smith, Noone House Press, 1966), p. 246.

5. The exchange of correspondence has been published by Gudrun Kaper, ed., *Eva, Wo Bist Du? Frauen i Internationalen Organisationen der Ökumene* (Berlin: Burckhardthaus-Laetare Verlag, 1981), p. 34.

6. W. A. Visser't Hooft, ed., *The First Assembly of the World Council of Churches, Amsterdam, 1948* (New York: Harper & Brothers, 1949), p. 148.

7. Ibid., p. 147.

8. Ibid., p. 149.

9. Ibid., pp. 147–48. Other recommendations urged that more women serve on WCC commissions and committees and that more information about women's activities appear in the Ecumenical Press Service and other WCC communication channels.

10. Kathleen Bliss, *The Service and Status of Women in the Churches* (London: SCM Press, 1952). This report evaluates information reported from fifty-eight countries regarding the status and roles of women. It points to the increasing number of churches that ordain women as well as to the influence on the churches of changes in the status of women in church and society. About ordination Bliss writes: "Why is the matter even discussed at all, seeing that for centuries the very idea of ordaining women to the ministry was unthought and unthinkable. . . . There is only one main reason

why a matter undiscussed for nineteen centuries is now a subject of serious study and lively debate, that is the radical change in the place of women in society in the last fifty years. The Churches have themselves helped to bring about that change, especially in their significant contribution to the education of women," p. 132.

11. W. A. Visser't Hooft, ed., *The Evanston Report: The Second Assembly of the WCC, 1954* (New York: Harper & Brothers, 1955). Dr. Madelein Barot's report was deferred to the evening session. She announced the new name of the department and defined its work "to promote the study of issues concerning the relationship and common service of men and women in the churches and in society, and to promote an ecumenical consciousness in church women's organizations," p. 61. The specific recommendation regarding promoting the recognition of women in the total life of the churches is in the report, p. 205.

12. Visser't Hooft, *The First Assembly*, p. 9, par. 2. This often-quoted sentence appears in "The Message of the Assembly."

13. Oliver S. Tomkins, ed., *The Third World Conference on Faith and Order, Held at Lund* (London: SCM Press, 1953), 27–38. Father Georges Florevsky, commenting on the Lund meeting at an evening session of the Evanston assembly, stated: "The greatest achievement of the ecumenical movement is the courage in acknowledging that there is a major disagreement," pp. 33–34 (Evanston report).

14. The woman ordained was the Rev. Florence Li-Lim Oi. Bishop Hall was censored for his action and this led Rev. Li-Lim Oi to resign her priesthood in 1946. At the Lambeth Conference of 1948, three Chinese bishops urged that ordaining women was an opportunity for national dioceses to express local autonomy. Their views did not prevail. It would be thirty years later at Lambeth 1978 before the ordination of women would be acknowledged as part of Anglican diversity in unity.

15. The first request for the ordination of women in Canada came in 1926. The first woman ordained was Lydia Gruchy, Saskatchewan Conference, 1936. Gruchy's ordination was requested in 1926 and turned down every two years until it was finally approved in 1936. Twenty years later, ordination of women became a subject of ecumenical discussion in Canada when the United Church of Canada and the Anglican Church of Canada began discussions of church union. See Stephen Neill, *The Church and Christian Union* (London: Oxford University Press, 1968), p. 233.

16. John E. Lynch, "The Ordination of Women: Protestant Experiences in Ecumenical Perspective," *Journal of Ecumenical Studies* 12/2 (Spring 1975): 180. Lynch states that in 1956 the Methodist discipline was changed to read: "Both men and women are included in all provisions of the Discipline which refer to the ministry" (no. 308.2).

17. *The Women's Pulpit* 38 (July–December 1960): 10. The article was taken from *The Manchester Guardian*, 16 April 1960. It is cited in Lynch, "Ordination of Women," p. 185.

18. W. A. Visser't Hooft, ed., *The New Delhi Report: The Third Assembly of the World Council of Churches, 1961* (New York: Association Press, 1962), p. 210.

19. Ibid., p. 170. Dr. George Johnston of the United Church of Canada urged that the study a) not be limited to Europe and b) be carried out in conjunction with the Department on Cooperation of Men and Women, p. 175.

20. In the negotiations for the establishment of the Church of South India, the Methodists were asked to relinquish the ordination of women to the diaconate. This was a concession to the Anglicans who would accept an order of deaconesses but not

of women deacons or priests. However, in Japan in 1951, with the establishment of the United Church of Christ in Japan (Anglicans were not involved), women's ordination, begun in 1933 by the Presbyterians, was continued. In 1984, 473 out of 2706 pastors are women. Of these, 175 serve in local churches: the majority work as evangelists, teachers, and associates. (Reported in *One World* [April 1984]: 9.)

21. Visser't Hooft, *New Delhi Report,* p. 217.

22. Ibid.

23. Ibid.

24. Ibid.

25. *Concerning the Ordination of Women, Geneva.* Published jointly by Faith and Order and the Department on Cooperation of Men and Women in Church, Family, and Society, 1964.

26. At the WCC Sixth Assembly in Vancouver, Dr. Marga Bührig was elected one of the seven presidents of the WCC, three of them women.

27. Marga Bührig, "The Question of the Ordination of Women in the Light of Some New Testament Texts," *Concerning the Ordination of Women,* pp. 41–56.

28. Ibid., pp. 55–56.

29. *Concerning the Ordination of Women,* p. 5.

30. Ibid., p. 6.

31. Ibid., p. 63. Kohre wanted to make clear that some women can be equal to men, but that their roles are different. He states:

> Although the Church has not yet yielded to the temptation of feminism in the form of its ministry, it extols certain women as the equals of the Apostles. The Holy Women were the first to see the open tomb and to announce the Resurrection to the Apostles. They received the Holy Spirit in the Upper Room. And one of them was considered worthy to bear the Word of life. The ministry of virginity is particularly theirs. They share with men in the glory of martyrdom. Woman is the sign of the religious life, because womanhood means sacrifice and self-surrender. The advent of woman is the advent of sainthood, which is a life hidden in God (Col. 3:3). If she removes the Veil behind which she lives a secret life with the Bridegroom, this does not constitute a progress of the human person within her.

32. Ibid., pp. 68–69. Quoted from E. L. Mascall, *Women and the Priesthood of the Church* (London: Church Literature Assoc.), p. 12.

33. Ibid., p. 68.

34. R. C. Rodgers and L. Vischer, eds., *The Fourth World Conference on the Faith and Order: Montreal, 1963,* Faith and Order Paper No. 42 (London: SCM Press, 1964), p. 26. The last discussion of this issue in Faith and Order was in Edinburgh in 1937: "The Unity of Mutual Recognition and Its Expression," in *The Meaning of Unity, Edinburgh, 1937* (New York: Harper & Brothers, 1937), pp. 17–25.

35. Ibid., pp. 63–64, pars. 83–88.

36. Ibid., p. 63, par. 84.

37. Ibid.

38. Ibid., p. 64, par. 89. Here the designations for the ordained person as prophet, priest, and king are used for the tasks of 1) proclaiming, 2) doing priestly service, and 3) guarding the unity of the church.

39. Ibid., p. 68, par. 102.

40. Faith and Order Commission, Montreal, Canada, 1963. Minutes of the Faith

and Order Commission, Faith and Order Paper No. 41 (Geneva: WCC, 1963), pp. 23–24. Also see Minutes of the Aarhus Standing Committee, 1964, Faith and Order Paper No. 44 where "ordination of women is referred to not under ministry but as a 'particular question,'" p. 52.

41. Stephen Neill, *The Church and Christian Union* (London: Oxford University Press, 1968), pp. 264–66.

42. Oliver S. Tomkins, ed., *The Third World Conference on Faith and Order, Lund* (London: SCM Press, 1952), p. 256.

43. *New Directions in Faith and Order, Bristol, 1967*, Faith and Order Paper No. 50 (Geneva: WCC, 1968), p. 148.

44. Margaret Nash, *Ecumenical Movement in the 1960's* (Johannesburg: Raven Press, 1975), p. 211.

45. Ibid.

46. *The Documents of Vatican II, 1963–65* (New York: Guild Press, 1966), "The Various Fields of the Apostolate," chapter 2, p. 500, par. 9.

47. Nash, *Ecumenical Movement in the 1960's*, p. 211.

48. Ibid., p. 221.

49. Norman Goodall, ed., *The Uppsala Report, 1968: Official Report of the IV Assembly of the World Council of Churches*, Uppsala, 4–20 July 1968 (Geneva: WCC, 1968), pp. 244–47.

50. Ibid., p. 225. The only reference to ordination of women at Uppsala appears in relation to a working paper on ordination prepared by Dr. Gerald Moede, Disciples Church, U.S.A. The paper was questioned by Professor John Meyendorff, Orthodox Church of America, for giving an "impression of being a consensus" when there were yet many disagreements, among them being the threefold ministry, the origin of the episcopate, and the ordination of women, p. 23.

51. Ibid., pp. 224–25.

52. Ibid., p. 250.

53. *The Ordination of Women to the Priesthood*, General Synod (Church of England)—A Consultative Document presented by the Advisory Council for the Church's Ministry, GS 104, prepared by Christian Howard, published by the Church of England, 1972, p. 2.

The Lambeth Conference of 1968 passed several resolutions regarding the ordination of women, stating that the theological arguments for and against are inconclusive, that each member church should study the question and submit their findings to the Anglican Consultative Council who will make them available to the entire Anglican Communion, and that, before any church should decide to ordain women, the advice of the ACC should be considered. (*The Lambeth Conference, 1968* [London: SPCK, 1968], Resolutions, 34–38, pp. 39–40).

The Lambeth Report stated:

It appears that the tradition flowing from the early fathers and the medieval church that a woman is incapable of receiving holy orders reflects biological assumptions about the nature of woman and her relation to man which are considered unacceptable in the light of modern knowledge and biblical study, and have been generally discarded today. If the ancient and medieval assumptions about the social role and inferior status of women are no longer accepted, the appeal to tradition is virtually reduced to the observation that there happens to be no precedent for ordaining women. (p. 106)

54. Brigalia Ban, ed., *What is Ordination Coming To?* Report of a Consultation on the Ordination of Women, Cartigny, Switzerland, 21–26 September 1970 (Geneva: WCC, 1971).

55. Ibid., p. 78.

56. Ibid., p. 70.

57. Ibid., p. 71.

58. Ibid., p. 63.

59. Ibid., p. 2.

60. Ibid., p. 39.

61. Ibid. Halkes recommends for the consideration of the consultation a study done in the Netherlands by R. J. A. Van Eyden, "The Request for the Ministerial Priesthood of Women in the Netherlands." Along with this study, other Roman Catholic research began to appear in Europe on this issue. The scholarly projects often referred to are Ida Raming's *Der Ausschluss der Frau von Priesterlichen Amt* (Wein: Böhlau Verlag, 1973) and Haye Van Der Meer's *Priestentum der Frau?* (Freiburg, 1969). Published in English as *Women Priests in the Catholic Church?* (Philadelphia: Temple University Press, 1973).

62. *National Catholic Reporter* (30 April 1971): 19.

63. Walter M. Abbot, *Documents of Vatican II* (New York: America Press, 1966), No. 29, pp. 227–28. Preceding this paragraph on the fundamental human rights of women is a paragraph on the theological justification for equality. It reads:

Since all men *(Homines:* human beings; not *vires)* possess a rational soul and are created in God's likeness, since they have the same nature and origin, have been redeemed by Christ, and enjoy the same divine calling and destiny, the basic equality of all must receive increasingly greater recognition.

64. *Pro Mundi Vita,* A Roman Catholic Center for Renewal of the Church, located in Belgium, has had four international consultations related to changing patterns of ministry: "New Forms of Ministries in Christian Communities" (Bulletin 50, 1974), "Women and Men as partners in Christian Communities" (Bulletin 59, 1976), "Mixed Pastoral Teams" (Bulletin 78, 1979), and "The Situation of Women in the Catholic Church" (Bulletin 83, 1980). The bulletins are published by PMV (Rue de la Limite 8, B–1030, Brussels, Belgium).

65. *Ordination of Women to the Priesthood: Pro and Con,* Authorized Study by the Anglican Church of Canada (Toronto: Anglican Book Centre, 1975), p. 9.

66. Michael P. Hamilton and Nancy S. Montgomery, *The Ordination of Women: Pro and Contra* (New York: Morehouse-Barlow, 1975). See Appendix B, "Orthodox Statement on Ordination of Women from the Orthodox-Anglican Consultation," 2 June 1973, pp. 175–76.

67. *Christianity and Crisis* 34/15 (16 September 1974): 185, 188. A week before their ordination the eleven women to be ordained from eight different dioceses sent a letter announcing the event. The letter states: "We know this ordination to be irregular. . . . We are certain that the Church needs women in priesthood to be true to the Gospel understanding of human unity in Christ." Quoted from Michael McFarlene Marrett, *The Lambeth Conference and Women Priests* (Smithtown, N.Y.: Exposition Press, 1981), p. 65.

68. *One Baptism, One Eucharist and a Mutually Recognized Ministry: Three Agreed Statements,* Faith and Order Paper No. 73 (Geneva: WCC, 1978), pp. 45–49, pars. 64–69.

69. *Commission on Faith and Order Minutes, Accra, 1974*, Faith and Order Paper No. 71 (Geneva: WCC, 1974), pp. 108–9. The first outline for the work of the community study appears here. It includes a) a theological study on "the fullness of diakonia, the ministry of the whole people of God, as it affects the relationship of men and women," b) "ordination of women as factor in the conversations and negotiations between the churches which do, and do not, ordain women," and c) questions of theological education and placement of women in the church, including in ordained ministries. One concrete suggestion was that a comparative study be undertaken of the ministry of women in the Church of Sweden where women are ordained and women in the Church of Finland where they are not.

70. Ibid., pp. 48–49.

71. David M. Paton, *Breaking Barriers: The Official Report of the Fifth Assembly of the World Council of Churches, 1975* (Grand Rapids: Wm. B. Eerdmans, 1976), p. 114.

72. Ibid.

73. Ibid., pp. 113–14.

74. Ibid., p. 68.

75. Ibid., pp. 62, 69, and 309.

76. Ibid., p. 303. Related discussion on pp. 62–64.

77. *Faith and Order, Louvain, 1971. Study Reports and Documents*, Faith and Order Paper No. 59 (Geneva: WCC, 1971), 240. The Louvain meeting challenged the traditional methodology of Faith and Order studies and urged the Commission to develop a new program that would include questions of the marks and boundaries of the church today in different societal contexts. It should explore how frames of reference "change and influence our thinking about the unity of the Church." Areas mentioned were 1) the place of conflict in community, 2) the significance of the struggle against racism in the search for unity, and 3) the meaning of weakness and the exercise of power in community.

78. Paton, *Breaking Barriers*, 109.

79. W. D. Pattinson, *General Synod*, GSM, sc. 53 (Church House, SW1), 26 July, "Letter from the Archbishop of Canterbury to His Holiness Pope Paul VI—Date 9th July, 1975," p. 3.

80. Pattinson, *General Synod*, "Letter from His Holiness Pope VI to the Archbishop of Canterbury—Date 30th November, 1975," p. 4.

81. Ibid.

82. Statement on *The Ordination of Women*, Anglican Orthodox Theological Consultation, 22–24 January 1976, par. 8.

83. *The Report of the Lambeth Conference, 1978* (London: CIO Co., 1978), pp. 45–46.

84. *Inter Insigniores*, Vatican Doctrinal Congregation's Declaration on the Question of Admission of Women to the Ministerial Priesthood, 15 October 1976. Made public, 27 January 1977. Leonard and Arlene Swidler edited a commentary on the declaration in which approximately fifty men and women theologians participated, *Women Priests: A Catholic Commentary on the Vatican Declaration* (New York: Paulist Press, 1977).

85. See article by The Rev. Hervé-Marie Legrand, "Views on the Ordination of Women," *Origins* 5 (November 1975): 459–68. Jean-Marie Aubert published *La Femme, antiféminisme et Christianisme* (Paris: Cerf, 1975), and earlier Yves Congar

published on the question in *La Maison Dieu* 103 (1970).

86. Legrand, "View on the Ordination of Women," p. 461. Quoted from *La Croix* (20 April 1974).

87. Legrand, "Views on the Ordination of Women," p. 460. In addition to grassroots movements, some national synods passed resolutions opening the way for a process of accepting the ordination of women in principle. Pastoral Synod of 1969 is one such initiative. In addition a number of bishops in Canada, Switzerland, West Germany, and Belgium urged consideration of the issue.

88. A. M. Gardiner, *Women and Catholic Priesthood: An Expanding Vision* (New York: Paulist Press, 1976). Two years later, a second conference was held and its report was published as *New Woman, New Church, New Priestly Ministry: Proceedings of the Second Conference on the Ordination of Roman Catholic Women,* 10–12 Nov., Baltimore (Rochester, N.Y.: Kirkwood Press, 1980). This was followed by a third conference, in October 1983, called "Woman Church Speaks" and organized by a coalition of Roman Catholic women's movements.

89. Legrand, "Views on the Ordination of Women," p. 460. In 1964, Roman Catholic Synods of West Germany and Austria urged the opening of the diaconate for women. Lambeth endorsed the principle of a diaconate for women in 1968.

90. *Research Report on Women in Church and Society* (The Catholic Theological Society of America, 1978), Appendix 2, p. 50. For further research on the topic see Max Thurian's chapter on "The Diaconate," in *Priesthood and Ministry: Ecumenical Research* (London: Mowbray, 1970, 1983), pp. 126ff. Also Michael A. Fahey, "Eastern Orthodoxy and the Ordination of Women," in *Women Priests,* pp. 107–113. A current work that challenges earlier scholarship on the role of women deacons in the early church is that by Elisabeth Schüssler Fiorenza, *In Memory of Her: A Feminist Theological Reconstruction of Christian Origins* (New York: Crossroad, 1983), pp. 285ff.

91. *Research Report,* pp. 50–51.

92. Legrand, "Views on the Ordination of Women," p. 461.

93. "Can Women be Priests? Biblical Commission Report," *Origins* 6 (1976): 92–96. Of the seventeen voting members the Commission voted 12–5 in favor of this statement. The report ends: "It does not seem that the New Testament by itself alone will permit us to settle in a clear way and once and for all the problem of the possible accession of women to the presbytery," p. 96.

94. Leonard and Arlene Swidler, *Women Priests: A Catholic Commentary on the Vatican Declaration,* p. 43, section 5, par. 27.

95. Paul K. Jewett, *The Ordination of Women* (Grand Rapids: Wm. B. Eerdmans, 1980), 80. From *Summa Theologica,* IIIa, q. 81, a. 7 ad 3 um.

96. *Los Angeles Times,* 18 March 1977.

97. Sister Elizabeth Carroll, RSM, "Women's Ordination and the Catholic Church," Washington, D.C.: Center of Concern, 18 February 1977 memo.

98. Leon McBeth, "The Ordination of Women," *Review and Expositor* 78 (Fall 1981): 515–30. Quotation from p. 517.

99. Ibid., pp. 519–20.

100. Ibid., p. 520.

101. *Sharing in One Hope,* Report and Documents from the Meeting of the Faith and Order Commission, 15–30 August 1978, Bangalore, India, Faith and Order Paper No. 92 (Geneva: WCC, 1978), p. 249.

The Commission at the Bangalore meeting could not resolve how to deal with the question of ordination of women. It agreed that the Community of Women and Men in the Church study would hold a special consultation on this issue. The agenda for the consultation would draw from considerations of the responses from the churches to the Accra document on *One Baptism, One Eucharist and a Mutually Recognized Ministry*. These were reported in Faith and Order Paper No. 84, *Towards an Ecumenical Consensus on Baptism, the Eucharist and the Ministry* (Geneva: WCC, 1977), Appendix, pp. 17–19.

102. *The Failure of the English Covenant* (London: British Council of Churches, 1982), p. 8. After about a decade of common work, the covenant was defeated in July 1982, in part due to the lack of agreement over the ordination of women between the free-churches and the Church of England.

103. Constance F. Parvey, ed., *Ordination of Women in Ecumenical Perspective*, Faith and Order Paper No. 105, pp. 54–59. The quotation (p. 59) is part of a critical response to par. 64 of *One Baptism, One Eucharist and a Mutually Recognized Ministry* which states: "Both men and women need to discover the full meaning of their specific contribution to the ministry of Christ. The Church is entitled to the style of ministry which can be provided by women as well as that which can be provided by men" (Faith and Order Paper No. 73, p. 45).

104. Parvey, *Ordination of Women*, pp. 57–58, par. 4.

105. Ibid., p. 58.

106. Constance F. Parvey, ed., *The Community of Women and Men in the Church: The Sheffield Report* (Philadelphia: Fortress Press, 1983), pp. 84ff.

107. Ibid., the Sheffield section report on "The Ordained Ministry." The report also notes that the question of the ordination of women needs sociological as well as theological clarification. It states:

> As our knowledge of sociology and theology develops, we are offered a chance to deepen our understanding and practice of ministry and our relations with one another.
>
> The issues involved in this matter touch us at our deepest level, embedded as they are in liturgy, symbolism, and spirituality. There can be no real progress if church, state, or any group within the church seeks to force a change in practice without taking this into account. At the same time we should never forget that all problems of the ministry are related to the social and cultural context where the identity of the church and of individual Christians is constantly being challenged. (pp. 129–30)

108. Point 3 recommended that Faith and Order undertake a study on "the possibility and implications of churches being in communion when they have different policies concerning the ordination of women" (Parvey, *Community of Women and Men*, p. 84).

109. Ibid., p. 90.

110. *World Council of Churches, Central Committee, Minutes of the Thirty-Third Meeting, Dresden, German Democratic Republic*, 16–26 August 1981 (Geneva: WCC, 1981), p. 29.

111. Ibid.

112. Ibid., p. 22.

113. Michael Kinnamon, ed., *Towards Visible Unity, Commission on Faith and*

Order. Vol. I: Minutes and Addresses, Faith and Order Paper No. 112 (Geneva: WCC, 1982), p. 128.

114. *Baptism, Eucharist and Ministry,* Faith and Order Paper No. 111 (Geneva: WCC, 1982).

115. Max Thurian, *Ecumenical Perspectives on Baptism, Eucharist and Ministry,* Faith and Order Paper No. 116 (Geneva: WCC, 1983). Quotation from the preface by Nikos Nissiotis, then moderator of the Faith and Order Commission, member of the Orthodox Church of Greece (p. xi).

116. Ibid., "The Ministry of Men and Women in the Church," p. 23, par. 18. This paragraph must be seen in tandem with par. 54, "Towards the Mutual Recognition of Ministries," p. 32.

117. Emmanuel Lanne, "Convergence and Ordained Ministry," in Thurian, *Ecumenical Perspectives,* p. 119.

118. Faith and Order Paper No. 111, p. 32, par. 54.

119. *Growing Towards Consensus and Commitment: Report of the Fouth Consultation of United and Uniting Churches, 1981,* Faith and Order Paper No. 110 (Geneva: WCC, 1981), p. 14. Also see recommendations 1 and 2 (p. 31) where the phrase "the urgent need to continue to search for a consensus on the ordination of women to the ministry of the Church" has not been included.

120. Ibid. This is a reference to the commentary on p. 25, par. 18, which reads:

> Those churches which do not practice the ordination of women consider that the force of nineteen centuries of tradition against the ordination of women must not be set aside. They believe that such a tradition cannot be dismissed as a lack of respect for the participation of women in Church. They believe that there are theological issues concerning the nature of humanity and concerning Christology which lie at the heart of their conviction and understanding of the role of women in the Church.

121. Thomas Hopko, ed., *Women and the Priesthood* (Crestwood, N.Y.: St. Vladimir's Seminary Press, 1983), p. 171.

122. J. Robert Wright, "Ordination in the Ecumenical Movement," *Review and Expositor* 78 (Fall 1981): 497–514. Wright discusses some of the problems raised by the issues of authority and order in the various ministries from the point of view of the Anglican tradition, within the ecumenical context. Fiorenza in *In Memory of Her* argues that the movement in the development of order and authority in the early church is from equality to patriarchalization. See "Patriarchal Household of God and the Ekklesia of Women," pp. 285–342.

123. This issue has not been a central focus in Faith and Order since the Faith and Order report on "Institutionalism" at the Montreal Conference in 1963. See Faith and Order Findings, *The Final Report of the Theological Commissions to the Fourth World Conference on Faith and Order, Montreal, 1963* (Minneapolis: Augsburg Publishing House, 1963), pp. 3–29.